Teaching and Learning

Essential Readings in Developmental Psychology

Series Editors: Alan Slater and Darwin Muir
Queen's University, Kingston, Ontario and the University of Exeter

In this series of nine books, Alan Slater and Darwin Muir, together with a team of expert editors, bring together selections of readings illustrating important methodological, empirical and theoretical issues in the area of developmental psychology. Volumes in the series and their editors are detailed below:

- Infant Development *Darwin Muir and Alan Slater*
- Childhood Social Development *Wendy Craig*
- Childhood Cognitive Development *Kang Lee*
- Adolescent Development *Gerald Adams*
- The Psychology of Aging *William Gekoski*
- The Nature/Nurture Debate *Steven Ceci and Wendy Williams*
- Teaching and Learning *Charles Desforges and Richard Fox*
- Language Development *Michael Tomasello and Elizabeth Bates*
- Children and the Law *Ray Bull*

Each of the books is introduced by the volume editor with a rationale behind the chosen papers. Each reading is then introduced and contextualized within the individual subject debate as well as within the wider context of developmental psychology. A selection of further reading is also assigned, making each volume an ideal teaching resource for both classroom and individual study settings.

Teaching and Learning
The Essential Readings

Edited by Charles Desforges and Richard Fox

Blackwell Publishers

© 2002 by Blackwell Publishers Ltd
a Blackwell Publishing company
except for editorial arrangement and introduction © 2002 by Charles
Desforges, Richard Fox, Darwin Muir and Alan Slater

Editorial Offices:
108 Cowley Road, Oxford OX4 1JF, UK
Tel: +44 (0) 1865 791100
350 Main Street, Malden, MA 02148-5018, USA
Tel: +1 781 388 8250

First published 2002 by Blackwell Publishers Ltd

Library of Congress Cataloging-in-Publication Data has been applied for

ISBN 0-631-21748-7 (hbk)
ISBN 0-631-21749-5 (pbk)

A catalogue record for this title is available from the British Library.

Set in 10.5 on 13 pt Photina
by Kolam Information Services Pvt. Ltd., Pondicherry, India
Printed and bound in Great Britain by MPG Books Ltd, Bodmin, Cornwall

For further information on
Blackwell Publishers, visit our website:
www.blackwellpublishers.co.uk

Contents

Acknowledgments

The editors and publishers gratefully acknowledge the following for permission to reproduce copyright material.

Text

Adey, P. and Shayer, M., "An exploration of long-term, far transfer effects following an extended intervention program in the high school science curriculum." *Cognition and Instruction*, *11*, 1, 1993.

Bryant, P., Maclean, M. and Bradley L., "Rhyme, language and children's reading." *Applied Psycholinguistics 11*, 1990 (©) Cambridge University Press.

Edwards, D., and Mercer, N., "Reconstructing content: the conventionalisation of classroom knowledge." *Discourse Processes 12*, 1989.

Entwistle, N. J., "Understanding academic performance at University: a research retrospective", from D. Shorrocks-Taylor (ed.), *New Directions in Educational Psychology* (Whurr Publishers Limited, London, 1998).

Ericsson, K. A., "Attaining excellence through deliberate practice: insights from the study of expert performance." From M. Ferrari (ed.), _The Pursuit of Excellence in Education_ (Erlbaum, Hillsdale, NJ, in press).

Rogers, C., "Teacher expectations: implications for school improvement." From D. Shorrocks-Taylor (ed.), _New Directions in Educational Psychology_ (Whurr Publishers Limited, London, 1998).

Saxe, G. B., "Candy selling and math learning." _Educational Researcher_ _17_, 6, 1988. Reprinted by permission of the American Educational Researcher Association.

Shepard, L. A., "The role of assessment in a learning culture." _Educational Researcher 28_, 7, 2000. Reprinted by permission of the American Educational Researcher Association.

Siegler, R. S., "The rebirth of children's learning." _Child Development_ _71_, 1, 2000. The University of Michigan Press, Ann Arbor.

Wood, D., Wood, H., Ainsworth, S. and O'Malley, C., "On becoming a tutor: toward an ontogenetic model." _Cognition and Instruction 13_, 4, 1995.

Figures

Figure 1.1 From "Expertise," by K. A. Ericsson and Andreas C. Lehmann, in press, _Encyclopedia of Creativity_. Copyright by Academic Press.)

Figure 1.2 From "Expertise," by K. A. Ericsson and Andreas C. Lehmann, in press. _Encyclopedia of Creativity_. Copyright by Academic Press.

Figure 1.3 From "The role of deliberate practice in the acquisition of expert performance," by K. A. Ericsson, R. Th. Krampe, and C. Tesch-Römer. 1993, _Psychological Review, 100_, 3, 379 and 384. Copyright 1993 by American Psychological Association. Adapted with permission.

Figure 1.4 Adapted from "The scientific study of expert levels of performance: General implications for optimal learning and creativity," by K. A. Ericsson in *High Ability Studies*, 9, 90. Copyright 1998 by European Council for High Ability.

Figure 1.5   Copyright 1999 by K. Anders Ericsson.

Figure 1.6   From "Can we create gifted people?" by K. A. Ericsson, R. Th. Krampe, and S. Heizmann in *The origins and development of high ability* (pp. 222–249), 1993, Chichester, UK: Wiley. Copyright 1993 by CIBA Foundation. Adapted with permission.

Figure 1.7   From "The scientific study of expert levels of perform-ance: General implications for optimal learning and creativity" by K. A. Ericsson in *High Ability Studies*, 9, p. 92. Copyright 1998 by European Council for High Ability.

Introduction
Education and Psychology
Charles Desforges and Richard Fox

We take psychology to be the science of mind. The main project for scientific psychology is to provide fundamental understanding of how human minds work. It is an act of faith that such understanding could provide a basis on which to improve the human condition. In this respect, teachers and psychologists have something in common. Both, in their different ways, are interested in how people think, learn and remember. They are also interested in people's feelings and attitudes, in what switches them on and in what keeps them going when things get difficult. Psychologists attempt to understand these processes of human action and interaction. Teachers attempt to manipulate these processes for learners' individual benefit and for the common social good.

Teachers in training often make a special study of aspects of psychology, in particular those dealing with learning, thinking, motivation and interpersonal dynamics, on the assumption that psychological research in these fields provides an appropriate knowledge base for teachers' planning and classroom interactions. That being said, the relationship between the science of psychology and the technology of teaching is hotly contested. It is difficult in any field of science and technology to develop practical applications from theoretical knowledge. It is predictably more difficult to do so in settings such as teaching and learning, which involve the rapid interplay of human action.

In the early days of psychology as a social science there was a widely held belief, or hope, that psychologists would create theories of learning and teaching which would then simply be applied to educational settings. However, this view is no longer seen as realistic. It is true that there remains a conceptual connection between psychology and education, in that educationists always have to make assumptions of some kind about the nature of learning and of teaching and about the nature of human beings. Moreover, it is still reasonable for them to look to psychology in the hope of basing such assumptions on the best available knowledge. But psychology is not the only resource to which they may turn. The other social sciences, notably sociology, also make important contributions to educational debates and educational research itself has become a partly independent enterprise, with teachers, for example, actively engaged in researching their own professional practice. Thus psychology has to earn its place as a contributor to the debate.

Teachers themselves are not simple technicians, applying known procedures from a rule book, but complex thinking agents, with their own conflicting values and aspirations, their own experiences, beliefs and intuitions. Teaching is thus neither exactly a science nor an art. On the one hand, teachers have to make frequent, rapid decisions that involve probabilistic calculations and trade-offs between competing aims. Teaching thus involves a degree of spontaneity and improvisation. On the other hand, teachers are not operating in the dark, purely on the basis of some kind of inspirational creativity. They learn to have expectations about what is practicable which are based on knowledge and experience. In this connection, systematic empirical research can lay claim to being a particularly valuable kind of knowledge. However, a further difficulty relates to the specificity of educational events. It is not always clear how far it is reasonable to generalize from the findings of research in one educational setting to the teachers and learners in another.

And if we turn to psychology itself we find that here, too, there are debates about its scientific credentials and character. How far should it be attempting to provide general causal explanations of human behaviour? And how far should it be seeking, rather, to produce specific, well-grounded interpretations of human actions in particular social contexts? Thus, underlying a book such as this are three important questions:

1   To what extent can teaching become an evidence-based profession?

2   To what extent will the evidence used be supplied from the concep-
    tual and empirical resources of psychology?
3   What sort of psychology will be used in this enterprise?

Notwithstanding these difficulties we are persuaded that psychology
has a great deal to offer those whose job it is to promote learning in
educational settings. This set of readings is intended to illustrate some
of the riches psychology has to offer. We have been spoiled for choice.
In making our selections we have focused on research into the fundamental processes of learning and teaching. We have organized the
readings accordingly into two sections, the first on learning and
the second on teaching, although we recognize that when one speaks
on either of the topics one raises matters related to the other.

Learning

Introduction to Part I

There is a vast and growing psychological literature on learning, much of it developed from laboratory studies aimed at developing detailed models of cognitive processes. In making our selections we have focused on work which has studied learning involving more complex skills or bodies of knowledge acquired in real life or authentic settings. In the first chapter, Ericsson discusses the acquisition of expertise in music, sport, and in several academic subjects. In the second chapter Bryant et al. report work on aspects of learning to read in young children. In the third chapter, Siegler discusses the general application of learning strategies by very young children while in the fourth chapter Saxe reports work on the exploration of how children learn arithmetic out of school while working as street traders. In contrast, in the last chapter of this section, Entwistle surveys decades of his work concerning how university undergraduates approach their studies.

The work reported in this section exhibits a very wide range of research methods including experimental and quasi-experimental work, qualitative and quantitative data collection, observation and case study. As we have noted earlier, there is no easy way of converting the powerful insights and conclusions from these studies into classroom action for teachers or tutors, but it is none the less clear that the research reported here has powerful implications for teaching.

Expert Performance

Introduction

Expert performers constitute the practical limit of human endeavour. Educational systems strive to achieve excellence and experts are the best practical definition of what this entails. Ericsson's paper is an extended review of research on the nature and acquisition of expertise.

The study of expertise has always been embedded in the nature/nurture debate. Does one need innate ability to achieve expertise in a given field or is expert status open to all who are prepared to work hard enough? What is the relationship (if any) between effort and giftedness?

Teachers' beliefs in regard to these questions in part shape their teaching behaviours. If teachers believe in a bell-shaped, normal distribution curve of 'natural talent' then this entails that some students will succeed and some will fail no matter what efforts the teacher makes. The nature of expertise and teachers' understanding of expertise are thus crucial issues in shaping both the goals and processes of teaching. In this review, Ericsson considers these questions, arguing strongly that expert performance is predominantly determined by particular kinds of deliberate practice. The implications for teaching are profound. In Ericsson's view, talent can be created.

ONE

Attaining Excellence through Deliberate Practice: Insights from the Study of Expert Performance

K. Anders Ericsson

Almost everyone can remember being awed by the public performances of elite musicians and athletes. All of us have looked at sculp-
tures and paintings and read novels that clearly transcend a level of
performance that we and other people in our immediate environment
could attain. For a long time it has been considered obvious that some
individuals' ability to achieve at a level superior to that of other
motivated individuals must reflect an unobtainable difference, some
genetically determined, and therefore innate, talent. If there were no
immutable inborn limit, why wouldn't every highly motivated individual reach the highest level?

The most obvious approach to determining how individuals excel is to
study those who have achieved mastery. As I will show by quoting
international masters discussing excellence later in this chapter, most
masters emphasize the role of motivation, concentration, and the willingness to work hard on improving performance. In contrast to the
general population and less accomplished performers, the masters seem
to consider inborn capacities and innate talent as relatively unimportant in comparison to their attained abilities and skills. However, most
people who have unsuccessfully pursued high excellence in a domain
find it very difficult to accept the masters' emphasis on motivation and
the continued need to work hard in improving performance. Many of us

have worked hard to improve a skill over a period of weeks without catching up or perhaps not even markedly gaining on the individuals who perform at the highest levels. Could it be that the masters were praising motivation and effort due to false modesty? Perhaps they simply do not know the critical factors that lead them toward excellence.

In this chapter I will demonstrate how the masters' descriptions of the critical role played by motivation and willingness to work can be understood as a manifestation of the specially designed training activities that my colleagues and I refer to as deliberate practice (Ericsson, 1996, 1997, 1998; Ericsson & Charness, 1994; Ericsson, Krampe & Tesch-Römer, 1993; Ericsson & Lehmann, 1996). In the first section, I will argue that once we define excellence as consistently superior achievement in the core activities of a domain, an interpretable picture emerges. Even the level of achievement of the most "talented" develops gradually and, with rare exceptions, it takes at least ten years of active involvement within a domain to reach an international level. However, the vast majority of active individuals in a domains such as golf and tennis show minimal performance improvements even after decades of participation. In the second section, I will discuss the difference between mere participation in domain-related activities and activities designed to improve performance – deliberate practice.

The Scientific Study of Expert Performance

Many of the most dazzling and amazing accomplishments of geniuses, such as those by the famous musician, Paganini, and the famous mathematician, Gauss, refer to events that cannot be independently verified (Ericsson, 1996, 1997, 1998). Our only knowledge about most of these achievements is based on reports by the exceptional persons themselves, often in the form of anecdotes about their childhood told by the famous individual at the end of their career. Under these circumstances it would be reasonable to expect distortions of memory and even exaggerations. To study exceptional achievement scientifically, it is necessary that we disregard questionable anecdotes and focus on the empirical evidence that reflects stable phenomena that can be independently verified and, ideally, reproduced under controlled circumstances. Once we restrict the research findings to this clearly defined empirical evidence then reviews (Ericsson & Lehmann, 1996;

Ericsson & Smith, 1991) show an orderly and consistent body of knowledge even for exceptional achievements and performance.

In most domains of expertise, individuals have been interested in assessing the level of performance under fair and controlled circumstances. In athletic competitions, this has resulted in highly standardized conditions that approach the controlled conditions used to study performance in the laboratory. In a similar manner, musicians, dancers, and chess players perform under controlled conditions during competitions and tournaments. These competitions serve several purposes beyond identifying the best performers and presenting awards. For younger performers, successful performance at competitions is necessary to gain access to the best teachers and training environments which, in turn, increases the chances of attaining one of the small number of openings as full-time professionals in the domain.

Ericsson and Smith (1991) discussed how one could use similar techniques to measure various types of professional expertise. More recent reviews show that efforts to demonstrate the superior performance of experts are not always successful. For example, highly experienced psychotherapists are not more successful in treatment of patients than novice therapists (Dawes, 1994). More generally, the length of professional experience after completed training has often been found to be a weak predictor of performance in representative professional activities, such as medical diagnosis (Norman, Coblentz, Brooks, Babcook, 1992; Schmidt, Norman & Boshuizen, 1990), auditing (Bédard & Chi, 1993; Bonner & Pennington, 1991), text editing (Rosson, 1985), and judgment and decision making (Camerer & Johnson, 1991; Shanteau & Stewart, 1992). If we are interested in understanding the structure and acquisition of excellence in the representative activities that define expertise in a given domain, we need to restrict ourselves to domains in which experts exhibit objectively superior performance.

If expert performers can reliably reproduce their performance in public, it is likely that they could do the same during training, and even under laboratory conditions, a finding confirmed by recent research (Ericsson & Lehmann, 1996). Unfortunately, the conditions of naturally occurring expert performance are quite complex and frequently differ markedly among performers within a domain. For example, musicians are allowed to select their own pieces of music for their performance and the sequence of moves chess players make in a game is never the same. However, most domains of expertise require that experts are able to excel at certain types of representative tasks or else they would not meet the definition of a true expert. Ericsson and Smith (1991) discussed how to identify representative tasks that capture the essence of expert performance in a domain and how to reproduce this performance under controlled laboratory conditions so that investigators could identify the responsible mediating mechanisms.

Figure 1.1 illustrates three types of tasks that have been found to capture the essence of expertise, where the measured performance is closely related to the level of naturally occurring performance. To study chess expertise, players at different skill levels are asked to generate the best move for the same unfamiliar chess positions. Typists are

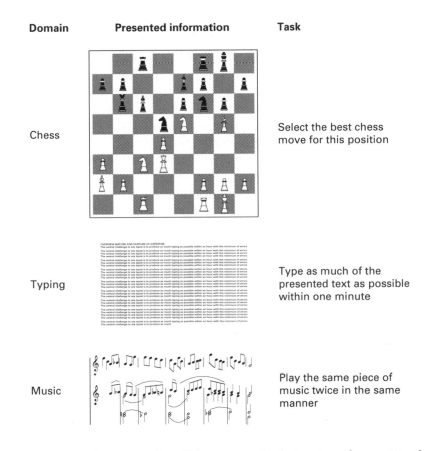

Domain   **Presented information**   **Task**

Chess — Select the best chess move for this position

Typing — Type as much of the presented text as possible within one minute

Music — Play the same piece of music twice in the same manner

Figure 1.1   Three examples of laboratory tasks that capture the consistently superior performance of domain experts in chess, typing and music

given the same material to type as fast as possible. Musicians are asked to play familiar or unfamiliar pieces, then asked to repeat their performance. When musicians are instructed to repeat their original performance, experts can do it with much less deviation than less skilled musicians, thus exhibiting greater control over their performance.

When we consider only the superior performance of experts, it is possible to identify several claims about expertise that generalize across domains. First, I will review evidence showing that superior expert performance is primarily acquired, and that extensive domain-related experience is necessary but not sufficient for its development. I will show that many thousands of hours of deliberate practice and training are necessary to reach the highest levels of performance. Then I will describe in depth the cognitive and physiological processes proposed to mediate the development of expert performance and show how deliberate practice optimizes the effect of these processes on performance.

The necessity of domain-specific experience

Recent reviews (Ericsson, 1996; Ericsson & Lehmann, 1996) show that extended engagement in domain-related activities is necessary to attain expert performance in that domain. What is the process in acquiring expertise? First, longitudinal assessments of performance reveal that performance improves gradually, as illustrated in Figure 1.2; there is no objective evidence for high initial level of performance without any relevant experience and practice nor for abrupt improvement of reproducible performance when it is regularly tested. Even the performance of child prodigies in music and chess, whose performance is vastly superior to that of their peers, show gradual, steady improvement over time. If elite performance was limited primarily by the functional capacity of the body and brain, one would expect performance to peak around the age of physical maturation – the late teens in industrialized countries. However, experts' best performance is often attained many years, and even decades, later, as illustrated in Figure 1.2. The age at which performers typically reach their highest level of performance in many vigorous sports is the mid- to late 20s; for the arts and science, it is a decade later, in the 30s and 40s (see Simonton, 1997, for a review). Continued, often extended, development of expertise past physical maturity shows that experience is necessary for improving the experts' performance. Finally, the most compelling evidence for the role of vast

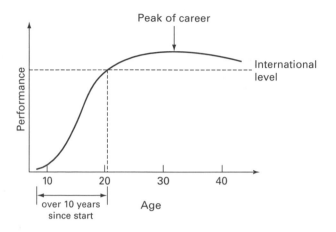

Figure 1.2   An illustration of the gradual increases in expert performance as a function of age in domains such as chess. The international level, which is attained after more than around ten years of involvement in the domain, is indicated by the horizontal dashed line

experience in expertise is that even the most "talented" need around ten years of intense involvement before they reach an international level, and for most individuals it takes considerably longer.

Simon and Chase (1973) originally proposed the ten-year rule, showing that no modern chess master had reached the international level in less than approximately ten years of playing. Subsequent reviews show that the ten-year rule extends to music composition, as well as to sports, science, and arts (Ericsson, Krampe & Tesch-Römer, 1993). In sum, the fact that engagement in specific, domain-related activities is necessary to acquire expertise is well established. Most importantly, given that very few individuals sustain commitment for more than a few months, much less years, most individuals will never know the upper limit of their performance.

Going beyond mere experience: activities that mediate improvements of performance

Extensive experience and involvement in a domain is necessary for the select group of elite individuals who steadily increase their perform-ance and reach very high levels. In contrast, the vast majority of individuals struggle to reach an acceptable level of performance, and having done so, allow their performance to remain relatively stable for years and even decades. Consider the example of recreational golfers, tennis players and skiers. The striking difference between elite and average performance seems to result not just from the duration of an individual's activity, but from the particular types of domain-related activities they choose.

From retrospective interviews of international-level performers in many domains, Bloom (1985) showed that elite performers are typically introduced to their future domain in a playful manner. As soon as they enjoy the activity and show promise compared to peers in the neighborhood, they are encouraged to seek out a teacher and initiate regular practice. Bloom and his colleagues show the importance of access to the best training environments and the most qualified teachers. The parents of the future elite performers spend large sums of money for teachers and equipment, and devote considerable time to escorting their child to training and weekend competitions. In some cases, the performer and their family even relocate to be closer to the teacher and the training facilities. Based on their interviews, Bloom (1985) argued that access to the best training resources was necessary to reach the highest levels.

Given the limited opportunities available to work with the best teachers and training resources, only the most qualified individuals are admitted at each stage. Could it be that the superior training resources do not really enhance the rate of improvement and the highly selected individuals would improve just as well by themselves? The best single source of evidence for the value of current training methods comes from historical comparisons (Ericsson et al., 1993; Lehmann & Ericsson, 1998). The most dramatic improvements in the level of performance over historical time are found in sports. In some events, such as the marathon and swimming events, many serious amateurs of today could easily beat the gold medal winners of the early Olympic Games. For example, after the IVth Olympic Games in 1908, they almost prohibited the double somersault in dives because they believed that these dives were dangerous and no human would ever be able to control them. Similarly, some music compositions deemed nearly impossible to play in the 19th century have become part of the standard repertoire today. Exceptional levels of performance are originally attained only by a single eminent performer. However, after some time other individuals are able to figure out training methods so they can attain that same level of performance. Eventually, this training becomes part of regular instruction and all elite performers in the domain are expected to attain the new higher standard. In competitive domains, such as baseball, it is sometimes difficult to demonstrate the increased level of today's performers because both the level of the pitcher and batter has improved concurrently (Gould, 1996).

If the best individuals in a discipline already differ from other individuals at the start of training with master teachers and coaches, how can we explain these differences in performance prior to this advanced level? Can we also explain individual differences in the rate of improvement among individuals in the same training environment? To determine which activities could improve individuals' performance development prior to advanced training, we should first consider activities with conditions beneficial to learning and effective performance improvement. A century of laboratory research has revealed that learning is most effective when it includes focused goals, such as improving a specific aspect of performance; feedback that compares the actual to the desired performance; and opportunities for repetition, so the desired level of performance can be achieved.

Based on interviews with expert violinists at the music academy in Berlin, my colleagues and I (Ericsson et al., 1993) identified activities for which we could trace the duration of the music students' engagement during the period prior to their entry in the music academy. We were particularly interested in those activities which had been specifically designed to improve performance, which we called deliberate practice. A prime example of deliberate practice is the music students' solitary practice in which they work to master specific goals determined by their music teacher at weekly lessons. We were able to compare the time use among several groups of musicians differing in their level of music performance, based on daily diaries and retrospective estimates. Even among these expert groups we were able to find that the most accomplished musicians had spent more time in activities classified as deliberate practice during their development (see Figure 1.3) and that these differences were reliably observable before their admittance to the academy at around age 18. By the age of 20, the best musicians had spent over 10,000 hours practicing, which is 2,500 and 5,000 hours more than two less

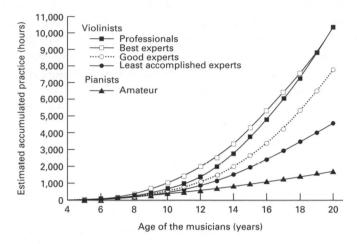

Figure 1.3 Estimated amount of time for solitary practice as a function of age for the middle-aged *professional* violinists (triangles), the *best* expert violinists (squares), the *good* expert violinists (empty circles), the *least accomplished* expert violinists (filled circles) and *amateur* pianists (diamonds)

accomplished groups of expert musicians, respectively, and 8,000 hours more than amateur pianists of the same age (Krampe & Ericsson, 1996).

Several studies and reviews have found a consistent relation between performance level and the quality and amount of deliberate practice in chess (Charness, Krampe & Mayr, 1996), sports (Helsen, Starkes & Hodges, 1998; Hodges & Starkes, 1996; Starkes et al., 1996) and music (Krampe & Ericsson, 1996; Lehmann & Ericsson, 1996; Sloboda, 1996). The concept of deliberate practice also provides accounts for many earlier findings in other domains, such as medicine, soft-ware design, bridge, snooker, typing, and exceptional memory performance (Ericsson & Lehmann, 1996), as well as for the results from the rare longitudinal studies of elite performers (Schneider, 1993).

When most people imagine a child practicing the piano, they tend to think of someone mindlessly repeating the same short piece, while the sound remains unmusical, aversive, and without any noticeable improvement. Nobody in their right mind would argue that poor or mediocre piano students could become outstanding musicians merely by spending more time on this type of mechanical practice. Mindless repetition is the direct opposite of deliberate practice, when individuals concentrate on actively trying to go beyond their current abilities. Consistent with the mental demands of problem solving and other types of learning, deliberate practice is done in limited periods of intense concentration. Diaries of the expert musicians revealed that they only engaged in practice without rest for around an hour and they preferred to practice early in the morning when their minds were fresh (Ericsson et al., 1993). Even more interesting, the best expert musicians were found to practice, on the average, the same amount every day, including weekends, and the amount of practice never consistently exceeded 4 to 5 hours per day. The experts told us during interviews that it was primarily their ability to sustain the concentration necessary for deliberate practice that limited their hours of practice. And their diaries reveal that the more the experts practiced, the more time they spent resting and sleeping – the increased sleep was primarily in the form of afternoon naps. Our review of other research (Ericsson et al., 1993) showed that the limit of 4–5 hours of daily deliberate practice or similarly demanding activities held true for a wide range of elite performers in different domains, such as writing by famous authors (Cowley, 1959; Plimpton, 1977), as did their increased tendency to take recuperative naps. Furthermore, unless the daily levels of practice were restricted, such that subsequent rest and nighttime sleep allowed the individual to restore their equilibrium, individuals would encounter overtraining injuries, and eventually incapacitating "burnout."

Do the best performers in a domain also need deliberate practice to perfect their skills, or are they fundamentally different? Fortunately, many of the famous musicians and acclaimed music teachers have been interviewed about the structure of their practice. Their answers are remarkably consistent and are eloquently summarized by one of the best-known violin teachers and virtuosi, Emil Sauer (1913, p. 238): "One hour of concentrated practice with the mind fresh and the body rested is better than four hours of dissipated practice with the mind stale and the body tired. . . . I find in my own daily practice that it is best for me to practice two hours in the morning and then two hours later in the day. When I am finished with two hours of hard study I am exhausted from close concentration. I have also noted that any time over this period is wasted."

It is clear that the need for specific types of practice, such as etudes and scales, diminishes for musicians who have already attained technical mastery, but not the need for deliberate practice in mastering new pieces: "With the limited time I have to practice nowadays, I apply myself immediately to works that I am preparing," writes Katims (1972, p. 238) and argues that mastering pieces for upcoming concerts presents the specific challenges that guide deliberate practice. Many elite musicians are able to engage in mental practice: "I have a favorite silent study that I do all of the time, I do it before I start practicing. I do it on the train during my travel, and before I come out on the platform. I do it constantly" (Primrose, 1972, p. 248). With such a generalized definition of practice, even the famous violinist, Fritz Kreisler (1972, p. 98), who claimed to have never "practiced," would have engaged in practice: "How sad it is that in these days the emphasis is on how many hours one practices. When the Elgar concerto was dedicated to me I never put a finger on the fingerboard. Then I saw a passage I thought I could improve, and spent six hours on it."

The necessity of concentration for successful practice is recognized by all adult performers and some of them can even recall when they gained that insight: "For the first five years of musical experience, I simply played the piano. I played everything, sonatas, concertos – everything; large works were absorbed from one lesson to the next. When I was about twelve I began to awake to the necessity for serious study; then I really began to practice in earnest" (Schnitzer, 1915, p. 217). In fact, many of the individual differences among young music students practicing the same amount of time may be attributable to differences in the quality of their practice. The famous violin teacher Ivan Galamian (1972, p. 351) argued: "If we analyze the development of the well-known artists, we see that in almost every case the success of their entire career was dependent upon the quality of their practicing. In practically each case, the practicing was constantly supervised either by the teacher or an assistant to the teacher. The lesson is not all. Children do not know how to work alone. The teacher must constantly teach the child how to practice."

Recent analyses of famous child prodigies in music showed that all of them had been closely supervised from a young age by skilled musicians (Lehmann, 1997; Lehmann & Ericsson, 1998). The supervising adult could then guide the young child's attention by appropriate activities and also help eliminate mistakes and poor technique. Equally important, the adult could monitor the child's attention and never push the child beyond their ability to sustain concentration. Thus, the training would be restricted to relatively brief periods at the start of systematic training. More generally, Starkes et al. (1996) showed that the duration of daily training given future expert performers was very similar across several domains, such as music and sports. During the first year, the daily level of practice was around 15–30 minutes, on average, with steady increases for each additional year, reaching 4–5 hours after around a decade. Starkes et al. found an intriguing similarity between increases in the amount of practice for sports when the athletes started practice around age 12, and music, when start of practice is closer to 6–7 years of age. If this pattern of results is found consistently across all domains, it would suggest that the level of increased training may require a slow physiological adaptation to the demands of sustained practice, which may be relatively insensitive to chronological age.

We have shown that the attainment of expert performance requires an extended period of high-level deliberate practice, where the duration of practice is limited by the ability to sustain concentration, a capacity which appears to increase as function of years of practice in the domain. Consequently, a certain amount of deliberate practice may be necessary to reach the highest performance levels, and individual differences, even among experts, may reflect differences in the amount and quality of practice. However, most people would argue that there are distinct limits to the influence of practice, and that inborn capacities and innate talent will play a very important role in determining performance, especially at the highest levels within a domain. It has even been proposed by Sternberg (1996) that individuals with more innate talent would be more successful during practice, and thus more willing to engage in practice – possibly explaining at least part of the relation between amount of deliberate practice and performance.

In the remainder of this chapter, I will propose how various types of training activities can, over time, change the body according to well-understood physiological principles and that expert performance can be viewed as the end product of an extended series of psychological modifications and physiological adaptations. Most proposed individual differences between elite performers that have been attributed to innate talent can more parsimoniously be explained as adaptations to extended, intense practice. Furthermore, I will explain how expert performance is mediated by complex memory mechanisms and representations which have been acquired as a result of practice, and how these mechanisms are critical to continued performance improvement.

Everyday skills and expert performance: the acquisition of integrated appropriate actions

Everyday skills and expert performance require that individuals efficiently generate appropriate actions when needed. A comprehensive theory needs to describe both the similarities and differences in the acquisition of everyday skills and expert performance. How individuals are able to acquire everyday life skills, such as typing, playing tennis, or driving a car, is extensively researched and well understood. It is therefore easiest to briefly review theories of everyday skill acquisition, then describe how the acquisition of expert performance differs.

The traditional theories of skill acquisition (Anderson, 1982, 1987; Fitts & Posner, 1967) propose that during the initial "cognitive" phase (see Figure 1.4) individuals learn the underlying structure of the activity and what aspects they must attend to. In the early stages of learning the activity, they get clear feedback about their misunderstandings as they make mistakes. Gradually they become able to avoid gross errors, and eventually, during the second "associative" phase, they can attain an acceptable level of performance. During the third and final "autonomous" phase, their goal is typically to achieve effortless performance as rapidly as possible. After some limited period of training and experience – frequently less than 50 hours for most recreational activities, such as skiing, tennis and driving a car – an acceptable standard of performance can be generated without much need for effortful attention. At this point, execution of the everyday activity has attained many characteristics of automated performance (Anderson, 1982, 1987; Fitts & Posner, 1967; Shiffrin & Schneider, 1977), and requires only minimal effort.

Figure 1.4 illustrates the transition from the first stage, when everyday performance initially improves as individuals expend effort to reach an acceptable level, to adaptation as their performance becomes automatized, and the performance level fixated, as individuals lose conscious control over intentionally modifying and changing it. Everyone can easily recall from their childhood and adolescence how many hours of rote memorization of the alphabet, the multiplication tables,

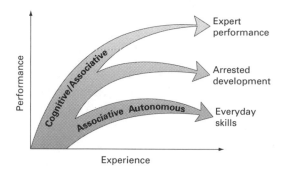

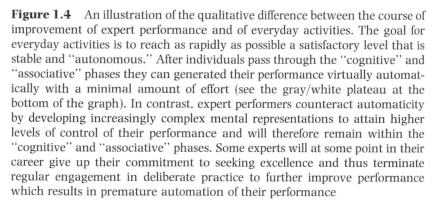

Figure 1.4 An illustration of the qualitative difference between the course of improvement of expert performance and of everyday activities. The goal for everyday activities is to reach as rapidly as possible a satisfactory level that is stable and "autonomous." After individuals pass through the "cognitive" and "associative" phases they can generated their performance virtually automatically with a minimal amount of effort (see the gray/white plateau at the bottom of the graph). In contrast, expert performers counteract automaticity by developing increasingly complex mental representations to attain higher levels of control of their performance and will therefore remain within the "cognitive" and "associative" phases. Some experts will at some point in their career give up their commitment to seeking excellence and thus terminate regular engagement in deliberate practice to further improve performance which results in premature automation of their performance

and foreign vocabulary items are necessary for direct retrieval from memory. Once this occurs, increased experience will not be associated with increased accuracy. Within this simple view of skill acquisition, it is inevitable that the major improvements are limited to the first phases, but then performance reaches a stable automatic level determined by factors that are believed to be outside the individuals' control. Individual differences are thus believed to reflect stable immutable differences, such as innate capacities and neural speed.

This popular conception of how everyday skills are acquired has little in common with our view of the acquisition of expert performance through deliberate practice. In contrast to the rapid automatization of everyday skills and the emergence of a stable asymptote for performance, expert performance continues to improve as a function of increased experience and deliberate practice, as a illustrated in Figure 1.4. One of the most crucial challenges for aspiring expert performers is to avoid the arrested development associated with generalized automaticity of performance and to acquire cognitive skills to support continued learning and improvement. Expert performers counteract the arrested development associated with automaticity by deliberately acquiring and refining cognitive mechanisms to support continued learning and improvement. These mechanisms increase experts' control and ability to monitor performance. The expert has to continue to design training situations where the goal is to attain a level beyond their current performance in order to keep improving. There are many methods for discovering new and higher levels of performance (Ericsson, 1996). One common method involves comparing one's performance to that of more proficient individuals in their domain of expertise. One can then identify differences and then attempt to reduce them gradually through extended deliberate practice.

In the next section I will show that expert performance is not fully automated. I will first briefly summarize empirical evidence demonstrating that experts retain cognitive control over detailed aspects of their performance at the highest levels and that experts rely on acquired representations to support planning and reasoning (Ericsson & Delaney, 1999). These cognitive representations allow the experts to generate internal images of a desired performance without having experienced it before and to design plans for producing a similar performance without having previously done so. In a second subsection I will then discuss how future experts acquire representations, and how these representations allow them to identify new goals so they can continue improving their performance. These representations form the foundation for continued learning without teachers, and ultimately, allow for the very best of them to make innovative creative contributions to their domain of expertise.

The cognitive mediation of expert performance

An everyday skill like driving one's car to work is typically viewed as a means to an end, where the goals of the activity concern safety and minimization of effort. These goals differ completely from those for expert-performance version of that activity, such as professionals driving race cars. Like other expert performers, race car drivers have to maintain full concentration as they try to push the limits of their best performance during training and competition without unduly increasing the risks for accidents.

To reach their highest possible level of performance, expert performers make adjustments appropriate to specific opponents or performance situations. For example, experts routinely make extensive adjustments to accommodate situational factors, such as weather and new equipment. A concert pianist will familiarize themselves with the piano and the acoustics of a concert hall. An expert billiard player will carefully examine any peculiarities of the billiard table before competing on it. Expert performers often study and prepare for competition against particular opponents, identifying their weaknesses to gain competitive advantage. As part of their expertise they are able to make fast, fluent adjustments to changes in their opponents' strategies. None of these adjustments would be possible if expert performance were fully automated. Furthermore, expert performers are well known for having accurate, detailed memories of their performance long after the competitions, which would be impossible if their performance during those events had been automated.

The most compelling scientific evidence for preserved cognitive control of expert performance comes from laboratory studies where experts reproduce their superior performance with representative tasks that capture the essence of expertise in their domain (Ericsson & Smith, 1991). In his pioneering work on expertise, de Groot (1946/1978) instructed good and world-class chess players to think aloud while selecting the best move to a set of unfamiliar chess positions. He found that the quality of selected moves was closely associated with the performers' chess skill. From verbal reports, he found that the chess players first perceived, then interpreted the chess position, and rapidly retrieved potential moves from memory. The moves were then evaluated by planning where the consequences of each move were explored by generating sequences of plausible counter moves using a mental representation of a chess board. During the course of this evaluation even the world-class players would discover better moves. Consequently, experts' defining ability to generate better moves for chess positions than less skilled players (see Figure 1.1) depends to a large extent on deliberate planning and reasoning, as well as on careful evaluation, in order to reduce the frequency of mistakes.

In sum, Ericsson and Lehmann (1996) found that experts' think-aloud protocols revealed how superior performance was mediated by deliberate preparation, planning, reasoning, and evaluation in a wide range of domains, such as medicine, computer programming, sports, and games. Therefore, the performance of experts cannot be completely automated, but remains mediated by complex control processes.

Recent reviews (Ericsson, 1996; Ericsson & Kintsch, 1995) show that individuals who perform at higher levels utilize specific kinds of memory processes. They have acquired refined mental representations to maintain access to relevant information and support more extensive, flexible reasoning about encountered tasks or situations. In most domains, better performers are able to rapidly encode, store, and manipulate relevant information for representative tasks in memory (Ericsson & Lehmann, 1996). To illustrate this ability, I will describe a couple of examples from two different domains. With increased skill, chess players are able to do deep planning, to mentally generate longer sequences of chess moves and evaluate their consequences (Charness, 1981). Chess masters are even able to hold the image of the chess position in mind so accurately that they can play blindfold chess – play without perceptually available chessboards.

Similar evidence for mental representations has been shown for motor-skill experts, such as snooker players and musicians. In a recent study, Lehmann and Ericsson (1995, 1997) had expert pianists memorize a short piece of music. The pianists were then given an unexpected series of tasks in which they were asked to reproduce the piece at the same tempo under changed conditions, such as playing every other measure, and playing notes with only one hand. Although reliable individual differences were observed, accuracy was uniformly very high. Many subjects were even able to accurately transpose the music into a different key at regular tempo when unexpectedly asked to do so. During accurate transposition performance, the pianists pressed different piano keys with new finger combinations, which demonstrates mediation of a flexible memory representation of the music. In sum, the essence of expert performance is a generalized skill at successfully meeting the demands of new situations and rapidly adapting to changing conditions.

Even expert performance in activities where superior speed is the criterion, such as typing (see Figure 1.1), appears to depend primarily on mediating representations rather than faster basic speed of neurons and muscles. The superior speed of expert typists is related to how far they look ahead in the text beyond the word that they are currently typing, as illustrated in Figure 1.5. With increased acquired skill, expert typists can look further ahead in the text so they can prepare

Typing expertise

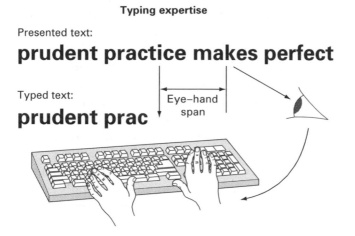

Figure 1.5 An illustration of how the eyes of expert typists fixate material in the text well in advance of the currently typed text in order to gain advantages by advance preparation

future keystrokes in advance, moving relevant fingers toward their desired locations on the keyboard. The importance of anticipatory processing has been confirmed by analysis of high-speed films of expert typists and experimental studies where expert typists have been restricted from looking ahead. Furthermore, the further someone looks ahead in a text when asked to read aloud rapidly, the higher their ability to read and the faster their silent reading speed (Levin & Addis, 1979).

Similarly, the rapid reactions of athletes, such as hockey goalies, tennis players and hitters in baseball, have been found to reflect skills acquired primarily to avoid time stress by successfully anticipating future events (Abernethy, 1991). This evidence supports the hypothesis that expert athletes have a learned, rather than a biological, speed advantage over their less accomplished peers. For example, when skilled tennis players are preparing to return a serve, they study the movements of the opponent leading up to contact between the ball and the racquet to identify the type of spin and the general direction. Given the ballistic nature of a serve, it is often possible for skilled players to accurately anticipate the consequences of these movements. It is important to note that novice tennis players use an entirely different strategy, and usually initiate their preparations to return the ball once it is sufficiently close to see where it will bounce. If the cues that immediately precede ball contact had become fully automated to guide the hitting of the ball, anticipatory perceptual skills would never develop. The anticipatory use of predictive cues must have been acquired later at more advanced level of skill. The superior anticipation of the ball trajectory has frequently been misinterpreted as evidence for superior basic perceptual capacity. It is a common misconception that elite athletes have more accurate vision that allows them to see the balls better, when, in fact, their performance reflects a highly specialized perceptual skill. Consistent with this hypothesis elite athletes are not consistently superior on standard vision tests compared to less accomplished performers and other control groups.

The increasingly refined representations allow expert performers to attain more control of relevant aspects of performance and greater ability to anticipate, plan, and reason about alternative courses of action. In addition to providing better control, these mental representations play an essential role in helping individuals continue improving their performance: setting new goals for improvement, monitoring their performance, and refining skills necessary to maintaining the integrity and fluency of their current level of superior performance during continued learning. How are these representations acquired during development? Are there special training activities that allow individuals to refine them?

The acquisition of representations that mediate the attainment of expert performance

The most important differences between autonomous everyday skills and expert performance are related to the experts' representations that allow them to keep controlling and monitoring their behavior. In an earlier section I showed that there is a natural tendency toward developing effortless automatized performance in which mediating representations are not required. Fluent repeated performance appears to become highly automated unless the individual actively resists. I will argue that experts and aspiring experts rely on deliberate practice to counteract complete automatization and to promote the development and refinement of representations. First, I will briefly discuss how the mediating representations are acquired from the start of supervised practice to the attainment of domain expertise. I will then discuss a few specific examples of how deliberate practice refines both representations and the associated skills to improve the integrated performance.

In many domains of expertise, individuals are introduced into the domain as children and after a short period of playful interaction the future expert performers start working with a teacher (see Figure 1.6 illustrating the three stages proposed by Bloom (1985)). The playful interaction will not stop but it will be augmented by deliberate practice. When beginners are initially introduced to practice in a domain, the teacher instructs them using very simple objectives and tasks and will explicitly guide the beginners' attention to specific aspects of the training situations as part of the instruction. The beginner – often aided by a parent – must learn to regenerate the goals of the training activity and sustain focus on attaining them through repeated attempts.

The assigned goal of the training activity also provides the beginners with a means to generate feedback about the correctness of their performance, which would imply some mental representation although not necessarily a sophisticated one. During development, teachers often help their students identify errors and make necessary changes and specific corrections. As the students' performance improves, they acquire more complex representations to monitor and control the aspects of performance targeted by the teacher for correction during solitary practice. As the complexity of the acquired performance level increases, so does the complexity of practice goals and the associated training activities. At higher levels, the teacher will provide primarily general instructions and feedback, which requires the students to monitor their own performance, to actively engage in problem solving as errors occur, and to make appropriate adjustments to their performance. Hence, parallel to improvement of their performance, students develop complex mental representations of the desired performance so they can monitor their concurrent performance to identify discrepancies between their desired and actual performance (Ericsson, 1996; Glaser, 1996). As students reach high levels of achievement, they will have acquired the knowledge of their teachers and have mental representations that enable them to independently monitor and improve their performance. They may also augment the training methods of their teachers by studying the performance and achievements of current and past

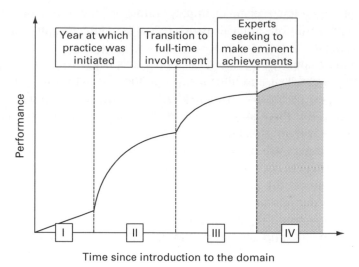

Figure 1.6 Three phases of acquisition of expert performance, followed by a qualitatively different fourth phase when, in order to make a creative contribution, experts attempt to go beyond the available knowledge in the domain

masters in their domain (Ericsson, 1996, 1997). When individuals have mastered all the knowledge and techniques of their domain (see the fourth phase in Figure 1.6), they are uniquely positioned to have a chance to make major creative contributions by adding something genuinely new, whether it is new idea, new training method or a new interpretation of past achievements. This type of creative expansion of the space of conceivable achievements and accumulated knowledge in a specific domain represent the supreme level of achievement in any domain.

We still have an incomplete understanding of representations, how they are acquired and refined, and their close connection to performance, but I will illustrate their involvement in deliberate practice with a few examples from chess, copying, and music.

Deliberate practice in chess: planning and anticipating the consequences of an opponent's actions

Once an individual has reached a level of proficiency in a domain, when they are better than everyone else in the chess club, for example, how can they be challenged to find increasingly better chess moves? Expert chess players have been shown to collect books and magazines with the recorded games of chess masters (Charness et al., 1996). They can play through the games to see if their selected moves correspond to those originally selected by the masters. If the chess master's move differed from their own, it would imply that they must have missed something in their planning and evaluation. Through careful, extended analysis the chess expert is generally able to discover the reasons for the chess master's move. Similarly, the chess player can read published analyses of various opening combinations and supplement their own knowledge by examining the consequences of new variations of these openings. Serious chess players spend as much as four hours every day engaged in this type of solitary study (Charness et al., 1996; Ericsson et al., 1993).

Deliberate practice in typing: a focus on improving copying speed

Once an individual has reached a stable typing speed, how can it be increased? During normal typing activities it is important to minimize errors and maintain a typing speed that can be sustained. On the other hand, typists can for short intervals sustain higher speeds with full concentration – at least 10 to 30% above normal rates. Consequently, the recommended practice to improve speed is setting aside time daily to type selected materials at the faster rate without concern about accuracy. Initially typists seem only to be able to sustain the concentration necessary to type 10 to 20% faster than normal speed for 10 to 15 minutes per day. After adaptation to this kind of regular practice, the duration of the training sessions can be increased (cf. the earlier discussion of the development of weekly practice time). When typists push themselves beyond the comfortable range of reliable typing, they will encounter key-stroke combinations that slow them down, causing hesitations or awkward motor movements. By eliminating the specific problems through better anticipation or coordination of motor behavior, these problems can be corrected. Typists can then iteratively confront remaining typing combinations that limit typing speed. The recommended training to improve speed in other perceptual motor activities shares many of these same methods of progressive improvement.

Deliberate practice in expert music performance: the importance of mental representations for monitoring performance

Let us consider the different types of mental representations that are necessary for advanced music performers. For example, musicians must be able to internally represent many aspects involved in mastering the interpretation of a new piece of music. Three of them are illustrated in Figure 1.7: the performer's image of how they want a given performance to sound to the audience, their plan of how the instrument should be played to achieve this goal, and their capacity to monitor the produced sound as they practice to produce the desired performance (Ericsson, 1997).

The importance of these representations and, in particular, the key role of critical listening to one's music performance, have been recognized and articulated by master teachers. "One of the greatest difficulties which stand in the way of progress is the failure to hear what one is doing at the piano . . . When the moment comes that the pupil actually hears what he is doing, consciousness is awakened and the progress begins" (Buhlig, 1917, p. 218). Critical listening remains equally important at advanced levels. "In his practicing, the real art is for the pupil to acquire the uncanny ability to listen to his own work, to discover his own minute failing" (Szigeti, 1972, p. 205). Even experts must be wary of the risk of reducing the level of concentration and lowering their performance criteria. "The habit of not listening becomes worse and worse, and in a short time the player is unconscious

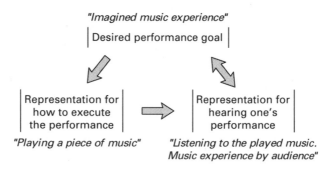

Figure 1.7 Three types of internal representations that mediate expert music performance and its continued improvement during practice

of the slight inaccuracies in pitch. There is listening, and listening *intently"* (Tertis, 1972, p. 267). Expert musicians actively try to counteract the threat of automaticity and reliance on habitual performance. The famous cellist Pablo Casals carefully prepared and studied even very familiar music pieces before playing them in public. "To play it perfectly every piece should be studied with the constant idea of improvement in mind, and it is seldom, working in this way, that I do not find that I can improve some one or another detail" (Casals, 1923, p. 234). Working out the intended music experience in detail allows the musician to carefully monitor their performance. "I try to form an ideal conception of the piece, work this out in every detail, then always endeavor to render it as closely like the ideal as possible" (Lerner, 1915, p. 46). And perfection is never permanently attained. "I never neglect an opportunity to improve, no matter how perfect a previous interpretation may have seemed to me. In fact, I often go directly home from a concert and practice for hours upon the very pieces that I have been playing, because during the concert certain new ideas have come to me" (Busoni, 1913, p. 106).

Individual differences in the acquired representations responsible for musical abilities, such as sight-reading, rapid memorization of music, and improvisation, are frequently attributed to musical talent, perhaps because it has been difficult to understand how such abilities are acquired (Bamberger, 1991). However, there are several theoretically and empirically supported accounts of how they are acquired through practice-related activities (Lehmann & Ericsson, 1993, 1995, 1996; Sudnow, 1978).

In sum, the superficial characteristics of deliberate practice are unimportant and differ greatly across as well as within domains but the defining common feature of deliberate practice refers to its ability to change and improve performance and will therefore depend on the desired changes in achievement. Once upon a time all effective methods for deliberate practice must have been discovered by individuals who experimented with different methods for practice. Today students do not need to rediscover these training techniques but they are passed along by their teachers and coaches. Recent accounts (Ericsson, 1996; Zimmerman, 1994) of the development of past and current masters describe how these individuals were able to invent techniques to increase their mastery of skilled activities with minimal instruction and external support. This type of extended self-guided search for effective practice methods in a domain is likely to foster the development of representations that benefit subsequent development of expertise supervised by skilled teachers.

Expert performers' learning: generalizable aspects and specific implementations

For anyone interested in general mechanisms mediating learning, the most striking findings from the study of expert performance concern its domain specificity and diversity. Not only does deliberate practice differ between domains, the particular training that would be optimal for individual experts within a domain will differ and depend on the individual's strengths and weaknesses. For this reason, training in most domains is designed to develop independent performers so they can find their own path toward expertise through reflective self-evaluation and problem solving. In fact, individual differences and diversity are encouraged at the highest levels to prepare elite performers to go beyond the accumulated knowledge in their domain and extend its boundaries through major innovations.

Is it possible to extract some generalizable principles for experts' learning in light of this striking variability and diversity? Many significant efforts have been made to extract concepts, mechanisms and characteristics of effective learning in the fields of education and professional development. Many of those findings capture several generalizable characteristics of experts' learning and deliberate practice: changes in behavior and performance are facilitated by setting specific attainable goals (Locke & Latham, 1984), effective students optimize improvement by designing and monitoring their learning activities (Schunk & Zimmerman, 1994), and learning should be mindful and reflective, striving toward genuine understanding, rather than mindless memorization (Langer, 1997). These three abstract characteristics reveal important higher-level differences between how experts and amateurs tend to learn, and focus on necessary characteristics of effective learning and thus explain why the learn ing of the amateurs tends to be limited. How much of the experts' efficient learning is explained by these characteristics? Would it be possible to induce effective learning by merely instructing the amateurs to change the methods for learning? If not, which conditions and prerequisites are necessary for efficient types of learning?

The study of the acquisition of expert performance gives us insight into these issues. The more we learn about the development of expert performance in specific domains, the better our understanding of prerequisites for effective learning. First, before reflective monitoring of behavior and learning in a domain can occur, the individuals have to have acquired appropriate knowledge and domain-specific representations. Use of reflective analysis and self-regulation is feasible only after prerequisite representations have been sufficiently developed at more advanced levels of performance. Given that these domain-specific representations are acquired to meet specific demands of reasoning in the domain, their transfer across domains seem to be quite limited (cf. Ericsson & Lehmann, 1996). To become an effective learner within a domain would appear to require a sustained commitment to acquiring the necessary representations and relevant knowledge.

Second, acquisition of complex representations for monitoring and evaluation (self-regulation) have to be closely intertwined with the acquisition of task-specific performance. Consequently, it may not be reasonable to try to distinguish these representations and associated learning activities from the structure of domain-specific performance (Ericsson & Kintsch, 1995). In complex skills it may be necessary that the same representations mediate the generation of the desired performance as well as the subsequent reflective analysis and modification of the actual performance. It is essential that structural changes made to improve performance during learning will not have any undesirable side effects on other aspects of performance. By using the same representation to monitor their performance during deliberate practice as they use to control the final public performance it is possible to make incremental adjustments without interfering with the integrity of the skill.

Finally, the research on deliberate practice has shown that concentration is necessary for optimal learning. Since most individuals seem to prefer less effortful activities that satisfy short-term learning goals, they must be motivated to attain high achievement in a domain before they will engage in sustained deliberate practice. Motivation is then an essential part of interventions to initiate acquisition of knowledge and representations that are necessary for effective learning. In sum, I believe that the study of expert performers will provide us with insights into the detailed structure of the complex, extended interactions required for the sustained efficient learning leading to mastery and expert performance.

Concluding Remarks on the Gradual Attainment of Excellence through Deliberate Practice

The general "law" of least effort predicts that activities are carried out with the minimum expenditure of effort. For this reason, the nervous system automates behavior whenever possible, and activities tend to be performed with the simplest possible mediating mechanisms. Individuals usually reach a satisfactory level of performance in most types of habitual everyday activities. At this level of achievement, repeating a similar series of actions doesn't change the structure of performance, it merely reduces the effort required for their execution. Any successful attempt to improve performance beyond this stable level thus requires active effort, changing the goal of performance, as well as designing new activities for training and improvement – deliberate practice. Depending on the domain, deliberate practice can range from simple repetitive activity aimed at increasing endurance or flexibility, to reflective analysis focused on identifying and improving aspects of skilled complex performance. Consequently, the specific activity of deliberate practice may differ dramatically across domains, but it always involves efforts to stretch performance toward higher, yet attainable, goals.

The emphasis on the sustained striving for improvement by expert performers may sound reminiscent of the arguments traditionally associated with motivational speakers advocating self-improvement. Both approaches agree that individuals tend to underestimate their achievement potential and that the first step in initiating change through training and practice requires that individuals are convinced that they capable of attaining their new goals. Beyond that, the resemblance is superficial. For example, where motivational speakers tend to be rather general about which attributes can be improved, accounts in terms of deliberate practice are limited to domains of expertise with reproducible superior performance. From laboratory analyses of the experts' superior performance, scientists have consistently found evidence for the acquired mediating mechanisms discussed above: very complex skills, highly refined representations, and large physiological adaptations. The complexity of these acquired mechanisms is consistent with the finding that not even the most "talented" can reach an international level of performance in less than a decade of dedicated practice. In this chapter I have shown how the acquisition of expert performance in several domains is closely related to engagement in deliberate practice. In particular I have focused on how well-understood mechanisms of skill acquisition and physiological adaptation can provide causal accounts of changes in the body and the nervous system that produce the desired improvements in performance.

The complex integrated structure of expert performance raises many issues about how these structures can be gradually acquired and perfected over time. It appears that teachers start guiding skill development from a child's initial introduction to training. The teacher knows the appropriate sequencing of skills and can provide training assignments of a challenging, yet attainable, difficulty level. Equally important, the teacher knows the future challenges at the highest levels and can therefore insist on mastery of the fundamentals during development to avoid the need for relearning at advanced levels. However, the best teachers in the world can never successfully train students without their full cooperation and active participation in the learning process. At all levels of performance, students who have representations supporting their planning, reasoning, and evaluation of the actual and intended performance will be better able to make appropriate adjustments to their complex skill. This advantage becomes absolutely essential at higher levels of achievement. Given that deliberate practice involves mastering tasks that students could not initially attain, or only attain imperfectly or unreliably, it is likely that more successful students acquire representations to support problem solving and learning through planning and analysis. Consequently, the faster learning of "talented" students might be explained by individual differences in acquired representations supporting effective learning.

Why would so many individuals engage in the strenuous, concentration-demanding activities of deliberate practice regularly over years and decades, when the research shows that the relaxed comfort zone provides the mood-enhancing effects of exercise and the states of high enjoyment associated with "flow" or the "runners' high"? An important part of the answer lies in their instrumentality: they offer the means to attaining superior performance with its many associated rewards and benefits, such as social recognition, relationships with teachers, playful interactions with like-minded peers, travel, scholarships and occupational opportunities and the other benefits associated with improved performance. The myth that hard work at the start will enable one to coast into future success is not supported by the evidence, and it most likely reflects confusion between merely maintaining a performance at a high level and continued further improvement of performance. In fact, as an individual's performance level improves, the demand for effort to further improve performance remains high. In support of this claim, the rated level of effort during training is greater, not less, for elite athletes than it is for amateurs.

From the perspective of deliberate practice, the rarity of excellence is primarily attributable to the environmental conditions necessary for its slow emergence, and to the years required to develop the complex mediating mechanisms that support expertise. Even individuals considered to have natural gifts gradually attain their elite performance by engaging in extended amounts of designed deliberate practice over many years. Until so-called ordinary individuals recognize that sustained effort is required to reach expert performance, they will continue to misattribute lesser achievement to lack of natural gifts, and will thus fail to reach their own potential.

The scientific study of expert performance and deliberate practice will increase our knowledge about how experts optimize their learning through the level of daily effort that they can sustain for days, months, and years. This knowledge should be relevant to any motivated individual aspiring to excel in any one of a wide range of professional activities. It is unlikely that we will ever be able to fully understand how excellence is acquired. Even if we were able to specify the exact path of development for the highest levels of performance at some point in time, such as today, excellence is protean, not static, and by the time we discovered that description expert performers will have reached even higher levels of performance. The highest levels of expertise and creativity will remain at the threshold of understanding, even for the masters dedicated to redefining the meaning of excellence in their domains.

References

Abernethy, B. (1991). Visual search strategies and decision-making in sport. *International Journal of Sport Psychology, 22*, 189–210.

Anderson, J. R. (1982). Acquisition of cognitive skill. *Psychological Review, 89*, 369–406.

Anderson, J. R. (1987). Skill acquisition: Compilation of weak-method problem situations. *Psychological Review, 94*(2), 192–210.

Bamberger, J. (1991). *The mind behind the musical ear: How children develop musical intelligence.* Cambridge, MA: Harvard University Press.

Bédard, J., & Chi, M. T. H. (1993). Expertise in auditing. *Auditing, 12*, (Suppl.), 1–25.

Bloom, B. S. (1985). Generalizations about talent development. In B. S. Bloom (Ed.), *Developing talent in young people* (pp. 507–549). New York: Ballantine Books.

Bonner, S. E., & Pennington, N. (1991). Cognitive processes and knowledge as determinants of auditor expertise. *Journal of Accounting Literature, 10*, 1–50.

Bouchard, C., Shephard, R. J., & Stephens, T. (Eds.) (1994). *Physical activity, fitness, and health: International proceedings and consensus statement.* Champaign, IL: Human Kinetics.

Buhlig, R. (1917). The value of learning to hear. In H. Brower (Ed.), *Piano mastery, Second series: Talks with master pianists and teachers* (pp. 215–223). New York: Frederick A. Stokes Company.

Busoni, F. B. (1913). Important details in piano study. In J. F. Cooke (Ed.), *Great pianists on piano playing: Study talks with foremost virtuosos* (pp. 97–107). Philadelphia, PA: Theo Presser Co.

Camerer, C. F., & Johnson, E. J. (1991). The process–performance paradox in expert judgment: How can the experts know so much and predict so badly? In K. A. Ericsson and J. Smith (Eds.), *Towards a general theory of expertise: Prospects and limits* (pp. 195–217). Cambridge: Cambridge University Press.

Casals, P. (1923). The newer cello technique. In F. H. Martens (Ed.), *String mastery: Talks with master violinists, viola players and violoncellists* (pp. 225–235). New York: Frederick A. Stokes Company.

Charness, N. (1981). Search in chess: Age and skill differences. *Journal of Experimental Psychology: Human Perception and Performance, 7*, 467–476.

Charness, N., Krampe, R. Th., & Mayr, U. (1996). The role of practice and coaching in entrepreneurial skill domains: An international comparison of life-span chess skill acquisition. In K. A. Ericsson (Ed.), *The road to excellence: The acquisition of expert performance in the arts and sciences, sports, and games* (pp. 51–80). Mahwah, NJ: Erlbaum.

Cowley, M. (Ed.) (1959). *Writers at work: The Paris review interviews.* New York: Viking.

Dawes, R. M. (1994). *House of cards: Psychology and psychotherapy built on myth.* New York: Free Press.

de Groot, A. (1978). *Thought and choice and chess.* The Hague: Mouton. (Original work published 1946.)

Elbert, T., Pantev, C., Wienbruch, C., Rockstroch, B. & Taub, E. (1995). Increased cortical representation of the fingers of the left hand in string players. *Science, 270*, 305–307.

Ericsson, K. A. (1996). The acquisition of expert performance: An introduction to some of the issues. In K. A. Ericsson (Ed.), *The road to excellence: The acquisition of expert performance in the arts and sciences, sports, and games* (pp. 1–50). Mahwah, NJ: Erlbaum.

Ericsson, K. A. (1997). Deliberate Practice and the Acquisition of Expert Performance: An Overview. In H. Jorgensen and A. C. Lehmann (Eds.), *Does practice make perfect? Current theory and research on instrumental music practice.* NMH-publikasjoner 1997:1. Oslo, Norway: Norges musikkhögskole.

Ericsson, K. A. (1998). The Scientific Study of Expert Levels of Performance: General Implications for Optimal Learning and Creativity. *High Ability Studies, 9*, 75–100.

Ericsson, K. A., & Charness, N. (1994). Expert performance: Its structure and acquisition. *American Psychologist, 49*, 725–747.

Ericsson, K. A., & Delaney, P. F. (1999). Long-term working memory as an alternative to capacity models of working memory in everyday skilled performance. In A. Miyake and P. Shah (Eds.), *Models of Working Memory: Mechanisms of Active Maintenance and Executive Control"* (pp. 257–297) Cambridge, UK: Cambridge University Press.

Ericsson, K. A., & Kintsch, W. (1995). Long-term working memory. *Psychological Review, 102*, 211–245.

Ericsson, K. A., Krampe, R. Th., & Heizmann, S. (1993). Can we create gifted people? In CIBA Foundation Symposium 178 *The origin and development of high ability* (pp. 222–249). Chichester, UK: Wiley.

Ericsson, K. A., Krampe, R. Th., & Tesch-Römer, C. (1993). The role of deliberate practice in the acquisition of expert performance. *Psychological Review, 100*, 363–406.

Ericsson, K. A., & Lehmann, A. C. (1996). Expert and exceptional performance: Evidence on maximal adaptations on task constraints. *Annual Review of Psychology, 47*, 273–305.

Ericsson, K. A., & Lehmann, A. C. (1998). Expertise. In M. A. Runco and S. Pritzer (Eds.), *Encyclopedia of Creativity*. San Diego, CA: Academic Press.

Ericsson, K. A., & Smith, J. (1991). Prospects and limits in the empirical study of expertise: An introduction. In K. A. Ericsson and J. Smith (Eds.), *Toward a general theory of expertise: Prospects and limits* (pp. 1–38). Cambridge: Cambridge University Press.

Fitts, P., & Posner, M. I. (1967). *Human performance*. Belmont, CA: Brooks/Cole.

Galamian, I. (1972). Ivan Galamian. In S. Applebaum and S. Applebaum (Eds.), *The way they play, Book I*, (pp. 240–351). Neptune City, NJ: Paganiniana Publications.

Glaser, R. (1996). Changing the agency for learning: Acquiring expert performance. In K. A. Ericsson (Ed.), *The road to excellence: The acquisition of
expert performance in the arts and sciences, sports, and games* (pp. 1–50).
Mahwah, NJ: Erlbaum.

Gould, S. J. (1996). *Full house: the spread of excellence from Plato to Darwin*. New
York: Harmony Books.

Helsen, W. F., Starkes, J. L., & Hodges, N. J. (1998). Team sports and the
theory of deliberate practice. *Journal of Sport and Exercise Psychology, 20,*
12–34.

Hodges, N. J., & Starkes, J. L. (1996). Wrestling with the nature of expertise:
a sport specific test of Ericsson, Krampe and Tesch-Römer's (1993) theory
of "Deliberate Practice," *International Journal of Sport Psychology*, 1–25.

Katims, M. (1972). Milton Katims. In S. Applebaum and S. Applebaum (Eds.),
The way they play, Book I, (pp. 233–242). Neptune City, NJ: Paganiniana
Publications

Krampe, R. Th., & Ericsson, K. A. (1996). Maintaining excellence: Deliberate
practice and elite performance in young and older pianists. *Journal of Experimental Psychology: General, 125,* 331–359.

Kreisler, F. (1972). Fritz Kreisler. In S. Applebaum and S. Applebaum (Eds.),
The way they play, Book I, (pp. 95–109). Neptune City, NJ: Paganiniana
Publications.

Langer, E. J. (1997). *The power of mindful learning*. Reading, MA: Addison-
Wesley.

Lehmann, A. C. (1997). Acquisition of expertise in music: Efficiency of deliberate practice as a moderating variable in accounting for sub-expert performance. In I. Deliege & J. A. Sloboda (Eds.), *Perception and Cognition of
Music* (pp. 165–191). Hillsdale, NJ: LEA.

Lehmann, A. C., & Ericsson, K. A. (1993). Sight-reading ability of expert
pianists in the context of piano accompanying. *Psychomusicology, 12,*
182–195.

Lehmann, A. C., & Ericsson, K. A. (1995). *Expert pianists' mental representation
of memorized music*. Poster presented at the 36th Annual meeting of the
Psychonomic Society, Los Angeles, CA, November 10–12.

Lehmann, A. C., & Ericsson, K. A. (1996). Music performance without preparation: Structure and acquisition of expert sight-reading. *Psychomusicology, 15,* 1–29.

Lehmann, A. C., & Ericsson, K. A. (1997). Expert pianists' mental representations: Evidence from successful adaptation to unexpected performance
demands. *Proceedings of the Third Triennial ESCOM Conference* (pp. 165–
169). Uppsala, Sweden: SLU Service/Reproenheten.

Lehmann, A. C., & Ericsson, K. A. (1998). The historical development of
domains of expertise: Performance standards and innovations in music. In

A. Steptoe (Ed.), *Genius and the mind* (pp. 67–94). Oxford, UK: Oxford University Press.

Levin, H., & Addis, A. B. (1979). *The eye-voice span.* Cambridge, MA: MIT Press.

Lerner, T. (1915). An audience is the best teacher. In H. Brower (Ed.), *Piano mastery: Talks with master pianists and teachers* (pp. 38–46). New York: Frederick A. Stokes Company.

Locke, E. A., & Latham, G. P. (1984). *Goal setting: A motivational technique that works!* Englewood Cliffs, NJ: Prentice-Hall.

Norman, D. A., Coblentz, C. L., Brooks, L. R., & Babcook, C. J. (1992). Expertise in visual diagnosis: A review of the literature. *Academic Medicine Rime Supplement, 67,* 78–83.

Plimpton, G. (Ed.) (1977). *Writers at work: The Paris review. Interviews, Second Series.* New York: Penguin.

Primrose, W. (1972). William Primrose. In S. Applebaum and S. Applebaum (Eds.), *The way they play, Book I* (pp. 243–261). Neptune City, NJ: Paganiniana Publications.

Robergs, R. A., & Roberts, S. O. (1997). *Exercise physiology: Exercise, performance, and clinical applications.* St. Louis, MO: Mosby-Year Book.

Rosson, M. B. (1985). The role of experience in editing. *Proceedings of INTER-ACT '84 IFIP Conference on Human-Computer Interaction* (pp. 45–50). New York: Elsevier.

Sauer, E. (1913). The training of the virtuoso. In J. F. Cooke (Ed.), *Great pianists on piano playing: Study talks with foremost virtuosos* (pp. 236–250). Philadelphia, PA: Theo Presser Co.

Schlaug, G., Jäncke, L., Huang Y., & Steinmetz, H. (1995). In vivo evidence of structural brain asymmetry in musicians. *Science, 267,* 699–701.

Schmidt, H. G., Norman, G. R., & Boshuizen, H. P. A. (1990). A cognitive perspective on medical expertise: Theory and implications. *Academic Medicine, 65,* 611–621.

Schneider, W. (1993). Acquiring expertise: Determinants of exceptional performance. In K. A. Heller, J. Mönks and H. Passow (eds.), *International handbook of research and development of giftedness and talent* (pp. 311–324). Oxford, UK: Pergamon Press.

Schnitzer, G. (1915). Modern methods in piano study. In H. Brower (Ed.), *Piano mastery: Talks with master pianists and teachers* (pp. 215–224). New York: Frederick A. Stokes Company.

Schunk, D. H., & Zimmerman, B. J. (Eds.) (1994). *Self-regulation of learning and performance: Issues and educational applications* (pp. 1–21). Hillsdale, NJ: Erlbaum.

Shanteau, J., & Stewart, T. R. (1992). Why study expert decision making? Some historical perspectives and comments. *Organizational Behaviour and Human Decision Processes, 53,* 95–106.

Shiffrin, R. M., & Schneider, W. (1977). Controlled and automatic human information processing: II. Perceptual learning, automatic attending and a general theory. *Psychological Review, 84,* 127–189.

Simon, H. A., & Chase, W. G. (1973). Skill in chess. *American Scientist, 61,* 394–403.

Simonton, D. K. (1997). Creative productivity: A predictive and explanatory model of career trajectories and landmarks. *Psychological Review, 104,* 66–89.

Sloboda, J. A. (1996). The acquisition of musical performance expertise: Deconstructing the "talent" account of individual differences in musical expressivity. In K. A. Ericsson (Ed.), *The road to excellence: The acquisition of expert performance in the arts and sciences, sports, and games* (pp. 107–126). Mahwah, NJ: Erlbaum.

Starkes, J. L., Deakin, J., Allard, F., Hodges, N. J., & Hayes, A. (1996). Deliberate practice in sports: What is it anyway? In K. A. Ericsson (Ed.), *The road to excellence: The acquisition of expert performance in the arts and sciences, sports, and games* (pp. 81–106). Mahwah, NJ: Erlbaum.

Sternberg, R. J. (1996). Costs of expertise. In K. A. Ericsson (Ed.), *The road to excellence: The acquisition of expert performance in the arts and sciences, sports, and games* (pp. 347–354). Mahwah, NJ: Erlbaum.

Sudnow, D. (1978). *Ways of the hand: The organization of improvised conduct.* Cambridge. MA: Harvard University Press.

Szigeti, J. (1972). Joseph Szigeti. In S. Applebaum and S. Applebaum (Eds.), *The way they play, Book I* (pp. 95–109). Neptune City, NJ: Paganiniana Publications.

Tertis, L. (1972). Lionel Tertis. In S. Applebaum and S. Applebaum (Eds.), *The way they play, Book I* (pp. 262–270). Neptune City, NJ: Paganiniana Publications.

Zimmerman, B. J. (1994). Dimensions of academic self-regulations: A conceptual framework for education. In D. H. Schunk and B. J. Zimmerman (Eds.), *Self-regulation of learning and performance: Issues and educational applications* (pp. 1–21). Hillsdale, NJ: Erlbaum.

Rhyme, Language, and Reading

Introduction

It is rare for breakthroughs to occur in our understanding of teaching and learning, but the following paper reports on a research programme that seems to justify the use of this term. One of the most controversial problems in education has concerned the question of how best to teach children to read. Psychology has been the discipline at the heart of research into this question and the research has contributed significantly both to our understanding of the fundamental perceptual and cognitive processes involved in reading and to the practical problems of teaching children to read (Adams, 1990; Beard, 1993).

When young children learn to read they are normally already fluent users of oral language. In order to recognize words in written texts they have to become familiar with the complex conventions which map speech sounds (phonemes) onto the letters of the alphabet and other symbols of our writing system (graphemes). Thus there are 44 distinct phonemes in spoken English, but only 26 letters in the alphabet with which to represent them. Vowels sounds, in particular, have complex and varied relationships with letters in the ways they are spelled in different English words. (Compare, for example, the sounds which correspond to the letter 'o' in the following words: hot, honey, hour, hoot and home). Peter Bryant and his colleagues have carried out a series of studies which show that one important aspect of the process of learning to read involves being able to hear, before one can read at all, some of the different sounds within spoken words. Without this capacity for 'phonological awareness' children struggle to make any sense of the matches between sounds and letters. Early phonological awareness tends to focus on the beginnings and ends of words and children of three and four years old can be taught to recognize rhyme (matching sounds at the ends of words) and alliteration (matching sounds at the beginnings of words).

Bryant's research shows that early ability to recognize rhyme and alliteration is a powerful predictor of success in early reading and spelling. The research has included longitudinal studies of children learning to read and write, and also training studies in which groups of children were taught to recognize patterns of sounds in words prior to learning to read. In the following paper, the authors report on their longitudinal study, showing that children's sensitivity to rhyme and alliteration at age four predicts their success in reading and spelling two years later, even when differences in measures of their IQ, social background and general linguistic abilities are statistically removed from the analysis.

References

Adams, M. J. 1990: *Beginning to Read*. Cambridge, MA, London: MIT Press.
Beard, R. (ed.) 1993: *Teaching Literacy: Balancing Perspectives*. London: Hodder & Stoughton.

Further reading

Bradley, L. and Bryan, L. 1999: *Categorising Sounds and Learning to Read – A Casual Connection*. Chapter 26 In A. Slater and D. Muir (eds), *The Blackwell Reader in Developmental Psychology*, London: Blackwell, ch. 26.

TWO

Rhyme, Language, and Children's Reading

Peter Bryant, Morag MacLean,
and Lynette Bradley

Preschool children are reasonably good at producing rhymes and at detecting whether words rhyme or not (Chukovsky, 1963; Dowker, 1989; Lenel & Cantor, 1981; MacLean, Bryant, & Bradley, 1987). Their ability to do so is interesting for two reasons. First, it demonstrates that preschool children can analyze the constituent sounds in words. If they understand that *cat* and *hat* rhyme, they recognize that these two words have a speech segment – the rime /at/ – in common.

The second reason why young children's rhyming abilities deserve attention is that there is a powerful connection between these abilities and the progress that children make later on when they learn to read and write. The performance of 3-, 4-, and 5-year-old children, who cannot yet read, in tests of sensitivity to rhyme and alliteration predicts their success in learning to read over the next three to four years even after controls for differences in intelligence, vocabulary, and social background (Bradley & Bryant, 1983, 1985; Bryant, MacLean, Bradley, & Crossland, 1990; Ellis & Large, 1987; MacLean et al., 1987). Furthermore, this connection is a specific one. The children's early rhyme scores predict their progress in reading and spelling later on but not in arithmetic (Bradley & Bryant, 1983; MacLean et al., 1987).

One possible reason for a connection between rhyme and reading is that children's experiences with rhyme allow them to form categories of words that share common sounds, and that later on they make a connection between these categories and words that share common spelling patterns. The knowledge that *light, fight,* and *might* rhyme might help children grasp the fact that the words share a common spelling sequence as well as a common rhyme. There is evidence that children do link rhyming categories with spelling categories as soon as they begin to learn to read and spell (Goswami, 1986, 1988).

The fact that measures of sensitivity to rhyme, taken before children learn to read, predict their progress in reading suggests a causal connection. The idea of a causal link is supported to some extent by the discovery that training in rhyme does have a beneficial effect on reading (Bradley & Bryant, 1983). However, it is always possible that a predictive relationship might not be a causal one: the relationship might be due to the fact that both the predicting and the predicted variables are determined by some other, unknown, and therefore unmeasured, factor.

Recently Bowey and Patel (1988) made the interesting suggestion that children's general language abilities might determine both children's sensitivity to rhyme and also their reading performance. They ran a correlational study with 60 children whose average age was 6 years. They gave these children an oddity rhyme and alliteration test based on the one used by Bradley and Bryant (1983). They also gave the children a syntactic awareness task, in which they had to "detect and correct" mistakes in ungrammatical sentences that were read to them. Bowey and Patel refer to the rhyme and alliteration tests and the syntax awareness task as "metalinguistic" tasks, since both involve a degree of awareness to an aspect of language. As well as this, the children were given two standardized linguistic tests, one a test of vocabulary (the well-known PPVT) and the other a sentence imitation test (a subtest of TOLD-P) in which they had to repeat a set of sentences of increasing semantic difficulty. Bowey and Patel also gave the children a standardized reading test. They did not measure the children's IQ.

The experimenters found a significant relationship between the two metalinguistic tests, rhyme and syntactic awareness, and the children's reading levels. But they also showed that this relationship was no longer significant when the effects of differences in the children's performance in the two linguistic tasks, vocabulary and sentence imitation, were partialled out. On the other hand, these two linguistic tests were significantly related to the children's reading comprehension even after differences in the two metalinguistic tasks were controlled.

Bowey and Patel concluded that the most important variable here was the children's general language ability, as measured by the two linguistic tests, and that this factor controlled the children's rhyming and syntactic abilities as well as their success in reading.

Bowey and Patel's data are extremely valuable and interesting, but they need to be extended. The children in Bowey and Patel's study were relatively old, and the study was not a longitudinal one. In studies that have shown a connection between rhyme and reading, the rhyme measures were given when the children were 3, 4, or 5 years old. There is also evidence from two studies (Lundberg, Frost, & Petersen, 1988; Stanovich, Cunningham, & Cramer, 1984) that by 6 years the relationship between scores in a rhyme task and in reading tests tends to be low. So it is quite possible that tests of rhyme given to 4-year-old children would continue to predict children's reading later on, even after the stringent controls for general language ability which are quite rightly advocated by Bowey and Patel.

We needed a study that measured children's sensitivity to rhyme (and also their ability to correct and detect mistakes in ungrammatical sentences) at an earlier age (say 4 years), which included measures of IQ and of social background, and which, *pace* Bowey and Patel, introduced a wide range of language measures including standardized tests of the children's receptive and expressive language, of their ability to understand sentences of varying grammatical complexity, and of their ability to imitate sentences.

We now report a longitudinal study of 65 children, which included all these tests as well as measures of the children's progress in reading and spelling over the following two years.

Methods

Subjects

Ages

There were 66 children in this project, but we shall report data on 65. One child left the country halfway through the project. All but one of the children came from native English-speaking backgrounds. The exception was a boy whose mother is Swedish; although English is the language spoken in his home, he knew a certain amount of Swedish as well.

At the time of the first tests that we shall report, the average age of the 65 children (31 boys, 34 girls) was 3;4 (*SD* = 2.8 months; range = 2;10–3;9). We shall report data over a period of 3 years; when the last measure was taken, the average age of the 64 children was 6;7 (range 5;9–6;10).

All the children were at school by the time the project ended. In all, the children were distributed over 28 different schools. The practices involved in teaching reading varied between schools and even between different classrooms in the same school. However, on the whole the teachers adopted a mixture of "phonic" and "whole word" approaches in teaching children how to read words.

Intelligence levels

At 4;3 the children were given the full WPPSI. The mean IQ was 111.1 (*SD* = 12.31). At 6;7 (range = 6;2–7;1) the children were given the short version of the WISC/R either just before or just after the final session. The four subtests given were Similarities, Vocabulary, Block Design, and Object Assembly. The mean IQ was 112.2 (*SD* = 16.49).

Social background

The children came from a wide range of backgrounds. Our measures of the home background included social class and the educational level of the parents. We decided to use mothers' educational level as our main measure of the children's background. We could not use social class because the project included several single-parent (mother) families to whom we decided not to apply the social class index because it is based on the father's occupation.

Procedure

The data for this article come from a longitudinal study of the 65 children, which started when their mean age was 3;4 and finished when it was 6;7. Parts of this study have been reported in other papers (Bryant et al., 1990; Kirtley, Bryant, MacLean, & Bradley, 1989; Mac-Lean et al., 1987). We shall report data from six sessions, when the children were 3;4, 3;5, 4;5, 4;7, 4;11, and 6;7.

In the first five of these sessions, we measured the children's linguistic abilities, and also their sensitivity to rhyme and alliteration and their awareness of syntax. In the last session we measured their reading and spelling levels.

We shall describe the three kinds of measures – of linguistic ability, of metalinguistic skills (rhyme, alliteration, and syntax awareness), and of reading and spelling levels – separately.

Linguistic measures

Vocabulary

When the children were 3;4, we administered the British Picture Vocabulary Scale (BPVS; the most modern British version of the Peabody Picture Vocabulary test, it is standardized in Britain). The mean ratio score for the group on the BPVS was 104.7 ($SD = 12.68$). The average for the population was 100.

Expressive and receptive language

One month later we administered the Reynell Developmental Language Scale (Reynell, 1983). This test assesses expressive language and receptive language (verbal comprehension) separately.

In the expressive part of the test, the child has to talk about scenarios acted out with toys or about scenes in pictures. For example, the child sees a boy who is sitting by a table being knocked off his chair and has to say what happened. The child's responses are scored in terms of their grammatical sophistication (the use of pronouns, prepositions, and tenses).

The receptive scale requires no speech from the child. The child is given some toys and has to respond to sentences of increasing difficulty about them. An example of a simple sentence is "Where is the chair?" In a slightly more complex question, "Which one do we cut with?", the child has to choose from a bed, chair, pot, pen, and knife. A difficult sentence is "Put one of the little pigs beside the man."

The mean standardized Expressive score was 0.937 ($SD = 0.797$) and the mean Receptive score was 0.988 ($SD = 0.863$). The average standardized score for the population was 0 in both cases.

Sentence imitation

When the children were 4;11 we gave them a sentence imitation task. We read out a series of 12 sentences of increasing complexity, beginning with "Dave likes cars" and ending with "Tom drank his milk because he likes to play with Bart when he's home." Our instructions to the child were: "I want you to say just what I say." This task was based on one devised by Jorm, Share, Maclean, and Matthews (1984) and differed from their task in one detail only. We substituted the sentence "He drank a glass of cold milk" for "He drank a glass of cold beer" because our children were younger than those tested by Jorm and colleagues and might have been less familiar with beer. The mean score in this task was 7.0 ($SD = 2.12$).

Metalinguistic measures

Rhyme and alliteration oddity tasks

In the session when the children were 4;7 we gave them a version of the rhyme oddity task that was used in a previous study (Bradley & Bryant, 1983). Before the trials began, we asked the children if they knew the nursery rhyme "Jack and Jill" and recited the first two lines: "Jack and Jill went up the...yes *hill, Jill, hill,* they sound the same, they rhyme, can you tell me another word that sounds like *hill?...fill.* Now we're going to play a game about words that sound the same, about words that rhyme."

In the test proper we used pictures in order to remove the memory load. This was necessary because each trial involved three words. The rhyme test consisted of two practice trials and then ten experimental trials. In each trial the child was given three words with pictures, two of which rhymed while the third did not (e.g., *peg, cot, leg; fish, dish, hook*). The children's task was to tell us the one that did not rhyme. Their mean scores were 6.22 ($SD = 2.63$) out of 10 in this test (chance level = 3.33).

We also measured the child's sensitivity to alliteration using the same methods. The children had to judge which of three words began with a different sound (e.g., *pin, pig, tree*). The children's mean scores were 6.53 ($SD = 2.44$) in this alliteration oddity test.

Syntax awareness

Our task was a slight adaptation of one developed by Tunmer, Nesdale, and Wright (1987), and it was very similar to the task used by Bowey and Patel (1988). The children were told "I've got some puppets here who haven't quite learned how to talk properly. What they say is wrong. I want you to show them what to say." They were then introduced to one puppet who produced eight sentences (two of which were practice items) in which there was a missing morpheme. Two such sentences were "Andrew drink juice every day" and "Sandra is paint a picture." After that they were introduced to another puppet who produced eight sentences in which the word order was incorrect (e.g., "Patted Bill the dog" and "Susan the bike rode").

Each trial was scored as correct or incorrect. We adopted Tunmer and colleagues' "strict" procedure. For example, for "Sandra is paint a picture" we accepted "Sandra is painting a picture" as correct, but judged "Sandra paints a picture" as incorrect because in this case the child did not produce the correct missing morpheme.

The missing morpheme questions were a great deal easier than the jumbled order questions. The mean scores for the two sets of questions were respectively 47.25% correct ($SD = 26.86$) and 31.57% correct ($SD = 25.50$). One possible reason for this difference is that the jumbled order questions make particularly difficult demands on the children's memory. We decided to combine the scores for the missing morpheme and jumbled order sentences for two reasons. One was that the distribution of the combined score was much nearer normality than the two separate scores. The second was that each of the separate scores was only based on six trials, and we felt that this was not a sufficient base for a predictive test. The mean combined score was 37.05% correct ($SD = 25.60$). Bowey and Patel (1988) combined missing morpheme questions with other questions in their test and used a combined score in their analyses.

Reading

When the children had a mean age of 4;5 (i.e., 2 months before we gave our first metalinguistic tests), we gave them some words to read to check whether any of them were precocious readers. The standardized reading tests were plainly too difficult to be appropriate, and so we gave the children 12 simple, highly frequent words to read. The words were: *on, the, car, dog, and, my, girl, was, boy, you, put*. Only 13 children could read any words at all. Of these, 5 could read one word only, and 8 could read three words or more.

In the final session (age 6;7) we gave the following three standardized tests:

1 France Primary Reading Test: a multiple choice test with 48 items arranged in ascending difficulty to assess the understanding of words and simple sentences. The items that involve sentences depend on the child understanding the meaning of these sentences, and so this test measures the child's comprehension as well as his or her ability to read single words. The group's mean reading age on the test was 7;6 (*SD* in months = 17.24).
2 Schonell Graded Word Reading Test: involved reading single words. The group's mean reading age on the test was 7;2 (*SD* in months = 15.27).
3 Schonell Spelling: tested spelling, using Form A. The group's mean spelling age on the test was 6;4 (*SD* in months = 14.4).

Results

Correlations

Our first step was to check that the individual phonological and linguistic tests that we gave the children in the first half of the project were related to their reading and spelling level at the project's end and to look at the other correlations between the different variables. Table 2.1 gives the correlation matrix. The table shows several interesting patterns.

First, the relations of the language measures, and particularly of the Expressive and Receptive (Reynell) scores, to the metalinguistic measures are quite high. This supports Bowey and Patel's suggestion that the metalinguistic tests may be no more than a measure of language proficiency.

The second interesting point is that the correlations between the metalinguistic variables and the reading/spelling measures were

Table 2.1 Correlations between the main variables in the study

	Wp	Ws	Voc	EL	RL	SI	SA	Al	Rh	R-F	R-S	Sp
Mother's education	0.62	0.47	0.43	0.58	0.50	0.44	0.65	0.53	0.59	0.63	0.58	0.61
WPPSI (WP)		0.71	0.35	0.64	0.57	0.43	0.66	0.66	0.58	0.71	0.67	0.66
WISC (WS)			0.33	0.47	0.40	0.34	0.59	0.60	0.59	0.67	0.68	0.67
Vocabulary (Voc)				0.38	0.31	0.34	0.45	0.29	0.31	0.45	0.41	0.39
Expressive language (EL)					0.70	0.48	0.64	0.55	0.52	0.59	0.55	0.47
Receptive language (RL)						0.50	0.59	0.36	0.44	0.46	0.40	0.34
Sentence imitation (SI)							0.57	0.51	0.45	0.50	0.51	0.45
Syntax awareness (SA)								0.59	0.53	0.63	0.63	0.63
Alliteration (Al)									0.75	0.77	0.80	0.73
Rhyme (Rh)										0.69	0.69	0.64
Reading (France) (R-F)											0.95	0.84
Reading (Schonell) (R-S)												0.89
Spelling (Sp)												

appreciably higher than the relationships between the language measures and reading and spelling. The correlations between the metalinguistic measures and reading and spelling varied in size from 0.63 to 0.80. The correlations of the language measures with reading and spelling ranged from 0.31 to 0.59. The relative strength of these correlations suggests that rhyme and alliteration should be related to reading and spelling even after controls for differences in the children's scores in the other linguistic tests.

Third, there is the question of whether the linguistic and the metalinguistic scores measure the same thing as intelligence tests. It should be noted that the two IQ scores correlate well with both kinds of measure, and with the reading and spelling scores as well. Thus, any relationship between the linguistic or metalinguistic measures and reading could be attributed to the variance that the linguistic and metalinguistic variables share with intelligence. As a result, it is essential to carry out fixed order multiple regressions that partial out the influence of differences in intelligence before charting the relationship between the linguistic and metalinguistic scores and reading.

Multiple regressions

Our next question was whether the children's early rhyme and alliteration scores and their performance in the syntax awareness test would predict their reading and spelling levels later on, even after the effects of differences in general linguistic ability had been partialled out. We ran two sets of multiple regressions to see whether this relation was significant.

Regressions without the social background and IQ scores

The regressions in the first set were very similar to the ones run by Bowey and Patel. They did not enter IQ or social background into their regressions and nor did we in this first set, which is presented in Table 2.2. The first five steps in all of these regressions were the same. We simply entered the children's age as the first step, and then we entered our four measures of general linguistic ability as the next four steps. The sixth and final step in each regression was one of the three metalinguistic measures – rhyme, alliteration, or syntax awareness.

Table 2.2 R^2 change in nine fixed order multiple regressions

Steps in regression	Outcome measure		
	Reading France test	Reading Schonell test	Spelling Schonell test
Extraneous variables			
1 Age at test of reading	0.003	0.031	0.39
Linguistic variables			
2 Vocabulary (BPVS)	0.201***	0.156***	0.141**
3 Language (Reynell) expressive	0.122**	0.115**	0.079*
4 Language (Reynell) receptive	0.114**	0.140***	0.102**
5 Sentence imitation	0.021	0.030	0.019
Final step			
6a Final step rhyme	0.144***	0.152***	0.149***
6b Final step alliteration	0.219***	0.251***	0.231***
6c Final step syntax awareness	0.046*	0.062*	0.120***

In each regression the children's general language scores are entered before the metalinguistic score. Each of the three outcome measures is analyzed three times; in each analysis one of the three metalinguistic measures represents the final step.
$*p < 0.05$; $**p < 0.01$; $*** p < 0.001$.

There were three different outcome measures, or dependent variables, which were the children's scores in the France reading test, in the Schonell reading test, and the Schonell spelling test when they were 6;7. This meant that there were nine fixed order multiple regressions in all (three different final steps with three different outcome measures).

Table 2.2 shows that our results are similar to Bowey and Patel's in one way but different in another. The results of the two studies are similar in that the linguistic measures in both predict reading well. Bowey and Patel reported that their linguistic measures accounted for 41% of the variance in one reading test and 29% in another. Our linguistic measures were even more powerfully connected to reading. As Table 2.2 shows, they accounted for 45.8% of the variance in the France reading test and 43.1% in the Schonell reading test. Ours probably accounted for more variance because they covered a wider range of linguistic behavior. All the linguistic tests were reasonable predictors of reading. The fact that the Sentence Imitation scores did not account for a significant portion of the variance in reading is merely a result of our entering it as the last linguistic measure in the regression. In other regressions we entered it at an earlier stage and then it became significant.

However, when we consider the final step in each of the multiple regressions, we can see that our results were quite different from Bowey and Patel's. Table 2.2 shows that all three metalinguistic scores did predict reading even after differences in the children's general linguistic abilities had been partialled out. There is a strong connection between 4-year-old children's sensitivity to rhyme, to alliteration, and to syntax and their reading two years later, which cannot be explained away as a mere symptom of a more general linguistic ability.

Regressions with the social background and IQ scores

However, this first set of regressions did not include IQ scores or measures of differences in social background, so it is possible that the connections between some of our measures and reading could simply have been a byproduct of differences in these important but extraneous variables. We needed multiple regressions in which these variables were entered before either the linguistic or the metalinguistic measures. The second set of nine multiple regressions, which are presented in Table 2.3, took this form.

The regressions had two extra steps. The children's social background (measured by their mothers' educational level) was entered as the second step. In these regressions we treated mothers' educational level as a categorical and not a continuous variable. The children's IQ was entered as the third step. We had two IQ scores for the group – the WPPSI scores when they were 4;3 and the WISC scores when they were 6;7. We decided to use the WPPSI scores because the test was given in the early part of the project at the time of the other predictive measures. (Table 2.1 shows that the WPPSI and the WISC scores were equally strongly related to reading.) Otherwise, the multiple regressions were the same as before.

It can be seen from Table 2.3 that the presence of the social background and the IQ measures in these regressions makes a striking

Table 2.3 R^2 change in fixed order multiple regressions in which social background and IQ are controlled as well as general language abilities

Steps in regression	Outcome measure		
	Reading France test	Reading Schonell test	Spelling Schonell test
Extraneous variables			
1 Age at test of reading	0.003	0.031	0.39
2 Mothers' educational level	0.444***	0.392***	0.413***
3 IQ (WPPSI)	0.178**	0.198***	0.158***
Linguistic variables			
4 Vocabulary (BPVS)	0.008	0.002	0.000
5 Language (Reynell) expressive	0.000	0.000	0.000
6 Language (Reynell) receptive	0.016	0.026	0.007
7 Sentence imitation	0.004	0.009	0.002
Final step			
8a Final step rhyme	0.048**	0.056**	0.034*
8b Final step alliteration	0.085***	0.110***	0.069***
8c Final step syntax awareness	0.001	0.000	0.000

Note: $*p < 0.05$; $**p < 0.01$; $***p < 0.001$.

difference in two ways. First, these two variables account for a large proportion of the variance. Second, the linguistic variables are no longer good predictors of reading and spelling. In fact, the vocabulary and the expressive and receptive language measures, which were significantly related to reading and spelling in the first set of regressions, now account for a tiny proportion of the variance in reading and spelling and fall far short of significance. So it seems that the previous connection between these linguistic measures and reading could simply have reflected differences in social background or in intelligence, since these variables were not controlled in the first set of regressions.

Exactly the same point can be made about one of the metalinguistic scores – syntax awareness. This was an excellent predictor of reading and spelling in the first set of regressions. In the second set it accounted for hardly any variance at all in the children's reading or in their spelling.

But our third point about these regressions is that the other metalinguistic measures – rhyme and alliteration – withstood the effect of partialling out differences in social background and IQ, as well as in general language abilities, extremely well. Even after controls for all these variables, both rhyme and alliteration accounted for a significant proportion of the variance in all three outcome measures. The children's alliteration scores were particularly powerful predictors of reading and spelling.

We should like to make a final remark about the second set of regressions. The combination of the "extraneous variables" and the linguistic and metalinguistic measures accounts for an impressive amount of the variance in the children's reading and spelling. For example, the multiple regressions in which the final step was the children's alliteration scores accounted for 73% of the variance in the France reading scores, 78% in the Schonell reading scores, and 68% in the Schonell spelling scores.

Precocious readers and outliers

Our main concern in this article has been with the possible importance of the age at which the children's sensitivity to rhyme is tested. Our argument is that tests given in the preschool years are likely to be more powerful predictors of reading than tests given after children have reached school. However, this raises the question whether tests of rhyme and alliteration are a powerful predictor of reading when they are given only to children who cannot yet read. It is certainly important to check whether the powerful relationships that we have reported between the rhyme and alliteration measures and reading two years later would be the same if we confined our analysis to children who could not read at the time of the original rhyme and alliteration tests. So we ran further analyses in which we excluded children who, on the basis of the results of the simple reading test that we gave to the children when they were 4;5, appeared to be precocious readers at the time of the original tests of rhyme and alliteration.

As we reported earlier, 8 children could read three or more words in our first reading test. We decided to exclude these 8 children from our analysis on the grounds that they must have made definite progress in reading in order to be able to read that many words. However we felt we could not count the 5 children who only managed to read one word in our test as precocious readers, because being able to read only one word of the simple and very common words in the test did not seem to us enough to warrant that description. So we did not exclude those 5 children from our further analyses, which were designed to establish whether the relationships between the metalinguistic measures and reading would be the same when the sample consisted only of children who had made no substantial progress in reading at the time of the metalinguistic tests. The new sample consisted of 57 children.

Table 2.4 gives the correlation matrix, and Table 2.5 gives the equivalent multiple regressions to those already presented in Table 2.3, for this reduced sample. The pattern of correlations in Table 2.4 was very similar to the correlations obtained from the total sample. The correlations between rhyme and alliteration were slightly smaller in the smaller sample, but still very strong. Table 2.5 shows that rhyme and alliteration continued to predict reading and spelling after the effects of differences in age, social background, IQ, and of the various linguistic measures were removed. Thus, the relationships that we found in our total sample are not the product of differences in reading skills in the preschool period.

Another possibility is that the very strong relation between our rhyme and alliteration scores and reading could be explained partly by the existence of "outliers," i.e., children not particularly representative of the rest of the sample. To find who could be counted as outliers, we used standardized residuals from the regression of the alliteration score and the Schonell reading level (the strongest relation of all in our total sample). This analysis produced 5 children who were clear outliers. We ran further analyses in which these 5 children were excluded.

The exclusion of these outliers led to even stronger correlations than before between rhyme and alliteration on the one hand and reading and spelling on the other. The correlations of rhyme to the France reading test, to the Schonell reading test, and to the spelling test were, respectively, 0.71, 0.73, and 0.68. The equivalent figures of alliteration were 0.79, 0.83, and 0.76. Not surprisingly, given these correlations, the exclusion of the five outliers in further multiple regressions made no difference to the relationships of rhyme and alliteration to reading or to spelling that we reported in Tables 2.2 and 2.3. These relationships cannot be attributed to the presence of outliers.

Table 2.4 Correlations between the main variables in the study after exclusion of precocious readers ($N = 57$)

	Wp	Ws	Voc	EL	RL	SI	SA	Al	Rh	R-F	R-S	Sp
Mother's education	0.58	0.61	0.35	0.55	0.53	0.36	0.61	0.40	0.50	0.50	0.43	0.50
WPPSI (WP)		0.67	0.31	0.62	0.56	0.38	0.63	0.61	0.53	0.69	0.63	0.67
WISC (WS)			0.26	0.42	0.38	0.26	0.56	0.49	0.51	0.56	0.57	0.60
Vocabulary (Voc)				0.32	0.38	0.33	0.43	0.16	0.23	0.36	0.31	0.34
Expressive language (EL)					0.74	0.47	0.66	0.51	0.49	0.59	0.55	0.51
Receptive language (RL)						0.49	0.59	0.36	0.44	0.49	0.40	0.33
Sentence imitation (SI)							0.54	0.46	0.40	0.45	0.46	0.41
Syntax awareness (SA)								0.55	0.49	0.60	0.58	0.59
Alliteration (Al)									0.70	0.71	0.74	0.70
Rhyme (Rh)										0.62	0.62	0.58
Reading (France) (R-F)											0.93	0.82
Reading (Schonell) (R-S)												0.87
Spelling (Sp)												

Table 2.5 R^2 change in fixed order multiple regressions of the 57 children who were not precocious readers

Steps in regression	Outcome measure		
	Reading France test	Reading Schonell test	Spelling
Extraneous variables			
1 Age at test of reading	0.000	0.011	0.001
2 Mothers' educational level	0.284***	0.216***	0.258***
3 IQ (WPPSI)	0.272**	0.287***	0.275***
Linguistic variables			
4 Vocabulary (BPVS)	0.005	0.001	0.003
5 Language (Reynell) expressive	0.030	0.030	0.017
6 Language (Reynell) receptive	0.001	0.002	0.029
7 Sentence imitation	0.003	0.009	0.004
Final step			
8a Final step rhyme	0.041**	0.060*	0.036*
8b Final step alliteration	0.090***	0.121***	0.076**
8c Final step syntax awareness	0.000	0.000	0.000

Social background and IQ are controlled as well as general language abilities. $^*p < 0.05$; $^{**}p < 0.01$; $^{***}p < 0.001$.

Discussion

Our study produced four main results. First, the measures that we gave the children when they were 3 and 4 years old accounted for an extremely high proportion of the variance in their reading single words, their comprehension, and their spelling at the age of 6;7.

Our second discovery was that the children's scores in rhyme and alliteration tests given to them at 4 years predicted their reading and spelling levels at 6 years after stringent controls for general language ability as well as for social background and intelligence. The connection between children's sensitivity to rhyme and alliteration at 4 years is not a mere byproduct of some broader linguistic ability.

Third, the children's scores in our other metalinguistic test – the syntax awareness task – were also related to their reading after the differences in general language ability had been partialled out, but this relationship dropped out when social background and IQ were entered into the equation. So we conclude that the connection between awareness of syntax and reading merely reflected differences in these extraneous variables.

Our fourth result concerns the linguistic measures (vocabulary, expressive and receptive language, and sentence imitation). The children's scores in these tests were related to their reading levels, but this relationship also became non-significant after the two extraneous variables, social background and intelligence, had been included in the regression. It seems that the connection between the linguistic measures and reading was simply due to the fact that both were determined by differences in intelligence and in background. Of course we cannot be sure whether the same pattern would have applied to the children tested by Bowey and Patel, because they gave their language measures to 6-year-olds, whereas we gave ours to 4-year-olds. There is a clear need to repeat Bowey and Patel's study with 6-year-olds, but this time to include measures of IQ and social background.

The clearest difference between our results and those of Bowey and Patel is in the power of the rhyme and alliteration tests as predictors of reading. Their rhyme and alliteration measures failed to predict reading after controls for general linguistic ability. In complete contrast, there was a highly significant relationship between our measures of rhyme and alliteration after similar controls. There seem to be two reasonable explanations for this difference. One, which we favor (mentioned in the introduction), is that our rhyme and alliteration measures were given to 4-year-olds, while Bowey and Patel's were given to 6-year-olds.

It may be much more important, from the point of reading, to know how aware a child is of rhyme at 4 years than at 6 years. Why should this be so? Our answer is that at 4 years one gets a relatively pure measure of the child's ability to categorize words by sounds, because he has not begun to read. At 6 years, on the other hand, the child will have had quite a lot of experience with reading, and his judgments about rhyme might now be affected by his knowledge about spelling. So, children might use their knowledge that two words do or do not have a common spelling pattern to help them judge whether the words rhyme. Thus, when the test is given to preschool children, one is measuring their ability to form categories that will help them to read later on, but when it is given to older children one might be picking up effects of the experience of reading as well.

The second possibility is that the difference in results is due to the fact that our tests of rhyme and alliteration took a different form than Bowey and Patel's. In our test the odd word had no phonemes in common with the other two words (*peg, cot, leg; pin, pig, tree*). In theirs, the odd word had one phoneme in common with the other words (*sun, gun, rub; hat, cot, pot; bun, rug, bus*). There is evidence that our version is easier than theirs (Lenel & Cantor, 1981), and our reason for adopting the easier version was that we were working with young children and wanted to be sure that the task would not be too difficult for them. The fact that we adopted an easy test of rhyme and alliteration, while Bowey and Patel adopted a hard one could explain the difference in results, but it is hard to see why. Neither study suffered from floor or ceiling effects, and there seems no reason why an easy test should be a better predictor of reading than a difficult one. In fact, the overall error rate in the rhyme and alliteration tasks seems to have been much the same in the two studies, presumably because the children in the Bowey and Patel study who were given the harder task were also two years older than the children in our study. So we prefer the first possible explanation to the second.

The fact that the odd word shared a phoneme with the other two in Bowey and Patel's task raises another issue. Throughout their paper, they refer to their rhyme and alliteration tests as "phonemic awareness" tests. They use this term because one phoneme told the odd word apart from the other two in their tests. For example with *sun, gun*, and *rub*, the first two words share a final phoneme /n/ which the other words does not possess. But, in our view, this does not mean that the children were responding to the presence or absence of a single phoneme. There is good evidence that children of this age are aware of a speech unit called the "rime" (Kirtley et al., 1989; Treiman, 1985). In single syllable words like *sun*, the rime consists of the vowel and the following consonant – *un*. Kirtley and colleagues (1989) showed that 6-year-old children find it extremely difficult to say which is the odd word in *mop, lead*, and *whip*, and yet quite easy in *top, rail*, and *hop*. In the former case, the odd word can be detected only on the basis of the fact that it lacks a single phoneme which is present in the other two. In *sun, gun*, and *rub* (the Bowey and Patel example) two words share a common rime that the odd word out does not possess. So it is likely that the children who produced the correct answer in Bowey and Patel's rhyme tasks did so on the basis of the words' rimes, which contained two phonemes, rather than on the basis of a single phoneme.

The point seems an important one to us, because we (Bryant et al., 1990) hold the view that awareness of rhyme makes a distinctive contribution to reading. Words that rhyme often share spelling sequences as well (e.g., *light, might, fight*). By forming categories of words that rhyme, the child might be preparing himself for learning spelling categories later on. Note that the unit here is not the single grapheme – phoneme relation. The connection is between sounds with more than one phoneme (rimes) and strings of letters. There is some evidence that this kind of association plays an important part in learning to read. We have shown (Bryant et al., 1990) that children's rhyme scores do make a separate contribution to children's reading even after their scores in phoneme detection tasks have been partialled out, which suggests that the connection between rhyme and reading concerns more than the learning of grapheme – phoneme correspondences. In addition, Goswami (1986, 1988) found that beginning readers make inferences about spelling patterns on the basis of rhyme. If they know how to read the word *beak*, for example, they will often use this knowledge to work out what a new word like *peak* means.

This idea is speculative. We still need to know a lot more about the relationship between the children's knowledge of spelling patterns and their judgments about rhyme. But our data certainly demonstrate that there is a powerful and specific connection between 4-year-old children's sensitivity to rhyme and the progress that they eventually make in reading and spelling. This connection is not a byproduct of differences in general linguistic ability.

References and further reading

Bowey, J. A., & Patel, R. K. (1988). Metalinguistic ability and early reading achievement. *Applied Psycholinguistics, 9*, 367–383.

Bradley, L., & Bryant, P. E. (1983). Categorising sounds and learning to read – A causal connection. *Nature, 301*, 419–521.

——(1985). Rhyme and reason in reading and spelling. *I.A.R.L.D. Monographs, 1*. Ann Arbor: University of Michigan Press.

Bryant, P. E., MacLean, M., Bradley, L., & Crossland, J. (1990). Rhyme and alliteration, phoneme detection and learning to read. *Developmental Psychology* (in press).

Chukovsky, K. (1963). *From two to five*. Berkeley: University of California Press.

Dowker, A. (1989). Rhymes and alliteration in poems elicited from young children. *Journal of Child Language, 16*, 181–202.

Ellis, N., & Large, B. (1987). The development of reading: As you seek so shall you find. *British Journal of Psychology, 78*, 1–28.

Goswami, U. (1986). Children's use of analogy in learning to read: A developmental study. *Journal of Experimental Child Psychology, 42*, 73–83.

——(1988). Children's use of analogy in learning to spell. *British Journal of Developmental Psychology, 6*, 21–33.

Jorm, A. F., Share, D. L., Maclean, R., & Matthews, R. (1984). Phonological confusability in short term memory for sentences as a predictor of reading ability. *British Journal of Psychology, 75*, 393–400.

Kirtley, C., Bryant, P., MacLean, M., & Bradley, L. (1989). Rhyme, rime and the onset of reading. *Journal of Experimental Child Psychology, 48*, 224–245.

Lenel, J. C., & Cantor, J. H. (1981). Rhyme recognition and phonemic perception in young children. *Journal of Psycholinguistic Research, 10*, 57–68.

Lundberg, I., Frost, J., & Petersen, O. (1988). Effects of an extensive program for stimulating phonological awareness in preschool children. *Reading Research Quarterly, 23*, 263–284.

MacLean, M., Bryant, P. E., & Bradley, L. (1987). Rhymes, nursery rhymes and reading in early childhood. *Merrill-Palmer Quarterly, 33*, 255–282.

Reynell, J. K. (1983). *Developmental Language Scales*. East Windsor: NFER-Nelson.

Stanovich, K. E., Cunningham, A. E., & Cramer, B. R. (1984). Assessing phonological awareness of kindergarten children: Issues of task comparability. *Journal of Experimental Child Psychology, 38*, 175–190.

Treiman, R. (1985). Onsets and rimes as units of spoken syllables: Evidence from children. *Journal of Experimental Child Psychology, 39*, 161–181.

Tunmer, W. E., Nesdale, A. R., & Wright, A. D. (1987). Syntactic awareness and reading acquisition. *British Journal of Developmental Psychology, 5*, 25–34.

Wise, B. W., Olson, D. K., & Treiman, R. (1990). Subsyllabic units as aids in beginning readers' word learning: Onset-rime versus post-vowel segmentation. *Journal of Experimental Child Psychology* (in press).

Learning and Development

Introduction

Learning is central to the aims of education. Developmental psychology has a long history of studying both children's learning and their more general cognitive development. Piaget's massive influence on the field, in particular, led to a sustained focus on children's developing conceptual knowledge. But while knowledge was put back 'into the frame', it was not always effectively connected to other closely related topics within psychology, such as learning, thinking, intelligence and memory. When Piaget's general stage theory of children's cognitive development came under increasing critical scrutiny in the 1970s, the search was on for alternative theories, not only of how cognition developed but of what it was, exactly, that developed.

Robert Siegler was a prominent exponent of the position which argued that it was not only children's specific knowledge which gradually improved as they got older but also their cognitive strategies for solving particular problems in any given domain. Siegler is concerned in this paper to make a close connection between learning and cognitive development. He first reviews some important contemporary ideas about children's learning and then focuses on his own particular area of interest: the varied strategies which children typically employ in solving problems. His 'overlapping waves theory' seems an important advance in our understanding both of the variability of children's problem-solving performances and of the detailed ways in which underlying strategies and knowledge are changing over time. He also addresses methodology, making a powerful case for the use of 'microgenetic' methods, that is, the intensive study of children's changing strategies and performances on a given type of problem over relatively short time periods. Finally, Siegler looks at four consistent findings about how change occurs, the last of which links up with the role of conceptual understanding.

The detailed analyses of learning supplied by Siegler and his colleagues appear to have great promise for teachers. They are supplying, perhaps for the first time, credible accounts of children's developing mastery of a range of problems commonly found in early years' classrooms, accounts which address the processes of change, the nature of changing competence and the varied constraints which operate on performance.

Further reading

For a more general summary of theories of cognitive development see, for example:

Demetriou, A. 1998: Cognitive Development. In A. Demetriou, W. Doise and C. van Lieshout (eds), *Life-Span Developmental Psychology*, Chichester: J. Wiley & Sons.

For a good collection of readings on cognitive development, see: K. Lee (ed.), *Cognitive Development*, in the present series.

For more detail on Siegler's own work see:

Siegler, R. 1996: *Emerging Minds: the process of change in children's thinking*. Oxford: Oxford University Press.

THREE

The Rebirth of Children's Learning

Robert S. Siegler

Introduction

At one time, children's learning was *the* central topic in developmental psychology. This has not been the case for many years, however. With the cognitive revolution in adult experimental psychology and the rise of Piaget's theory within developmental psychology, the emphasis shifted from learning to thinking. This shift laid the foundation for a rich and vibrant field of cognitive development. The gains, however, came at a cost. We now know quite a bit about children's thinking at different ages, but we know little about how they get from here to there. In a sense, we threw out the baby of learning with the bath water of associationism.

The movement away from studying children's learning reflected more than a shift in interest; it also reflected an assumption that development and learning are fundamentally different processes. Piaget frequently distinguished between development, by which he meant the active construction of knowledge, and learning, by which he meant the passive formation of associations. Active developmental processes were of interest; passive learning processes were not. This distinction was valuable in focusing attention on children's efforts to make sense of the world and in exposing hidden assumptions that had shaped previous research on children's learning. However, Piaget's stance had the unfortunate side effect of producing skepticism about the importance of any kind of learning for development. This led to a drastic decline in studies of children's learning. As Stevenson (1983) commented:

> By the mid-1970s, articles on children's learning dwindled to a fraction of the number that had been published in the previous decade, and by 1980, it was necessary to search with diligence to uncover any articles at all. . . . The discussion of children's learning had been displaced by a newfound interest in cognitive development (p. 213).

Prominent successors to Piaget's theory, in particular neonativist and theory–theory approaches, also have focused on children's thinking, largely to the exclusion of their learning. The research that they have inspired has expanded our understanding of development by revealing substantial, domain-specific, cognitive capabilities that children possess from early in life and by demonstrating the key roles of causal connections, often mediated by unobservable constructs, in these early understandings. Like Piaget's theory, however, they have told us little about how children come to have these understandings.

It is no accident that recent theories have focused more on the ways children typically think at particular ages than on the processes by which they learn to think in more advanced ways. Intellectually, it makes sense to map out landmarks within the developmental progression before trying to specify the mechanisms by which children move from here to there. Logistic factors militate in the same direction; simply put, it is easier to determine what children know at different ages than to determine how they acquire the knowledge. Research approaches also create their own momentum; the great recent progress in understanding certain topics that have been in vogue, such as understanding of other people's minds and of living and nonliving things, has raised numerous interesting questions regarding alternative interpretations and potential extensions of previous findings.

Arrayed against these varied factors that exert pressure toward continuing to focus on how children think, rather than on how they learn, is one central fact: learning is a central part of children's lives. Learning probably is even more central in the lives of children than in the lives of adults. Adults frequently have considerable expertise with the tasks they undertake. As they gain experience, they continue to learn, but much of the learning involves relatively small refinements of existing competencies rather than acquisition of new capabilities. In addition, how well they perform in their jobs and in their other everyday tasks such as driving is important to their own and other people's well-being. Thus, performance is very important in adults' lives, relative to learning.

In contrast, childhood is a period of life in which learning plays a particularly large role relative to performance. Infants, toddlers, and preschoolers frequently need to acquire new capabilities; their ability to learn is very important. On the other hand, how well they perform any given task at a given time ordinarily is unimportant. The quality of the pictures they draw, their skill at playing games, and their knowledge of songs and television characters matters little. What is important is that they, and school-age children, learn to act in ways that will allow them to perform effectively in future settings. Five hundred years ago, 14-year-olds were adults, because they had learned enough that they could function as adults; today, they are children, because they need to learn so much more before they can function in adult capacities. Thus, although learning is important for adults, it plays an even larger role in the lives of children. Any theory of development that has little to say about how children learn is a seriously limited theory of development.

The importance of children's learning for a coherent understanding of development has led a small but increasing number of investigators to take on the challenges associated with studying it directly. These investigators come to the task from a variety of theoretical backgrounds: neo-Piagetian (e.g., Fischer & Biddel, 1998; Karmiloff-Smith, 1992), cultural contextualist (Ellis & Gauvain, 1992; Granott, 1993), dynamic systems (Thelen & Ulrich, 1991; van Geert, 1998), and information processing (Johnson & Morton, 1991; Munakata, 1998; Siegler, 1996). They do not study learning of paired associates or nonsense syllables. Instead, they investigate how children learn meaningful concepts and skills such as object permanence, reaching, face recognition, scientific and mathematical problem solving, arithmetic, and so on. Thus, the new field of children's learning, unlike the old one, emphasizes acquisition of concepts and skills that are important in children's lives.

Despite differences in the investigators' theoretical orientations, modern investigations of children's learning have yielded highly similar results. Such commonalities are especially encouraging, because they suggest that the regularities in children's learning are sufficiently strong that they shine through differences in investigators' preconceptions and specifics of tasks, content domains, and populations.

The empirical studies that have revealed the commonalities in children's learning rest on a foundation of recent theoretical and methodological advances. The next two sections of this article examine these theoretical and methodological advances; the following section highlights four findings that have emerged consistently from the empirical research; and the final section focuses on two key issues for future consideration: the relation between learning and development and educational implications of current research on children's learning.

Emerging Theories of Children's Learning

In the past few years, theoretical proposals regarding children's learning have increased considerably in both number and precision. A wide range of theoretical approaches have contributed to this trend, as is apparent in the chapters of the most recent *Handbook of Child Psychology* (Damon, 1998). In a chapter focused on information processing approaches, Klahr and MacWhinney (1998) noted that beneath the superficial differences between connectionist and symbolic information processing models of children's learning, there are important similarities. Both types of models indicate that learning involves considerable parallel processing; that it influences the activations of many local units rather than being limited to high-level changes such as those envisioned in stage approaches; and that it produces qualitative as well as quantitative change.

Rogoff (1998) emphasized that within sociocultural approaches to development, learning involves not just increasing knowledge of content but also incorporation of values and cultural assumptions that underlie views about how material should be taught and how the task of learning should be approached. Case's (1998) examination of neo-Piagetian theories provides a third example. He proposed that children learn new information by organizing it to fit central conceptual structures for thinking about number, space, and other domains. To cite a fourth example, Gelman and Williams (1998) examined constraints on learning. They argued that all theories of cognitive development posit that learning is constrained, that almost all of the theories recognize that many of the posited constraints help rather than hinder learning, and that the theories vary more in their views regarding the specificity and origins of the constraints than in whether learning is constrained. Finally, Spelke and Newport (1998) proposed that innate knowledge provides the building blocks from which more refined and culturally contingent learning is later created. Thus, although neither neo-Piagetian nor information processing nor sociocultural nor neonativist theories have focused primarily on how children learn, all are devoting increasing attention to it.

One theory that does focus primarily on children's learning is the overlapping waves theory (Siegler, 1996). This theory is based on three assumptions: (1) children typically use a variety of strategies and ways of thinking, rather than just a single one, to solve a given problem; (2) the diverse strategies and ways of thinking coexist over prolonged periods of time, not just during brief transition periods; (3) experience brings changes in relative reliance on existing strategies and ways of thinking, as well as introduction of more advanced approaches.

A schematic illustration of these assumptions is provided in Figure 3.1. Examination of any vertical slice of the figure indicates that multiple approaches are used at one time. Comparing several vertical slices indicates that relative frequencies of strategies shift continuously

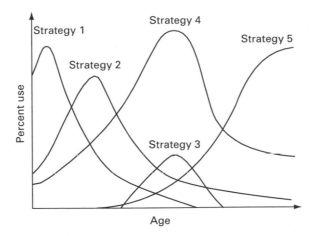

Figure 3.1   Schematic depiction of the overlapping waves model

over time, with new strategies sometimes being added and older strategies sometimes ceasing to be used. Following the curve for a given strategy indicates that a single strategy will often be used for a protracted period, even after later-developing, more advanced approaches are also known.

The cognitive diversity postulated by overlapping waves theory appears to be present at every level of analysis. It is present within individuals as well as across them; in studies of arithmetic, serial recall, spelling, time telling, and other tasks, most children used at least three strategies (Siegler, 1996). The variability also is evident within an individual solving the same problem on two occasions close in time; presented the same simple addition problem or the same time on an analog clock, one third of children used different strategies on two presentations within a one-week period (Siegler & McGilly, 1989; Siegler & Shrager, 1984). The variability is even present within a single trial. Children sometimes express one strategy in speech and a different one in gesture on the same trial (Goldin-Meadow, Alibali, & Church, 1993). Other times, verbalizations alone reveal multiple strategies; for example, children frequently use category naming and rehearsal on a single free recall trial (Coyle & Bjorklund, 1997).

This last phenomenon – cognitive variability within a single trial – raises interesting challenges for formal models of strategy choice. To date, such models have focused on situations in which a single strategy is chosen on a given trial (e.g., Siegler & Shipley, 1995). However, the models could be extended in any of three ways to choosing among multiple strategies on a single trial. One possibility is that two or more strategies could be organized into a linked unit, and the linked unit could be chosen; thus, children might on one trial choose "name a category and rehearse its members," though on another trial they might choose one of the component strategies (e.g., "name the category") alone. A second possibility is the separate strategy choices could be made at different times within a trial; children might first choose category naming as a strategy and later in the trial choose rehearsing the members of the category. A third possibility, especially applicable to cases where different strategies are expressed in different modalities, is that strategy choices could be made in parallel in the two modalities; thus, children might choose one strategy in gesture and simultaneously choose one a different one in speech. These possibilities are not exclusive; all are plausible, and all may be used.

Overlapping waves theory also specifies four dimensions along which learning occurs: acquistion of novel ways of thinking, more frequent use of the more effective ways of thinking from among the existing possibilities, increasingly adaptive choices among alternative ways of thinking, and increasingly efficient execution of the alternative approaches.

The most obvious dimension of learning is acquisition of new, more advanced ways of thinking. Such acquisition can occur through drawing analogies to better understood problems, through direct verbal instruction, through forming mental models of the situation and reasoning about them, or through observations during the course of problem solving (Anderson, 1991; Sternberg, 1985). Acquisition of new strategies involves a mix of associative and metacognitive processes, and also a mix of conscious and unconscious processes. In at least some cases, new strategies are constructed on an unconscious level before people are aware of doing anything different than they had done previously; behavioral indices show that new approaches are being used, although verbal reports of use of the new strategy lag slightly behind (Siegler & Stern, 1998). Thus, discovery is not exclusively a metacognitive process, nor is it exclusively an associative process. Both types of processes are crucial.

Although important, acquiring new ways of thinking is not the only way learning occurs. A second dimension of learning involves increasing reliance on the more advanced alternatives within the set of approaches that children already know. This is a more common vehicle of cognitive growth than is commonly recognized. For example, Lemaire and Siegler (1995) found that from the end of the first week of instruction to the end of the year, French children who were learning single-digit multiplication used the same set of strategies. The frequency of the most advanced strategy (retrieval of the answer from memory) increased considerably during this period, and the frequency of the least advanced strategy (adding one of the multiplicands the number of times indicated by the other) decreased considerably, but most children used the same set of strategies throughout the period.

Learning also can occur through increasingly precise fitting of strategy choices to the demands of problems and situations. Even if both the set of strategies and the frequency of use of each strategy remain the same, each strategy can be chosen increasingly often in those cases in which it is the best available alternative. Such changes also were present in the Lemaire and Siegler (1995) study. Over the course of the year, children fit their strategy choices increasingly precisely to the demands of problems and to the limits of their own knowledge. In particular, they used retrieval increasingly consistently on the easiest problems, problems on which they usually could retrieve the correct answer, and they increasingly limited use of repeated addition to the most difficult problems, problems on which retrieval was less accurate.

Another dimension along which learning occurs is improved execution of existing approaches. Even without changes along the other three dimensions, children's performance can improve greatly as they become increasingly skillful in executing each approach. In the Lemaire and Siegler (1995) study, for example, on those problems on which children retrieved answers to a given multiplication problem at all three times of measurement, percentage of errors decreased from 23% to 2%, and mean solution time decreased from 4 s to 2 s.

Data consistent with the overlapping waves model have been obtained across such varied tasks as toddlers' locomotor activity, preschoolers' arithmetic, and elementary and high school children's scientific experimentation (see Siegler, 1996, for a recent review of these studies). In all of these areas, children have been found to use multiple strategies at any given age, with variability existing within individual children as well as between children. In each area, children also have been found to rely increasingly on the relatively advanced approaches as they learn more about the domain. These same features are characteristic of adults' thinking and learning, as has been demonstrated in such domains as multidigit mental arithmetic, sentence–picture verification, and spatial reasoning (LeFevre, Sadesky, & Bisanz 1996; Marquer & Pereira, 1990; Newton & Roberts, in press).

These findings regarding children's and adults' learning have formed the basis for computer simulation models that use a common set of principles to account for cognitive growth from early childhood through adulthood (Shrager & Siegler, 1998; Siegler & Shipley, 1995). These simulation models suggest that the overlapping waves pattern arises through the workings of several learning processes. Problem-solving experience leads to an increasingly extensive database becoming associated with both strategies and problems. This database includes information on the speed and accuracy of each strategy on problems in general, problems with particular features, and specific problems. Experience using each strategy also leads to its execution becoming increasingly automatized. The increasingly extensive database on characteristics of strategies and problems makes possible increasingly refined choices among strategies and increasing reliance on the most advanced strategies. The increasing automatization of the strategies leads to increasingly fast, accurate, and effortless execution of strategies.

An interesting aspect of the most recent of these computer simulations, SCADS (Strategy Choice and Discovery Simulation; Shrager & Siegler, 1998) is that within it, discovery of new strategies arises through the interplay of associative and metacognitive learning processes. Automatization of execution of strategies leads to the freeing of cognitive resources that previously had been needed to monitor execution of the strategies. Some of these freed cognitive resources are used to search for redundant processing within existing strategies. If such redundancies are found, strategy discovery heuristics are used to generate potential strategies from the components of previous ones. These potential strategies are then evaluated against conceptual constraints on legitimate strategies in the domain. If the potential strategy is consistent with the conceptual constraints, it is tried. With each use of the new strategy, speed and accuracy characteristics become associated with it. This emerging database and the databases of the prior strategies together determine when the new approach is used. Thus, newly discovered strategies that are more effective than known alternatives are used increasingly, and new strategies that are inferior to known alternatives come to be used less or not at all.

The fact that learning within the Shrager and Siegler (1998) model involves an interaction between metacognitive and associative processes is unlikely to be unique to the specific model or content domain. Rather, children's learning in most domains seems likely to reflect the interaction of associative and higher level processes. The reason why developmental psychologists could at one time focus on associative processes and at a later time on higher level processes is that both are important parts of cognition and learning. Focusing on one to the exclusion of the other yields a one-sided picture of cognitive growth.

Other models of children's learning, such as those constructed within dynamic systems theories (Smith, Thelen, Titzer, & McLin, 1999; van Geert, 1998), differ in their particulars but they share with overlapping waves theory a number of assumptions about how learning occurs. Within both approaches, children learn by doing;

learning occurs through performance. Another shared assumption is that variability is a central characteristic of the cognitive system, rather than reflecting measurement error. A third shared assumption is that learning comes about through many simultaneously changing aspects of the system rather than through any one central change that moves the system as a whole from one state to another. A fourth shared assumption is that a wide variety of constraints – anatomical, physiological, environmental, and cognitive – guide the form of learning.

Together, these theories converge on a new agenda for studying children's learning. Rather than trying to identify *the* age at which children develop a given capability, we would trace over time the set of approaches that they use. In other words, we would examine changing distributions of existing approaches as well as emergence of new ones. Another priority would be to examine changes that occur with age and experience in children's choices among alternative approaches, that is, in ability to flexibly adjust what they do to the demands of the problem and situation. A third priority would be to examine the circumstances surrounding new forms of behavior – what leads up to discoveries and how they are generalized once they emerge. Fortunately, all of these issues can be addressed through use of a particular method for studying children's learning, the microgenetic approach.

Microgenetic Methods for Studying Children's Learning

The central questions within prevailing theories influence, and are influenced by, prevailing research methods. Standard cross-sectional and longitudinal methods, which sample the thinking of children at different ages, fit well with theories that emphasize such questions as "When do children understand —" and "What is the developmental sequence of knowledge states by which children come to understand —."

In contrast, if a central theoretical question is "Through what processes do children learn —," standard cross-sectional and longitudinal methods are less useful. The problem is that within these methods, observations of emerging competence are spaced too far apart in time to yield detailed information about the learning process. They lack the temporal resolution needed to indicate how change occurs.

This is where microgenetic methods are particularly useful – for answering questions about learning processes. As noted by Siegler and Crowley (1991), such methods have three main properties:

1 Observations span the period of rapidly changing competence.
2 Within this period, the density of observations is high relative to the rate of change.
3 Observations are analyzed intensively, with the goal of inferring the representations and processes that gave rise to them.

The second property is especially important. Densely sampling changing competence during the period of rapid change provides the level of temporal resolution needed to understand the learning process. If children's learning usually proceeded in the most straightforward way possible, such dense sampling of ongoing changes would be unnecessary. We could examine their thinking before and after changes occurred, identify the shortest path between the two states, and infer that children moved in a beeline from the less advanced one to the more advanced one. Such beelines are the exception rather than the rule, however. Cognitive changes involve regressions as well as progressions, odd transitional states that are present only briefly but that are crucial for the change to occur, generalization along some dimensions from the beginning of learning but lack of generalization along other dimensions for years thereafter, and many other surprising features. Simply put, the only way to find out how children learn is to follow them closely while they are learning.

Four Lessons from Recent Studies of Children's Learning

In the past decade, microgenetic methods have been used to study an increasing range of populations and content domains: infants' learning of reaching and locomotor skills (Adolph, 1997; Thelen & Ulrich, 1991), preschoolers' learning of attentional strategies and number conservation (Miller & Aloise-Young, 1996; Siegler, 1995), elementary schoolers' learning of memory strategies, mathematical principles, analogical reasoning, and pictorial representation (Alibali, & 1999; Bjorklund, Coyle, & Gaultney, 1992; Chen & Klahr, 1999; Goldin-Meadow, Alibali, & Church, 1993), and adolescents' and adults' learning of scientific experimentation skills (Kuhn, Garcia-Mila, Zohar, & Andersen, 1995; Schauble, 1996). Despite varying theoretical predispositions of the investigators, diverse content domains of the tasks, and widely separated ages of the children studied, the descriptions of learning that have emerged from microgenetic studies are strikingly similar. Consider four of the most consistent findings.

Change is gradual

In the large majority of studies of children's learning, researchers have found change to be gradual. Older, less powerful ways of thinking about a task often continue to be employed for a long time after newer, more advanced ways of thinking about it are also available (Kuhn, 1995; Schauble, 1990, 1996; Siegler, 1994). Change is especially likely to be gradual in cases where the new approach is not hugely advantageous relative to existing approaches. This is often the case, because early approaches tend to be reasonably effective. Counting from one generally yields correct solutions to arithmetic problems (Siegler & Jenkins, 1989), unsystematic scientific experimentation strategies often allow identification of causal relations (Schauble, 1996), inefficient map drawing strategies usually get the ambulance to the hospital (Karmiloff-Smith, 1979), and so on. Even when a new approach eventually offers large advantages, it may not do so at first, because children cannot execute it effectively (Bjorklund, Miller, Coyle, & Slawinski, 1997; Miller & Seier, 1994). When a new way of thinking is much more effective than any previous approach, it sometimes becomes dominant quite quickly (Alibali, 1999; van Geert, 1998), but more often change is gradual.

Discoveries follow success as well as failure

A second consistent characteristic of children's learning is that children discover new strategies when they have been succeeding on a task as well as when they have been failing (Karmiloff-Smith, 1992; Miller & Aloise-Young, 1996; Siegler & Jenkins, 1989). Necessity sometimes is the mother of invention, but at other times, invention occurs without external pressure. Children frequently generate novel strategies after having solved several problems correctly and on problems that they have previously solved correctly. This finding is in accord with the everyday observation that many discoveries arise in situations with minimal external demands: taking a shower, driving to work, taking a walk, and so on.

Early variability is related to later learning

A third common finding from microgenetic studies is that the initial variability of thinking is positively related to the subsequent rate of learning. In many studies, the greater the initial variability, the more likely that children will generate useful problem solving strategies and abandon ineffective older ones (Alibali & Goldin-Meadow, 1993; Graham & Perry, 1993; Perry & Lewis, 1999; Siegler, 1995). Several specific forms of initial cognitive variability have been found to be positively related to subsequent learning: number of strategies used over a set of problems, frequency of shifting from one strategy to another within a single trial, frequency of self-corrections and deletions in verbal descriptions of strategies, and frequency of expressing one strategy in speech and another in gesture on a single trial.

Not all types of variability are positively related to learning. For example, Coyle and Bjorklund (1997) found that changes in strategy use from one trial to the next were negatively related to percent correct recall. This may have reflected children adopting a win-stay-lose-shift approach, in which they tended to shift strategies from one trial to the next when recall on the earlier trial was incorrect but tended to maintain the same strategy if it yielded correct recall. Consistent with this possibility, McGilly and Siegler (1989) found that strategy shifts on a serial recall task occurred more often following incorrect recall than following correct recall. More generally, because cognition is variable in so many different ways, it will be important to examine the relation between initial variability and subsequent learning using a variety of measures of both variability and learning.

Discoveries are constrained by conceptual understanding

A fourth consistent finding is that discovery of new strategies is guided by conceptual understanding of the domain (Coyle & Bjorklund, 1997; Gelman & Gallistel, 1978; Granott, 1993; Schauble, 1990, 1996). The novel strategies that children attempt generally make sense; they are not generated via blind trial and error. Newly generated strategies do not always yield correct solutions to the problems that elicited them, but they usually are reasonable efforts in that direction. It is important to note that there certainly are times when children generate conceptually flawed strategies. These can arise either through children having an incomplete understanding of the goals that legitimate strategies in the domain must meet or through the situation requiring children to generate an answer even though they do not know any plausible strategy for doing so. Despite these exceptions, it is striking how often newly discovered strategies conform to the principles underlying legitimate strategies in the domain.

The consistent phenomena that have arisen from microgenetic studies have given rise to a set of intriguing proposals regarding the processes that produced the changes. To account for the persistent use of nonoptimal strategies despite more effective strategies being known, the construct of utilization deficiency has been proposed (Bjorklund, Miller, Coyle, & Slawinski, 1997; Miller & Seier, 1994). To account for discoveries being made in the absence of external pressure, the SCADS computer simulation progressively frees attentional resources as it gains experience executing existing strategies, thus activating strategy discovery heuristics (Shrager & Siegler, 1998). To account for positive relations between initial variability and subsequent learning, investigators have focused on the ways variable behavior reveals the possibilities inherent in the task environment (Neuringer, 1993; Stokes, 1995). To account for how children discover legitimate addition strategies without ever trying illegal ones, the idea of goal sketches has been proposed (Siegler & Jenkins, 1989), tested and supported through empirical experiments (Siegler & Crowley, 1994), and formally specified as a part of the SCADS model (Shrager & Siegler, 1998).

The connection between the microgenetic studies and the detailed ideas about mechanisms is no coincidence. Microgenetic studies yield sufficiently detailed information both to suggest ideas about how the data were generated and to rule out many otherwise plausible alternative accounts. To cite one such case, prior to the first microgenetic study of single-digit addition, the prevailing model (Groen & Resnick, 1977) was that children first solved such problems by counting from one (the *sum strategy*), then by counting from the first addend, and then by counting from the larger addend (the *min strategy*). That is, children were hypothesized first to solve problems such as $3 + 5$

by counting "1, 2, 3—1, 2, 3, 4, 5—1, 2, 3, 4, 5, 6, 7, 8"), then by counting "4, 5, 6, 7, 8," and then by counting "6, 7, 8." Although this model seemed plausible, a microgenetic study of development of single-digit addition disconfirmed it; children discovered the min strategy without ever having counted from the first addend. Conversely, the microgenetic study indicated that shortly before children discovered the min strategy, they began to use a different transitional approach that had not been hypothesized. This was the shortcut sum strategy; children using it would solve 3 + 5 by counting "1, 2, 3—4, 5, 6, 7, 8." In retrospect, the shortcut sum strategy made sense as a transitional approach. As in the less advanced sum strategy, children count from 1; as in the more advanced min strategy, children count each number only once, rather than twice as in the sum strategy. However, it was not until the microgenetic study of addition that the shortcut sum strategy was identified as a transitional approach. The example illustrates how microgenetic data constrain ideas about transition mechanisms, both in the negative sense of ruling out otherwise plausible accounts and in the positive sense of documenting the path of change.

Learning and Development

As noted earlier, the movement away from studying children's learning was fueled in large part by the view that learning and development were fundamentally different processes. Recent studies of children's learning provide reason to rethink this conclusion. As Kuhn (1995) commented:

> In the 1960s and 1970s, development was contrasted to a simplistic, nonrepresentational conception of learning that has little relevance today. Modern research has made it clear that learning processes share all of the complexity, organization, structure, and internal dynamics once attributed exclusively to development. If the distinction has become blurred, it is not because development has been reduced to "nothing but" learning, but rather because we now recognize learning to be more like development in many fundamental respects (p. 138).

Findings from cognitive developmental neuroscience provide additional support for the view that learning and development are both similar and inseparable. Regardless of whether the change is species-typical, such as development of stereopsis in response to binocular exposure to patterned light, or idiosyncratic, as when a rat learns to turn left in a maze to obtain food, synaptic changes involve a cycle of proliferation and pruning (Greenough, Black, & Wallace, 1987). First, there is a burst of formation of new synaptic connections; then, experience prunes away those synapses not involved in subsequent processing. The terms "learning" and "development" are used differently, with development referring to changes that are more universal within the species, that occur over longer time periods, and that occur in response to a broader variety of experiences. At the level of process, however, the two have a great deal in common.

Increasing our focus on children's learning will yield a more comprehensive understanding of development; it also may yield valuable educational applications. It is no secret that many children do not learn well in school. Rigorous developmental analyses of how children learn – and fail to learn – reading, writing, and mathematics may produce better understanding of the learning difficulties and may contribute to better programs for remedying them. This is already starting to happen. Geary (1994) identified a number of contributors to mathematics disability: limited early exposure to numbers, poor working memory capacity for numerical information, and limited conceptual understanding of arithmetic operations and counting. Similarly, Griffin (in press) formulated a neo-Piagetian analysis of how children learn basic numerical concepts and applied it to the task of helping low-income first graders master these basic concepts, with impressive results.

Microgenetic analyses of learning may prove especially helpful for indicating how instructional procedures exercise their effects, and thus for designing more effective future instructional procedures. For example, recent studies indicate that asking children to explain both why correct answers are correct and why incorrect answers are incorrect produces greater learning than only asking them to explain why correct answers are correct (Siegler, in press). Microgenetic analyses of the learning process indicated that part of the reason for this advantage was that asking children to explain both correct and incorrect answers led to their adopting new strategies that were more widely applicable, ones that would generate correct answers not only on the original problem set but also on types of problems that were not initially presented. The practical implication is that when students have a tendency to respond to instruction by adopting overly narrow strategies, it may be particularly useful to ask them to explain both why correct answers are correct and why incorrect answers are incorrect. More generally, as these examples illustrate, the rebirth of children's learning promises not only to create a more exciting field of cognitive development but also to help children learn.

References

Adolph, K. E. (1997). Learning in the development of infant locomotion. *Monographs of the Society for Research in Child Development, 62*(3, Serial No. 251).

Alibali, M. W. (1999). How children change their minds: Strategy change can be gradual or abrupt. *Developmental Psychology, 35*, 127–145.

Alibali, M. W., & Goldin-Meadow, S. (1993). Gesture-speech mismatch and mechanisms of learning: What the hands reveal about a child's state of mind. *Cognitive Psychology, 25*, 468–523.

Anderson, J. R. (1991). Is human cognition adaptive? *The Behavioral and Brain Sciences, 14*, 471–484.

Bjorklund, D. F., Coyle, T. R., & Gaultney, J. F. (1992). Developmental differences in the acquisition and maintenance of an organizational strategy: Evidence for the utilization deficiency hypothesis. *Journal of Experimental Child Psychology, 54*, 434–438.

Bjorklund, D. F., Miller, P. H., Coyle, T. R., & Slawinski, J. L. (1997). Instructing children to use memory strategies: Evidence of utilization deficiencies in memory training studies. *Developmental Review, 17*, 411–441.

Case, R. (1998). The development of conceptual structures. In D. Kuhn & R. S. Siegler (Eds.), W. Damon (Series Ed.), *Handbook of child psychology: Vol. 2. Cognition, perception, and language* (5th ed., pp. 745–800). New York: Wiley. Chen, Z., & Klahr, D. (1999). All other things being equal: Children's acquisition of the Control of Variables Strategy. *Child Development, 70*, 1098–1120.

Coyle, T. R., & Bjorklund, D. F. (1997). Age differences in, and consequences of, multiple-and variable-strategy use on a multitrial sort-recall task. *Developmental Psychology, 33*, 372–380.

Damon, W. (Series Ed.). (1998). *Handbook of child psychology* (5th ed., Vols. 1–4), New York: Wiley.

Ellis, S., & Gauvain, M. (1992). Social and cultural influences on children's collaborative interactions. In L. T. Winegar & J. Valsiner (Eds.), *Children's development within social context* (Vol. 2, pp. 155–180). Hillsdale, NJ: Erlbaum.

Fischer, K. W., & Biddel, T. R. (1998). Dynamic development of psychological structures in action and thought. In R. M. Lerner (Ed.), W. Damon (Series Ed.), *Handbook of child psychology: Vol. 1. Theoretical models of human development* (5th ed., pp. 467–562). New York: Wiley.

Geary, D. C. (1994). *Children's mathematical development: Research and practical implications.* Washington, DC: American Psychological Association.

Gelman, R., & Gallistel, C. R. (1978). *The child's understanding of number.* Cambridge, MA: Harvard University Press.

Gelman, R., & Williams, E. (1998). Enabling constraints for cognitive development and learning: Domain specificity and epigenesis. In D. Kuhn & R. S. Siegler (Eds.), W. Damon (Series Ed.), *Handbook of child psychology: Vol. 2. Cognition, perception, and language* (5th ed., pp. 575–630). New York: Wiley.

Goldin-Meadow, S., Alibali, M. W., & Church, R. B. (1993). Transitions in concept acquisition: Using the hand to read the mind. *Psychological Review, 100,* 279–297.

Graham, T., & Perry, M. (1993). Indexing transitional knowledge. *Developmental Psychology, 29,* 779–788.

Granott, N. (1993). Patterns of interaction in the co-construction of knowledge: Separate minds, joint effort, and weird creatures. In R. Wozniak & K. W. Fischer (Eds.), *Development in context: Acting and thinking in specific environments* (pp. 183–207). Hillsdale, NJ: Erlbaum.

Greenough, W. T., Black, J. E., & Wallace, C. S. (1987). Experience and brain development. *Child Development, 58,* 539–559.

Griffin, S. A. (in press). Evaluation of a program designed to teach number sense to children at risk for school failure. *Journal of Research in Mathematics Education.*

Groen, G. J., & Resnick, L. B. (1977). Can preschool children invent addition algorithms? *Journal of Educational Psychology, 69,* 645–652.

Johnson, M. H., & Morton, J. (1991). *Biology and cognitive development: The case of face recognition.* Oxford: Blackwell.

Karmiloff-Smith, A. (1979). Micro- and macro-developmental changes in language acquisition and other representational systems. *Cognitive Science, 3,* 91–118.

Karmiloff-Smith, A. (1992). *Beyond modularity: A developmental perspective on cognitive science.* Cambridge, MA: MIT.

Klahr, D., & MacWhinney, B. (1998). Information processing. In D. Kuhn & R. S. Siegler (Eds.), W. Damon (Series Ed.), *Handbook of child psychology: Vol. 2. Cognition, perception, and language* (5th ed., pp. 631–678). New York: Wiley.

Kuhn, D. (1995). Microgenetic study of change: What has it told us? *Psychological Science, 6,* 133–139.

Kuhn, D., Garcia-Mila, M., Zohar, A., & Andersen, C. (1995). Strategies of knowledge acquisition. *Monographs of the Society for Research in Child Development, 60*(4, Serial No. 245).

LeFevre, J. A., Sadesky, G. S., & Bisanz, J. (1996). Selection of procedures in mental addition: Reassessing the problem-size effect in adults. *Journal of Experimental Psychology: Learning, Memory, and Cognition, 22,* 216–230.

Lemaire, P., & Siegler, R. S. (1995). Four aspects of strategic change: Contributions to children's learning of multiplication. *Journal of Experimental Psychology: General, 124,* 83–97.

Marquer, J., & Pereira, M. (1990). Reaction time in the study of strategies in sentence-picture verification: A reconsideration. *The Quarterly Journal of Experimental Psychology, 42A,* 147–168.

McGilly, K., & Siegler, R. S. (1989). How children choose among serial recall strategies. *Child Development, 60,* 172–182.

Miller, P., & Aloise-Young, P. (1996). Preschoolers' strategic behaviors and performance on a same-different task. *Journal of Experimental Child Psychology, 60,* 284–303.

Miller, P. H., & Seier, W. L. (1994). Strategy utilization deficiencies in children: When, where, and why. In H. W. Reese (Ed.), *Advances in child development and behavior* (Vol. 25, pp. 108–156). New York: Academic Press.

Munakata, Y. (1998). Infant perseveration and implications for object permanence theories: A PDP model of the AB task. *Developmental Science, 1,* 161–184.

Neuringer, A. (1993). Reinforced variation and selection. *Animal Learning and Behavior, 21,* 83–91.

Newton, E., & Roberts, M. (in press). An experimental study of strategy selection and strategy development. *Memory and Cognition, 29,* 565–573.

Perry, M., & Lewis, J. L. (1999). Verbal imprecision as an index of knowledge in transition. *Developmental Psychology, 25,* 749–759.

Rogoff, B. (1998). Cognition as a collaborative process. In D. Kuhn & R. S. Siegler (Eds.), W. Damon (Series Ed.), *Handbook of child psychology: Vol. 2. Cognition, perception, and language* (5th ed., pp. 679–744). New York: Wiley.

Schauble, L. (1990). Belief revision in children: The role of prior knowledge and strategies for generating evidence. *Journal of Experimental Child Psychology, 49,* 31–57.

Schauble, L. (1996). The development of scientific reasoning in knowledge-rich contexts. *Developmental Psychology, 32,* 102–119.

Shrager, J., & Siegler, R. S. (1998). SCADS: A model of children's strategy choices and strategy discoveries. *Psychological Science, 9,* 405–410.

Siegler, R. S. (1994). Cognitive variability: A key to understanding cognitive development. *Current Directions in Psychological Science, 3,* 1–5.

Siegler, R. S. (1995). How does change occur: A microgenetic study of number conservation. *Cognitive Psychology, 28,* 225–273.

Siegler, R. S. (1996). *Emerging minds: The process of change in children's thinking.* New York: Oxford University Press.

Siegler, R. S. (in press). Microgenetic studies of self-explanations. In N. Granott & J. Parziale (Eds.), *Microdevelopment: Transition processes in development and learning.*

Siegler, R. S., & Crowley, K. (1991). The microgenetic method: A direct means for studying cognitive development. *American Psychologist, 46,* 606–620.

Siegler, R. S., & Crowley, K. (1994). Constraints on learning in non-privileged domains. *Cognitive Psychology, 27,* 194–227.

Siegler, R. S., & Jenkins, E. A. (1989). *How children discover new strategies.* Hillsdale, NJ: Erlbaum.

Siegler, R. S., & McGilly, K. (1989). Strategy choices in children's time-telling. In I. Levin and D. Zakay (Eds.), *Time and human cognition: A life span perspective* (pp. 185–218). The Netherlands: Elsevier Science.

Siegler, R. S., & Shipley, C. (1995). Variation, selection, and cognitive change. In T. Simon and G. Halford (Eds.), *Developing cognitive competence: New approaches to process modeling.* Hillsdale, NJ: Erlbaum.

Siegler, R. S., & Shrager, J. (1984). Strategy choices in addition and subtraction: How do children know what to do? In C. Sophian (Ed.), *The origins of cognitive skills* (pp. 229–293). Hillsdale, NJ: Erlbaum.

Siegler, R. S., & Stern, E. (1998). A microgenetic analysis of conscious and unconscious strategy discoveries. *Journal of Experimental Psychology: General, 127,* 377–397.

Smith, L. B., Thelen, E., Titzer, R., & McLin, D. (1999). Knowing in the context of acting: The task dynamics of the A-not- B error. *Psychological Review, 106,* 235–260.

Spelke, E. S., & Newport, E. L. (1998). Nativism, empiricism, and the development of knowledge. In R. M. Lerner (Ed.), W. Damon (Series Ed.), *Handbook of child psychology: Vol. 1. Theoretical models of human development* (5th ed., pp. 275–340). New York: Wiley.

Sternberg, R. J. (1985). *Beyond IQ: A triarchic theory of human intelligence.* New York: Cambridge University Press.

Stevenson, H. (1983). How children learn: The quest for a theory. In W. Kessen (Ed.), P. H. Mussen (Series Ed.), *Handbook of child psychology: Vol. 1. History, theory, and methods* (pp. 213–236), New York: Wiley.

Stokes, P. D. (1995). Learned variability. *Animal Learning & Behavior, 23,* 164–176.

Thelen, E., & Ulrich, B. D. (1991). Hidden skills. *Monographs of the Society for Research in Child Development*, 56(1, Serial No. 223).

van Geert, P. (1998). A dynamic systems model of basic developmental mechanisms: Piaget Vygotsky, and beyond. *Psychological Review*, *105*, 634–677.

Maths Learning

Introduction

Children learn both inside and outside classrooms. In fact the cultural context of learning has turned out to be a potent influence on exactly what is learned where. As Siegler (this volume) argues, children often develop more than one strategy for solving a given type of problem and select strategies to fit different contexts and purposes. In the following study, Saxe was able to investigate how a group of Brazilian children, who sold candy (sweets) on the streets, had worked out strategies for dealing with arithmetic calculations to do with currency recognition, pricing and profits. He also considers the influence of schooling on the calculations of those who had attended school, and the comparable performance of same-aged children who attended school but were not involved in street selling. Although experience of mathematics in school is shown to have some effects it had little influence on the street-sellers' success in solving the sorts of problems they faced in their day-to-day work.

The study illustrates how strategy learning often relies on the observation of more experienced peers, or adults, and on practical problem solving, rather than on direct instruction or practice with pencil- and-paper problems. In pre-industrial human societies, the basic way of life used to be acquired by children mainly through observation, trial and error and some form of apprenticeship in adult roles. The advent of specialized schools and teachers, using instruction and texts as their main tools, is comparatively recent in human cultural history. While schools have enormous advantages for the learner, in terms of their focused aims, resources and expertise, they also have some disadvantages, including being relatively remote from the cultural sites where most knowledge will eventually be applied. There is also a strong risk that young children will approach school-based learning as a specialized kind of work which belongs only in classrooms. This may often lead to their making little connection between such school-based work and their problem solving out of school. The transfer of learning between contexts is thus a major educational problem.

Further reading

Rogoff, B. 1990: *Apprenticeship in Learning*. New York: Oxford University Press.

Rogoff, B. and Chavajay 1995: What's Become of Research on the Cultural Basis of Cognitive Development? *American Psychologist*, 50, 10, 859–77.

Kirshner, D. and Whitson, J. (eds), 1997: *Situated Cognition*. Mahwah NJ: L. Erlbaum Associates.

FOUR

Candy Selling and Math Learning

Geoffrey B. Saxe

It is a common belief that the principal context in which children learn mathematics is school. Clearly, this belief has merit when we consider that over the course of our social history, from pre-Babylonian times to today, civilizations have produced an immense legacy of complex mathematical systems and procedures, a legacy that children could not invent on their own. In school we attempt to teach this legacy, and children's acquisition and use of these systems have generally become identified in everyday language with *mathematics learning*.

Despite its merits, the view that children learn mathematics principally in school has been increasingly questioned. Anthropologists, psychologists, and educators have joined ranks in the study of the kinds of knowledge children acquire outside of school. They have found that children gain mathematical understandings in out-of-school contexts, but the mathematics may only on occasion resemble that of the classroom. This recent work has expanded our conceptions of what counts as mathematics as well as opened up important new questions about how children acquire basic mathematical concepts.

One context in which researchers have documented out-of-school mathematics learning is in the everyday activities of the preschooler. In a recent investigation, colleagues and I found that young children from both middle and working class homes are typically engaged with a remarkable array of activities involving number, including games of mothers' and children's own invention, like counting stairs; store-bought games involving number; and educational television shows, like Sesame Street (Saxe, Guberman, & Gearhart, 1987). The numerical understandings that children generate in these activities are remarkable, and, in some respects, they are different from those they later acquire in school In our own research and in the work of other investigators, we find that even 2- and 3-year-olds have considerable competence in counting objects (Fuson, 1988; Gelman & Gallistel, 1978; Gelman & Meck, 1983; Greeno, Riley, & Gelman, 1984; Schaeffer, Eggleston, & Scott, 1974). Further, by 4 years of age, most children extend their early counting knowledge to comparing and reproducing sets (Ginsburg & Russell, 1981; Saxe, 1977; Saxe, 1979) as well as to addressing simple arithmetical problems with small sets (Groen & Resnick, 1977; Klein & Starkey, 1988).

Unlike school math, the preschooler's mathematics is not linked to an orthography for number; the very young child's mathematics may even be based on an idiosyncratic list of number words rather than our standard one (Fuson, Richards, & Briars, 1982; Gelman & Gallistel, 1978).

Other contexts in which out-of-school mathematics has been investigated are the activities of children and adults who have limited formal schooling. Children and adults construct complex strategies to address arithmetical problems that emerge in everyday commercial transactions (Carraher, Carraher, & Schliemann, 1985; Carraher, Schliemann, & Carraher, 1988; Guberman, 1987; Pettito, 1982; Posner, 1982; Saxe, 1982) and in work activities such as tailoring (Lave, 1977) or loading cartons (Scribner, 1984). Individuals also develop concepts of measurement and of mathematical progression in doing tasks like weaving (Greenfield & Childs, 1977; Saxe & Gearhart, in preparation; Saxe & Moylan, 1982), pottery making (Price-Williams, Gordon, & Ramirez, 1969), grocery shopping (Lave, Murtaugh, & De la Rocha, 1984) and even weight watching (de la Rocha, 1983). Like the preschoolers' math, this mathematics often has only a distant resemblance to classroom mathematics; individuals usually do not use a written symbol system to produce mathematical computations but rely, instead, on invented procedures that may include mentally regrouping terms to arrive at sums or manipulating objects in computations. Perhaps an extreme instance of the invention of a system of mathematics has been documented among unschooled Oksapmin adults from a remote and recently contacted group in Papua New

Guinea. The Oksapmin are adapting their traditional 27 body-part counting system to solve new problems that arise in the commercial transactions introduced by a money economy (Saxe, 1982).

What comes out of the accumulating research on out-of-school practices is the view that mathematics learning is not limited to acquisition of the formal algorithmic procedures passed down by mathematicians to individuals via school. Mathematics learning occurs as well during participation in cultural practices as children and adults attempt to accomplish pragmatic goals. The contrast between a school mathematics linked to Western cultural history and a mathematics linked to out-of-school activities is remarkable. It prompts fundamental questions about how children come to develop mathematical forms so pervasive in everyday life and whether there is an interplay between children's constructions of these forms and their developing understandings of school mathematics.

This chapter presents a research approach to these issues through a summary of some of my recent work with child candy sellers who live in an urban center in northeastern Brazil (Saxe, 1991). These candy sellers are a population in which the questions raised by the accumulating research are extraordinarily amenable to study.

As an inherent part of candy selling, children must construct fairly complex mathematical goals, goals that take form in a web of such sociocultural processes as an inflating monetary system, practice-linked conventions, and patterns of social interaction. Observing sellers, who range in age from 5 to 15, enabled me to document how children's mathematical goals emerge in the practice and to gain some appreciation of the interplay between social and developmental processes in the emergence of these goals. Additionally, interviewing experienced sellers about their mathematical understandings provided a basis for addressing a number of central issues.[1] Contrasting the mathematical understandings of unschooled sellers and nonsellers revealed the nature of sellers' understandings and indicated whether playing their trade led children to form particular kinds of mathematical concepts. Further, contrasting the mathematics of unschooled sellers at different age levels produced insight into how sellers' mathematics came to take the form it did. Finally, the interviews allowed understanding the interplay of schooling and selling experience. Some candy sellers did attend school; contrasting the way same-aged sellers with different amounts of schooling addressed practice-linked problems revealed whether the children had incorporated school-linked math forms into the math for selling candy. Conversely, contrasting the way both nonsellers and sellers who attended school addressed school-linked mathematics problems showed whether sellers had incorporated understandings constructed in candy selling into school mathematics.

The Candy Sellers' Practice

To learn about the mathematical goals that sellers form in the practice required an analysis of the social processes of the practice and how sellers goals are interwoven with them. To accomplish this, I conducted a series of observational studies of sellers as they conducted their trade (Saxe, 1991).

Figure 4.1 contains a schematic of the candy selling practice. The practice has a cyclical structure, depicted by the inner rectangle in the figure. To sell candy, one must accomplish four basic tasks. During a *purchase phase* (left upper corner of inner rectangle), sellers must buy one or more boxes of candy from one of about 30 wholesale stores, boxes that may contain any one of a wide variety of candy types. In a *prepare-to-sell phase*, sellers must price their candy for sale in the streets, a task in which they must mark-up the wholesale price for a multi-unit box to a retail price for units. In a *sell phase*, children must exchange

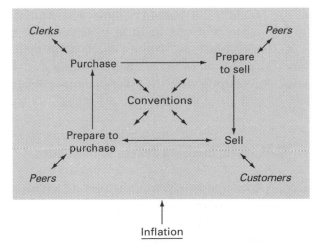

Figure 4.1 The candy selling practice and related social processes

their goods for currency with customers. In a *prepare-to-purchase phase*, sellers must prepare for the purchase of a new box of candy, a task that may involve estimating what candy types are most in demand and coordinating those considerations with possible comparative pricing at different wholesale stores.

Three social processes depicted in Figure 4.1 influence the form sellers' mathematical goals take in each phase of the practice. Brazil's *inflation* rate, which was 250% at the time of the study, is a socioeconomic process that not only affects the magnitude of the values that sellers address in their everyday calculations (a box of candy ranged between Cr$ 3600 [3600 cruzieros] and Cr$20,000 over the course of the study), but also produces a need for children to adjust for inflation in retail pricing. Social *conventions* that have emerged over the history of the practice may simplify some types of mathematical problems but complicate others. For instance, the price ratio convention of selling a fixed number of candy units for a specific bill denomination (e.g., 3 bars for Cr$1000) simplifies on-the-spot computations because it reduces the likelihood of computations involving change (and odd values in computation); however, the convention also leads to ratio comparison problems that arise when a seller contrasts his or her own price ratio with another seller's or when he or she chooses to sell for more than one price ratio (e.g., 3 lifesavers for Cr$500 and 7 for Cr$1000). Finally, *social interactions* further modify the nature of the mathematical problems of the practice. For instance, some wholesale store clerks occasionally help sellers with the math in their purchase by reading the prices of candy boxes or aiding sellers with their mark-up computations. Other pertinent interactions include the sellers' collaborations on price setting and their bargaining transactions with customers.

Methods for Studying Sellers' Mathematics

To understand sellers' mathematics, tasks and interview procedures were designed to document four general areas of sellers' practice-linked understandings: (a) representation of large numerical values, (b) arithmetical manipulation of large values, (c) comparison of ratios, and (d) adjustment for inflation in wholesale to retail markups. In this summary, I sketch some of the methods and the results for the first three of these four mathematical domains.

Representation of large numerical values

There are two ways that sellers could represent large numerical values in the practice. One is through our *standard orthography*. The prices of candy are often posted in the wholesale stores, and the ability to read these values would be useful to sellers. Further, in various phases of the practice, sellers must solve arithmetical problems containing large values, and the standard number orthography would be useful in solving such problems. An *alternative system* to represent large numbers in problem solving would be to use currency units as tokens for number by identifying the numerical values of currency units on the basis of their different figurative characteristics (e.g., colors, pictures) and manipulating these units in problem solving. Such an alternative system coupled with the assistance of store clerks and peers to help read prices could also serve as a representational vehicle in solving practice-linked problems.

To determine the sellers' competence with both representational systems, I developed assessment tasks. For the *standard orthography task*, they were asked to read and compare 20 multidigit numerical values, values that were within the range that they addressed in their practice. To determine their ability to use currency as an alternative system for large number representation, I constructed two types of additional tasks. In *bill identification tasks*, the sellers were presented with 12 bills (or printed bill values) in each of three conditions (see Figure 4.2a): i. standard bills, ii. bills with their numbers occluded by tape, iii. photocopies of cutouts of the numbers. They were required to identify the values of the bills or numbers in each condition. In the *currency comparison tasks*, they were presented with 14 pairs of

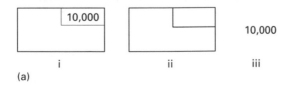

(a)

Figure 4.2a   Bill identification conditions

(b)

Figure 4.2b   Currency comparison conditions

currency units and asked to tell which was the larger of the two (e.g., bills of Cr$200 and Cr$1000) as well as the multiplicative relations between units, that is, how many of the smaller units were equivalent to the larger unit (see Figure 4.2b). If sellers can identify currency units and compare them numerically, they have the basis for a representational system to manipulate large numerical values, a system that would serve them well in their everyday computations.

Arithmetic with large currency units

The ability to produce arithmetical computations with large sums of currency is an achievement of central importance to the selling practice. To assess this ability, I created tasks that required sellers to add and subtract large sums. In one addition problem, for example, sellers were handed a stack of 17 bills (in a standard but haphazard order) totalling Cr$17,300 and told "Suppose you started the day with this amount. Would you add the money for me?" In another, they were asked to produce change for a purchase of Cr$7600 for a bill of Cr$10,000.

Comparison of ratios

In presenting their merchandise to potential customers, sellers often use more than one pricing ratio. For instance, a seller may offer 5 bars for Cr$1000 and 2 bars for Cr$500. Although the use of multiple ratios should increase sales by providing customers with lower prices for larger quantities, it also increases the complexity of the mathematics of selling. Clearly, the ability to produce ratio comparisons would be important for sellers who are considering using multiple prices for their candy.

To assess their understanding of ratio comparisons, sellers were presented with problems in which they had to determine which of two pricing ratios would yield a larger profit. For instance, a seller was told, "Suppose that you bought this bag of Pirulitos, and you must decide the price you will sell the units for in the street. Let's say that you have to choose between two ways of selling: selling 1 Pirulito for Cr$200 or selling 3 for Cr$500 (1 Pirulito was placed next to a Cr$200 bill and 3 were placed next to a Cr$500 bill). Which way do you think that you would make the most profit?" Children were also asked, if they did not do so spontaneously, to justify their choice.

Studies of Sellers' Mathematics

The battery of assessment tasks provided tools to address questions reviewed earlier about properties of sellers' mathematics, the way this mathematics develops, and the way children may use understandings developed in one context (school or the practice) to address problems that emerge in the other.

Influence of selling on children's mathematics

My first question was whether sellers were constructing mathematical understandings linked to their practice. To this end, I interviewed 23 10- to 12-year-old candy sellers who had minimal schooling[2] and I contrasted their performances with two groups of nonsellers who were matched with the sellers for age and schooling level, a group of 20 urban children from the same commercial environment as the sellers and a group of 17 rural children who use the same currency system but whose level of exposure to commercial transactions was more limited. I reasoned that if engagement with the practice-linked mathematical goals was leading sellers to construct specific forms of mathematical understandings, then we should observe a particular pattern of findings in children's performances. Because children had limited, if any, schooling, I suspected that all would perform poorly on the standard orthography tasks. For those problems that were common to all groups, like using currency to represent large values, group performance should not appreciably differ. For problems more specific to frequent commercial transactions, however, problems like bill arithmetic and ratio comparisons, performances should show differences as a function of level of involvements with these problem types.

The results of children's performances for each general type of problem, as a function of population group, are summarized in Figure 4.3a. Clearly, performance varied across groups for some problem types but not others, and these variations largely corresponded to expectation.[3]

Children's performances on the two number representation task types, the standard orthography tasks and the alternative representation tasks (bill identification and currency comparison), differed markedly. On the standard number orthography tasks, few performed well; the highest performing group, the urban nonsellers, read only one-half of the values correctly. In contrast, on the alternative representation tasks, virtually all performed at or near ceiling. The lack of group differences on these tasks indicates that children growing up in Brazil, with minimal education, regardless of selling experience, develop an understanding of the organization of the currency system to a

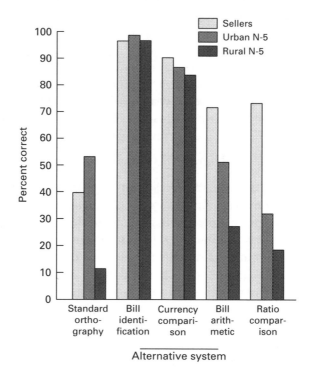

Figure 4.3a Percent of items correct as a function of problem type and population group

sufficient extent to use it to represent and compare large numerical values.

Children's performances on the problems more closely linked to the selling practice, the bill arithmetic tasks and the ratio comparison tasks, show that sellers more frequently demonstrated adequate solutions than urban or rural nonsellers, and that the urban nonsellers, in turn, demonstrated more adequate solutions than the rural nonsellers. For the arithmetical problems, differences were moderate, whereas, for the ratio tasks, differences were more extreme.

Children's solution strategies on these more complex tasks reveal the character of sellers' mathematics. Typical solution strategies on addition problems were to manipulate bill values into convenient groups. In such manipulations, a child might shift an order of bills from Cr$500, 200, 500, 200, 100 into [500 + 500] [200 + 200 + 100]. Though this was a common strategy, many of the sellers were capable of producing accurate summations without such manipulations. Virtually none used paper and pencil solution strategies to solve any of the addition or subtraction problems. For the ratio problems, children's adequate solutions were accompanied by an explanation in which they equated ratios by reference to a common term. For instance, in determining the ratio that would yield a larger profit, 3 for Cr$500 or 1 for Cr$200, they might argue that 1 for Cr$200 was the more profitable ratio, because 1 for Cr$200 would yield Cr$600 for the equivalent number of candies.

Sellers' mathematics as a function of age

Having established that children develop specific forms of mathematical understandings as a function of their engagement in the candy selling practice, my next concern was to understand the changing character of sellers' mathematics as a function of their age. On the basis of the observational studies, it was clear that the practice itself has considerable tolerance for sellers of varying levels of mathematical competence. For instance, upon questioning about how they priced their boxes for retail sale, the younger (6- to 7-year-old) sellers said that an older person (e.g., mother, older sibling, older peer) told them what retail price to use, whereas older sellers typically performed the calculation themselves (or received some assistance in their calculations from others). Further, the young children typically sold their candy for only one ratio and thus did not confront problems of ratio comparison, whereas older children sold their candy for more than one pricing ratio and did address ratio comparison problems in their practice. Finally, wholesale store clerks sometimes aided sellers with their calculations, aid that was typically prompted by sellers' requests for help.

Such forms of social supports mean that the central mathematical goal of the practice for the young seller may be merely that of appropriately identifying a many-to-one ratio between candy units and bill denominations in retail sales transactions with customers (for example, making an exchange of three candy bars for a Cr$1000 bill). Although using only one price ratio may have handicapped some younger sellers in accomplishing sales, it was compensated by customers' tendency to extend more sympathy to younger sellers; indeed, 6- to 7-year-old sellers accomplished about twice as many sales transactions per time interval than did the 12- to 15-year-old sellers.

To determine the character of sellers' developing mathematical knowledge as a function of age, sellers from three age groups, none of whom had progressed beyond the 2nd grade, were interviewed individually using the tasks outlined. The groups consisted of 5- to 7-year-olds,[4] 8- to 11-year-olds, and 12- to 15-year-olds. The observations noted suggested that young sellers may perform well on the alternative representational system tasks, but performances on the other tasks may be quite limited. With age, sellers' participation with the more complex problems of the practice increases, and we should observe corresponding developments in their solutions to these problems. Figure 4.3b contains a summary description of the three groups' performances, which bore out these expectations.

For the standard orthography tasks, the young children identified virtually no values correctly. Although their knowledge of the standard orthography improved with age, sellers' performances remained at relatively low levels, even in the oldest age group. In contrast, for the alternative representation system tasks, they performed at or near ceiling, an ability that would serve them well in exchanges with customers.

Age differences on the mathematically more complex problems of the practice, currency arithmetic and ratio comparison, also show the anticipated trends. In the currency arithmetic problems, some of the young children appeared not to identify the goal of the task as defined by the interviewer. For instance, on the bill addition task, several interpreted the problem as involving merely an enumeration of bills and

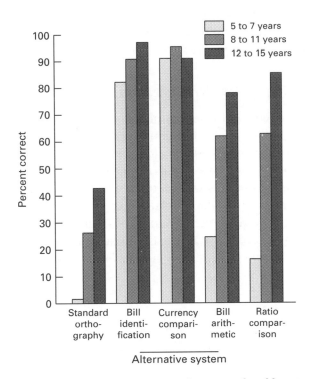

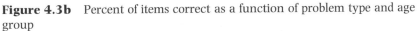

Figure 4.3b Percent of items correct as a function of problem type and age group

counted them, whereas others treated the task as involving recognition of currency denominations and identified the values of the bills sequentially. For the ratio comparison tasks, younger sellers typically understood the problem as merely one of identifying the larger currency unit. With age, sellers showed increasingly sophisticated means of both producing arithmetical computations with bills and comparing ratios.

The Interplay Between Math Learning in School and Math Learning in Selling Candy

The mathematics of the selling practice clearly differs in form from the orthography-based mathematics of school, a mathematics that is linked to the place–value structure of our notational system for number and to associated procedures for computation (e.g., carrying and borrowing algorithms). In the following two sets of analyses, my concern was to understand whether children were using mathematical knowledge constructed in one context to address problems in the other.

Schooling and sellers' practice-linked mathematics

To study the influence of schooling on the mathematics children develop in the candy selling practice, I contrasted the performances of three groups of sellers approximately matched for selling experience and age (ranging from 12- to 15-years old) who differed in the extent of their school experience (never attended, to attended through 2nd grade; attended up to 3rd or 4th grade; and attended up to 5th through 7th grade).

The contrasts between performances of sellers with different extents of school experience on the practice-linked tasks are illustrated in Figure 4.3c. Clearly, sellers with greater levels of schooling achieved

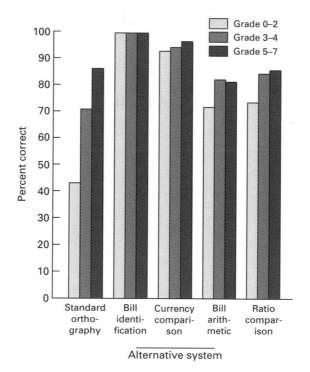

Figure 4.3c   Percent of items correct as a function of problem type and level of schooling (sellers only)

higher levels of performance on the number orthography tasks. A related difference in performance, not represented in the figure, was in schooled sellers' use of the standard orthography in solving the practice-linked problems. For instance, for the subtraction problems of the bill arithmetic tasks, schooled sellers more frequently made use of the standard orthography than those with less schooling; they used standard notation to represent and sometimes to solve the problems. There was, however, no statistically significant difference in sellers' accurate solutions of currency arithmetic and ratio comparison tasks as a function of schooling experience. Thus, although schooling may have influenced the way some sellers addressed and solved mathematical problems emerging in the practice, there was no evidence in this study that schooling led sellers to achieve more correct solutions of practice-linked problems.

Practice participation and sellers' school-linked mathematics

To study the influence of the children's participation in the selling practice on their performance with problems typical of school, the performances of sellers who attended school were contrasted with those of nonsellers who attended school. In this study, rather than administering practice-linked problems, a new set of assessment procedures was devised to study properties of the mathematics children use in school contexts. These assessment procedures consisted of 12 arithmetical problems, some presented in computational (column) format and others in word problem format.

To determine whether participation in the selling practice influenced children's solution of school-linked mathematics tasks, the school problems were administered to 2nd and 3rd grade sellers and nonsellers who were about the same age. I reasoned that if participation in the selling practice influenced the way children solved school mathematics tasks, we should observe that children with selling experience would use different strategies to solve the school problems and achieve higher levels of accuracy.

Children's solutions were coded both for correctness and strategy. Strategies were coded as one of two basic types: *algorithmic strategies*, in which children used school-linked algorithms to solve the problems (e.g., proceeding by column right to left); and *regrouping strategies*, in which they formed convenient values by regrouping the terms of a problem (e.g., $28 + 26 =?$ became $(20 + 20) + (8 + 6) =?$), a strategy analogous to that used in currency arithmetic to solve practice-linked addition problems.

The tabulation of the strategies used to achieve accurate solutions is presented in Figure 4.4. Clearly, at 2nd grade, sellers more frequently achieved accurate solutions. Further, the strategies that sellers used to achieve these solutions were almost exclusively regrouping ones and likely reflected ways of doing bill arithmetic in their practice. By 3rd grade, these differences in accuracy and strategy type were attenuated, an attenuation that suggests that school had begun to have an equalizing effect on children's mathematical competence.

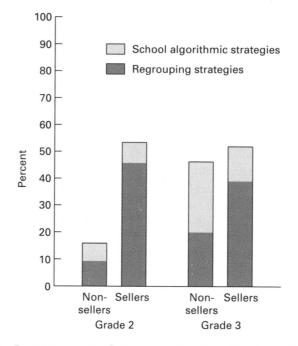

Figure 4.4   Percent correct solutions as a function of grade level and selling experience

Cognition in Context

These studies highlight an interplay between social and developmental processes in candy sellers' mathematics learning. Through practice participation, these children construct and operate on mathematical problems that are influenced by social conventions (like pricing ratios), artifacts of culture (like the inflated currency), and social interactions (like assistance with computations provided by clerks). Moreover, the way these social processes influence sellers' construction of mathematical problems shifts with their ages: Young sellers typically use only a single pricing ratio and thus avoid problems of ratio comparison, whereas their older peers use multiple pricing ratios and are engaged with ratio comparison problems. Young sellers typically identify bill denominations in transactions with customers but are not involved with complex arithmetical problems with large values, whereas older sellers are involved with such computations in their transactions. Finally, younger sellers receive considerable assistance in pricing their goods for retail sale, whereas older sellers more frequently attempt these calculations on their own.

In dealing with practice-linked problems, unschooled candy sellers develop a mathematical system, one that their nonselling peers do not achieve at the same age, if at all. For the young sellers as well as the nonsellers, the early manifestation of the system is their use of the medium of exchange, Brazilian currency, as a representational system for number. Both the ability to identify currency values and knowledge of the numerical relations between values provide an alternate to our standard orthography that is effective in retail exchanges with customers. As sellers become involved in the more complex problems of the practice, their mathematical system becomes increasingly distinct from that of their nonselling peers. Sellers use their knowledge of bill values and relations between them to develop arithmetical problem solving strategies that draw on the structure of the currency system. More and more, they construct concepts of ratio, knowledge forms linked to pricing conventions that have emerged over the history of the practice. Thus, sellers develop a mathematics that is adapted to the practice and, over time, manifests mathematical operations of increasing complexity and power.

The sellers' practice-linked mathematics thus appears to be tightly interwoven with sociocultural artifacts and supports. This apparent interdependence between cognition and context could indicate that sellers' understandings have limited generality. However, the findings on the interplay between sellers' knowledge constructed in the practice and in school show that individuals can make use of knowledge formed in one context to address problems in the other. We saw that sellers who attended school worked towards adjusting practice-linked re-grouping strategies to solve school linked mathematical problems. We also saw some evidence that the process works in the opposite direction; sellers who had more school experience had greater know-ledge of the standard orthography for number and on occasion adjusted the orthography-based column arithmetic that they had ac-quired in school to practice-linked problems, though these efforts at transfer from school to practice did not influence the accurateness of sellers' solutions. In both cases, the character of children's solution strategies on the mathematics tasks is evidence that such processes of transfer are often protracted ones, ones in which sellers increasingly specialize and adjust strategies formed in one context to deal ad-equately with problems that emerge in another (see Saxe, in press).

Sellers clearly draw on what they have constructed through plying their trade to address the mathematical problems of the classroom. Research in other cultural settings shows that such adaptations are not limited to candy sellers but may be a very common phenomenon (Baroody, 1987; Saxe, 1985). These uses of out-of-school mathematics in school, whether finger counting strategies to solve an arithmetic problem presented in a 1st grade classroom or sophisticated regroup-ing strategies to solve multidigit multiplication problems later, could be viewed as the intrusion of inappropriate and primitive strategies that should be adaptively replaced by the formal mathematics of the class-room. However, many researches now recognize the pedagogical im-portance of using linkages as means of strengthening children's mathematical intuitions (Ginsburg & Asmussen, 1988; Carraher, Schliemann, & Carraher, 1988; Hiebert, 1984; Hatano, 1988; Hughes, 1986) and recommend appropriate classroom techniques to facilitate and build on these linkages (Baroody, 1987). Clearly, we would profit from systematic empirical work exploring ways we may help children to use what they know to decipher the mathematics of school instruction.

The bridges that children build from the mathematics of the classroom to the problems that emerge in out-of-school activities are no less important concerns for educational practice. Indeed, a worthy instructional objective is for children to feel some ownership of classroom mathematics, a possibility only if classroom mathematics becomes transparent and functional to them. While they were subjects in the interview study, some sellers did use math linked to school to address out-of-school problems, however, the influence of schooling on sellers' out-of-school mathematics was not major. Indeed, the greatest effect of instruction found in this study was to improve children's ability to decode the standard number orthography. The breach between school mathematics and the mathematics used in everyday tasks is probably not unique to candy sellers. These results, like the accumulating research on children's and adults' out-of-school mathematics, point to the need to examine how we can better make classroom mathematics more readily accessible and transparent to children as they approach and pursue problems in the course of their everyday out-of-school activities.

Notes

1 Sellers interviewed all had worked at their practice for a minimum of 3 months (often 7 days-a-week), but most sellers who participated in this study had considerably more experience.
2 Minimal schooling was defined as never having attended school beyond 2nd grade (public school).
3 A more detailed analysis of these data is presented in Saxe (in press-a).
4 The 5- to 7-year-olds were a heterogeneous group because only a small number of candy sellers in this age range could be found. Although all children in this group were involved in commercial activities, only 6 were actually candy sellers. The remaining children helped their parent(s) in selling such commodities as vegetables and may be better defined as "seller-initiates."

References

Baroody, A. J. (1987). *A guide to teaching basic mathematics in the primary grades*. Boston, MA: Allyn and Bacon.

Carraher, T. N., Carraher, D., & Schliemann, A. D. (1985). Mathematics in the streets and in schools. *British Journal of Developmental Psychology*, 3(1), 21–29.

Carraher, T. C., Schliemann, A. D., & Carraher, D. W. (1988). Mathematical concepts in everyday life. In G. B. Saxe & M. Gearhart (Eds.), *Children's mathematics. New directions in child development*. San Francisco, CA: Jossey-Bass.

de la Rocha, O. (1983, November). The reorganization of arithmetic practice in the kitchen. Paper presented at the 82nd annual meeting of the American Anthropological Association. Chicago, Illinois.

Fuson, K. C. (1988). *Children's counting and concepts of number*. New York: Springer-Verlag.

Fuson, K. C., Richards, J., & Briars, D. J. (1982). The acquisition and elaboration of the number word sequence. In C. Brainerd (Ed.), *Children's logical and mathematical cognition: Progress in cognitive development* (pp. 33–92). New York: Springer-Verlag.

Gelman, R., & Gallistel, C. R. (1978). *The child's understanding of number*. Cambridge, MA: Harvard University Press.

Gelman, R., & Meck, E. (1983). Preschoolers' counting: Principles before skill. *Cognition, 13*, 343–359.

Ginsburg, H. P., & Asmussen, K. A. (1988). Hot mathematics. In G. B. Saxe & M. Gearhart (Eds.), *Children's mathematics. New directions in child development* (pp. 89–112). San Francisco, CA: Jossey-Bass.

Ginsburg, H. P., & Russell, R. L. (1981). Social class and racial influences on early mathematical thinking. *Monographs of the Society for Research in Child Development, 46*(6, Serial No. 193).

Greenfield, P. M. & Childs, C. P. (1977). Weaving, color terms, and pattern representation: Cultural influences and cognitive development among the Zincantecos of Southern Mexico. *Interamerican Journal of Psychology, 11*, 23–48.

Greeno, J. G., Riley, M. S., & Gelman, R. (1984). Conceptual competence and children's counting. *Cognitive Psychology, 16*, 94–134.

Groen, G. J., & Resnick, L. B. (1977). Can preschool children invent addition algorithms? *Journal of Educational Psychology, 69*, 645–652.

Guberman, S. R. (1987). Arithmetical problem-solving in commercial transactions of Brazlian children. Presented at 1987 Meetings of the Society for Research in Child Development, Baltimore, Maryland.

Hatano, G. (1988). Social and motivational bases for mathematical understanding. In G. B. Saxe & M. Gearhart (Eds.), *Children's mathematics. New directions in child development* (pp. 55–70). San Francisco, CA: Jossey-Bass.

Hiebert, J. (1984). Children's mathematics learning: The struggle to link form and understanding. *Elementary School Journal, 84*, 497–513.

Hughes, M. (1986). *Children and number: Difficulties in learning mathematics*. Oxford: Basil Blackwell, Inc.

Klein, A., & Starkey, P. (1988). Universals in the development of early arithmetic cognition. In G. B. Saxe & M. Gearhart (Eds.), *Children's mathematics. New directions in child development*. San Francisco, CA: Jossey-Bass.

Lave, J. (1977). Tailor-made experiments and evaluating the intellectual consequences of apprenticeship training. *Quarterly Newsletter of the Institute for Comparative Human Development*, 1(2), 1–3.

Lave, J., Murtaugh, M., & de la Rocha, O. (1984). The dialectic of arithmetic in grocery shopping. In B. Rogoff & J. Lave (Eds.), *Everyday cognition: Its development in social context* (pp. 67–94). Cambridge, MA: Harvard University Press.

Pettito, A. L. (1982). Practical arithmetic and transfer: A study among West African tribesmen. *Journal of Cross-cultural Psychology, 13*, 15–28.

Posner, J. (1982). The development of mathematical knowledge in two West African societies. *Child Development, 53*, 200–208.

Price-Williams, D., Gordon, W., & Ramirez, M. (1969). Skill and conservation: A study of pottery-making children. *Developmental Psychology, 1*, 769.

Saxe, G. B. (1977). A developmental analysis of notational counting. *Child Development, 48*, 1512–1520.

Saxe, G. B. (1979). Developmental relations between notational counting and number conservation. *Child Development, 50*, 180–187.

Saxe, G. B. (1982). Developing forms of arithmetic operations among the Oksapmin of Papua New Guinea. *Developmental Psychology, 18*(4), 583–594.

Saxe, G. B. (1985). The effects of schooling on arithmetical understandings: Studies with Oksapmin children in Papua New Guinea. *Journal of Educational Psychology, 77*(5), 503–513.

Saxe, G. B. (1988). The mathematics of child street venders. *Child Development*.

Saxe, G. B. (in press). The interplay between learning in formal and informal social contexts. In M. Gardner, J. Greeno, F. Reis, & A. Schoenfeld (Eds.), *Toward a scientific practice of science education*. Hillsdale, NJ: Erlbaum.

Saxe, G. B. (1991). Culture and cognitive development: Studies in mathematical understanding. Hillsdale, NJ: Erlbaum.

Saxe, G. B., & Gearhart, M. (1990). The development of typological concepts in unschooled straw weavers. *British Journal of Development Psychology, 8*, 251–258.

Saxe, G. B., Guberman, S. R., & Gearhart, M. (1987). Social processes in early number development. *Monographs of the Society for Research in Child Development, 52*, (2, Serial No. 216).

Saxe, G. B., & Moylan, T. (1982). The development of measurement operations among the Oksapmin of Papua New Guinea. *Child Development, 53*, 1242–1248.

Schaeffer, B., Eggleston, V. H., & Scott, J. L. (1974). Number development in young children. *Cognitive Psychology, 6,* 357–379.

Scribner, S. (1984). Studying working intelligence. In B. Rogoff & J. Lave (Eds.), *Everyday cognition: Its development in social context* (pp. 9–40). Cambridge, MA: Harvard University Press.

Learning in Higher Education

Introduction

In this paper Entwistle reviews work on teaching and learning in higher education. He draws mainly on his own, highly influential, body of research accumulated over decades. Entwistle takes students' conceptions of and approaches to learning to be the key mediating variables between teaching and learning in this sector of education. He identifies how these processes operate and how they are shaped by teaching arrangements in university departments.

These approaches to learning can vary markedly, some leading to a surface approach concentrating on the ability to reproduce taught material in tests and others leading to a deep approach aimed at personal understanding.

The work described has achieved high levels of national and international recognition for its authenticity and validity and yet it, along with other research on teaching and learning, has had little if any impact on the practice of teachers. In education, there is a huge, knowledge transformation gap between the valid description of current processes and evidence-based improvement of practice.

Further reading

For international developments in this field see Dart, B. and Boulton-Lewis, G. (1998) *Teaching and Learning in Higher Education*. Melbourne: Australian Council for Educational Research. For the latest developments in the application of the work reported here see www.ex.ac.uk/ESRC-TLRP/.

FIVE

Understanding Academic Performance at University: a Research Retrospective

Noel J. Entwistle

The Prediction of Academic Performance

The attempts in the late 1960s to understand differences in students' academic performance were directed towards its more accurate prediction. The rather weak predictive power of measures of school achievement, such as 'A' level or Highers grades, led to a search for more accurate selection instruments, drawing on the experience of using the Scholastic Aptitude Tests in the USA (Choppin, 1973). But it was realised that other influences on academic performance might also have to be taken into account to achieve substantially higher levels of prediction. In a large scale follow-up study at Lancaster University, a national sample of first-year students was followed through to graduation in an attempt to identify factors related to academic success (Entwistle and Wilson, 1977). Besides using a scholastic aptitude test, additional measures of personality, values, social attitudes, motivation, and study methods were also included in a test battery. These predictive variables from the first year were then compared with levels of degree performance three years later.

Simple correlations confirmed that 'A' level grades correlated with degree performance to only a modest extent (0.29 in pure science down to 0.11 in social science, although higher levels were found in smaller samples of applied scientists and mathematicians). Higher correlations were actually found with scores on an inventory of motivation and study methods (0.33 in pure science and 0.21 in social science). Multivariate analyses of the data were then undertaken. Regression analyses using the whole set of variables in combination to predict degree performance increased the correlations to only a limited extent (0.38 in pure science and 0.25 in social science). Motivation and study methods contributed most to that prediction, along with achievement and intellectual measures.

Factor analysis was then used to make sense of the whole pattern of intercorrelations. One factor was found to distinguish between arts and science, indicating that students in the different subject areas had contrasting sets of characteristics. The other two factors summarised the relationships with academic performance; one factor was defined in terms of high levels of school attainment combined with hard work and an avoidance of social distractions, while motivation and organised study methods were linked to low levels of both anxiety and radicalism in the other factor.

A different form of multivariate analysis was also explored in this study. Cluster analysis brings together individuals whose responses to the tests are similar (as opposed to factor analysis which groups similar variables). In this way, it was possible to identify groups of individuals. Some of the differences reflected contrasting areas of study, but other differences indicated quite different ways of studying. Four of the clusters are of particular interest.

- *Highly motivated, stable scientists* (the most successful group of all). This group contained students with high 'A' level grades who were satisfied with their courses . . . They were highly motivated and had good study methods. In personality they were emotionally stable and had high scores on theoretical and economic values, linked to a tendency towards tough-minded conservatism. This combination of characteristics suggests a rather cold and ruthless individual, governed by rationality and spurred on by competition to repeated demonstrations of intellectual mastery.
- *Hard-working, syllabus free arts students* (the most successful Arts group). These students did not have outstandingly high 'A' level grades, although their verbal aptitude scores were well above average. High motivation, good study methods and long hours of

study were linked with syllabus-freedom. There were no defining characteristics in terms of personality, but high aesthetic values were associated with radical attitudes.

- *Anxious students who work long hours* (mixed success – scientists doing well). The main defining features (of this group) were high scores on neuroticism and syllabus-boundness, and low scores on both extraversion and (the competitive form of) motivation. They saw themselves as neither likeable nor self-confident. They had no active social life and few aesthetic interests. It is tempting to see these students as being motivated by 'fear of failure'.

- *Students with low motivation and poor study methods* (poor performance). This group contains students who came up to university with below average 'A' level grades, but their ... ability appeared to be equivalent to (that of highly successful students) ... Their theoretical values were (however) low ... (They) showed a marked deterioration in performance after the first year and ... had (consistently) low motivation and study method scores ... They spent little time on studying and rather more on leisure pursuits. (Many also came) from lower social class backgrounds. (Entwistle and Wilson, 1977, pp. 129–32)

The particular value of these cluster analyses was the way in which they retained full information about links between cognitive, personality and other variables in describing linkages. These links were lost in the factor analyses, through the process of merging and simplification of factor structures. The fuller picture offered by the cluster descriptions provided valuable suggestions about reasons for success and failure.

The link between study methods, motivation, and personality was explored further by John Wilson in a separate study at Aberdeen University (Entwistle and Wilson, 1977, p. 76). Combining scores on motivation and study methods, and examining levels of degree performance for each of four personality 'types', it was clear that consistent relationships came only from extraversion (relationships with neuroticism varied by subject area). It was found that 45 per cent of extroverts had low combined scores on motivation and study methods, compared with 23 per cent of introverts, who also obtained a somewhat higher proportion of 'good' degrees (68 per cent compared with 63 per cent of extroverts). Clearly, personality was related to both study methods and degree performance. However, it was found that the combined scores on motivation and study methods showed a much closer relationship with academic success than had personality (76 per cent of students with high scores had good degrees compared with 50 per cent of those with low scores). Further analyses showed a very similar proportion of extroverts and introverts, who also had high scores on motivation and study methods, obtaining good degrees (extroverts 77 per cent; introverts 75 per cent).

This finding had a substantial influence on the future direction of the research group at Lancaster. It suggested that variables which directly described behaviour and attitudes within the academic context were likely to be much better predictors than more general psychological variables.

As we saw earlier, regression analyses had indicated that a combination of ability with motivation and study methods made the best combined predictor of academic achievement. Besides this quantitative study, however, an interview study was also carried out which contrasted students with different forms of motivation, and that, combined with the cluster descriptions, led to a realisation that different students perceived their academic environments in very different ways.

> Students of differing personality and motivational types not only tackle their academic work in different ways but, from their descriptions of their university experience, they evidently perceive themselves to be in differing environments. (Entwistle, Thompson and Wilson, 1974, p. 393)

The other outcome of this longitudinal study was a growing conviction that correlational studies did not suggest, in any convincing way, what might be done to improve teaching and learning in higher education. The emphasis on prediction suggested ways of selecting students more accurately in terms of their academic potential, and yet there was so much variance unaccounted for that selection alone was not an appropriate response. We needed to see what could be done to help students study more effectively and to suggest to lecturers better ways of encouraging high quality learning. The advice which Charles Carter, the then Vice-Chancellor of Lancaster University, gave to educational researchers at about that time was forthright. He said:

> The purpose of research into higher education, for most of us, is a practical one. We do not want merely to describe the quaint or awful

things which are going on: we want to make things better ... So I hope that ... you will ... refrain from chasing along familiar paths and surrounding what you find with a spurious erudition; and see if your colleagues can be helped with some of the simple and obvious faults which have persisted in higher education for too long. (Carter, 1972, pp. 1–3)

This injunction struck home. It coincided with our own dissatisfactions with the previous focus of our work and led to a change in direction – an attempt to understand the processes of studying – and not just to describe correlates of different outcomes of learning.

Study Strategies and the Processes of Student Learning

The search for concepts having greater ecological validity in describing the processes of student learning did not take long, as the work of Marton and his colleagues was being published as our first survey was being written up (Marton and Säljö, 1976; Svensson, 1977). With the description of the contrasting approaches to learning, we were able to shift our focus to the processes of learning. Initial studies showed that these categories were just as powerful in distinguishing quite different ways of studying in Britain as they had been in Sweden (Entwistle, Hanley and Ratcliffe, 1979). An SSRC research programme was then undertaken which followed both quantitative and qualitative tracks (Entwistle and Ramsden, 1983).

Interviews in the early stages of the qualitative study indicated that besides deep and surface approaches to learning, there was also a strategic approach to studying, depending on well-organised studying and an alertness to assessment criteria. These three categories provided the conceptual underpinning for the quantitative study. The initial interviews had also indicated that there was indeed a certain consistency in the approach, or combination of approaches, to studying adopted by students. It thus made sense to measure typical approaches to studying, at least within a specific course, through an extension of the inventory previously used to measure study methods and motivation. After substantial development work, the *Approaches to Studying Inventory* (ASI) (Entwistle and Ramsden, 1983) was produced. The inventory was given to a national sample of 2208 students from

66 departments drawn from six contrasting subject areas. Factor analyses suggested the existence of four main *study orientations*:

- *meaning* (incorporating the deep approach)
- *reproducing* (surface approach)
- *achieving* (strategic approach)
- *non-academic* (later called *apathetic*, involving disorganised studying and negative attitudes).

Biggs (1976) had independently been developing a *Study Processes Questionnaire*. Factor analyses produced three main dimensions describing study processes which were subsequently seen to cover deep, surface, and achieving approaches to studying (Biggs, 1987). It was particularly interesting to find that both inventories had independently produced three main factors in which a learning process or strategy was associated with a distinctive form of motivation:

- deep/meaning with interest and active engagement with course content (a form of intrinsic motivation)
- surface/reproducing with anxiety about coping with course requirements (fear of failure)
- strategic/achieving with a self-confident and competitive form of motivation (need for achievement). (Entwistle, 1988; Biggs, 1993)

It was also interesting to find a close correspondence between the four orientations and the four clusters described above which came from a quite different set of variables.

The combination of learning process and distinctive motivation within both factors and clusters was readily understandable in both theoretical and experiential terms. Moreover, this combination can now be seen as containing two of the three components of what has since been called a disposition (Perkins *et al.*, 1993). In more recent work, the third element of the dispositional triad has also appeared in findings which indicate that students adopting deep or surface approaches also seem to have different sensitivities towards their learning environment (Meyer, Parsons and Dunne, 1990; Entwistle and Tait, 1990; Meyer, 1991). Certainly, students adopting deep approaches are better able to identify, and to appreciate, types of teaching which are designed to support understanding. Approach to studying, as derived from quantitative analyses at least, can thus be seen as a disposition, describing a relatively stable characteristic of the individual student in relation to learning in a specific academic context.

Having data on 66 departments enabled analyses of the ASI also to be carried out with the department as the unit of analysis. These analyses looked at mean scores on approaches to studying in relation to descriptions of departments provided by a *Course Perceptions Questionnaire* developed by Paul Ramsden (Entwistle and Ramsden, 1983). Conclusions from those analyses have recently been summarised in the following way:

> Departments which were perceived to provide good teaching (and particularly help with studying) combined with freedom in learning (offering choice of study method and content) were more likely to have students reporting an orientation towards meaning. Reproducing orientations were more commonly found in the departments perceived to combine a heavy workload with a lack of choice over content and method... Some departments seem to induce surface approaches in a direct way. Other departments appear to provide contexts within which students find it easier to develop an interest in the subject matter and to use approaches aimed at understanding. The influence is, however, less easy to predict, depending presumably more on individual students... (who) differ markedly in what they want to achieve from their studying. If they *want* to make the academic content personally meaningful, these departments will facilitate such development. (Ramsden, 1997, pp. 213–4)

In subsequent work, the idea of providing an effective learning environment, seen as a coherent, mutually supporting whole, was developed into a conceptual overview of the teaching–learning process in higher education (Entwistle, 1987), which has been developed further as a result of more recent research (for a full description, see Entwistle, in press). The model (see Figure 5.1) indicates how the outcomes of learning depended on an interaction between the characteristics of the individual student, the teaching provided by the lecturer (focusing mainly on lecturing, for simplicity), and the context provided by departmental practices. It focuses on learning strategies and the learning outcomes, and these are placed at the centre of the diagram. Around the outside are the influences on those processes and outcomes. The characteristics of the student are described broadly in terms of

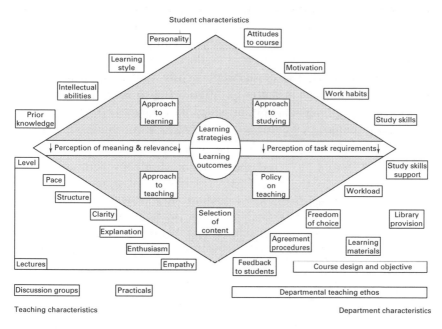

Figure 5.1   A conceptual overview of the teaching–learning process

variations in approaches to learning – deep/surface – (on the left) and approaches to studying – strategic/apathetic (on the right). The outer set of concepts are narrower in focus and have been shown to be related to these two approaches (Entwistle and Ramsden, 1983). The way students react to the learning environment depends on their perceptions of the teaching and general departmental policies on teaching which they are experiencing – perceptions of the meaning and relevance evoked by the content presented by the lecturer or tutor and of the task requirements which depend on departmental policies on assessment.

Trigwell, Prosser and Taylor (1994) have described three main conceptions of teaching – transmitting information, helping students to acquire the concepts of the discipline, and helping students to develop and change their own conceptions. But underlying these conceptions of teaching are two contrasts. First, there is a distinction between viewing teaching from the perspective of staff and institution, and from that of the student. Then there is a related contrast between seeing teaching as transmitting information and as encouraging learning. These differing conceptions affect the overall way in which the lecturer approaches teaching, from the choice and organisation of course material to the specific teaching methods adopted in class.

The approach to teaching can be disaggregated into aspects of 'good teaching' as perceived by students. Taking lecturing as an example, it can be described in terms of the seven components at the bottom left-hand side of the model. These aspects have been identified both in interviews with students (Entwistle and Ramsden, 1983) and from dimensions found to underlie student feedback questionnaires (Marsh, 1987). In the model, the positioning of these elements to some extent parallels equivalent student characteristics linked to the approach to learning (e.g. level at which the lecture is pitched should depend on the prior knowledge of the students; pace depends on intellectual abilities). Other methods of teaching could be disaggregated in a similar way, but there is currently insufficient research evidence to make this convincing.

Finally, other influences on learning outcomes, less directly under the control of the lecturer, are shown in the bottom right of Figure 5.1. Of these, assessment procedures have the most direct and immediate impact on the approach to studying, but it is also influenced by helpful feedback on assignments, freedom in the choice of topics and courses for students, a timetable and workload which is not too demanding, and appropriate support in the development of study skills. These components of departmental provision are backed up by provision of library materials and other learning materials (resource- or technology-based). These specific aspects are incorporated into an overall course design and stem from the overall departmental teaching ethos.

The model was designed to illustrate some of the main influences on the quality of learning which need to be borne in mind in designing curricula, and to emphasise the need to provide a learning environment specifically intended to support a deep approach (Entwistle, Thompson and Tait, 1996). But more recently the focus of our research has shifted to look in more detail at that determination to extract meaning and reach a thorough understanding of course material which lies at the heart of the deep approach. Qualitative methods, similar to phenomenography, have been used to explore students' experiences of developing their understandings.

The Nature of Academic Understanding

A recent description of the defining features of the three approaches to learning describe the deep approach as depending on an interplay between an adventurous relating of ideas (holist strategy) and a cautious examination of evidence in relation to conclusions (serialist strategy) (Entwistle, 1995a). This description echoes the earlier idea of the *reasonable adventurer* (Heath, 1964).

> In the pursuit of a problem, (the Reasonable Adventurer) appears to experience an alternation of involvement and detachment. The phase of involvement is an intensive and exciting period characterised by curiosity, a narrowing of attention towards some point of interest . . . This period of involvement is then followed by a period of detachment, an extensive phase, accompanied by a reduction of tension and a broadening range of perception . . . Here [the Reasonable Adventurer] settles back to reflect on the meaning of what was discovered during the involved stage. Meaning presumes the existence of a web of thought, a pattern of ideas to which the 'new' element can be related . . . We see, therefore . . . a combination of two mental attitudes: the curious and the critical. They do not occur simultaneously, but in alternation. (pp. 30–1)

The next stage of our research investigated the experiences of students as they actively sought understanding and produced an alternative way of conceptualising the 'web of thought' or 'pattern of ideas' developed by students as they made use of both holist and serialist thinking in preparing for finals.

So far, we have carried out a series of small-scale studies of students mainly from psychology, social history and zoology. Hour-long interviews were transcribed and analysed, not only to identify categories of description, but also to investigate their meaning in relation to previous research findings, and the inter-relationships between them. It became clear early in our analyses of the interviews that, while most students talked about how they were trying to understand their notes, they were describing very different forms of understanding. Those differences we came to describe in terms of breadth, depth and structure. Breadth described the amount of material the student had sought to incorporate in the understanding. Depth indicated the amount of time and effort put in considering what the material meant, while five different ways of structuring the understanding could be seen in the students' responses, varying from no structure at all, through structures which were tied closely to the perceived assessment demands, to structures which represented individual conceptions of the discipline (Entwistle and Entwistle, 1992, 1997).

Although the students differed markedly in the sophistication of the understanding they were seeking, they all tended to describe the experience of reaching understanding in rather similar terms. Repeatedly, they mentioned feelings of connectedness, coherence and confidence in explaining.

> (Understanding?) It's an active process; it's constructive...(It's) the interconnection of lots of disparate things – I think that's probably the best way to describe it – the way it all hangs together, the feeling that you understand how the whole thing is connected up – you can make sense of it internally. You're making lots of connections which then make sense and it's logical...It is as though one's mind has finally 'locked in' to the pattern. Concepts seem to fit together in a meaningful way, when before the connections did not seem clear, or appropriate, or complete...like jigsaw pieces, you know, suddenly connect, and you can see the whole picture...It's (also) the act of being able to construct an argument from scratch. I think if you are able to reconstruct it by yourself, that shows you understood it. (Adapted from extracts reported in Entwistle and Entwistle, 1992)

Several students referred specifically to how they were able to visualise – or almost visualise – their understanding through the revision notes they had prepared. They could visualise the pattern they had made to summarise the main topics, but not the words or details. The notes encapsulated students' understanding within a structure which had a mnemonic function for them. Students remembered the structure of their understanding, and they were aware that there was much more detailed knowledge associated with the 'nodes' of that structure which would pull in additional information as they needed it. This can be illustrated by comments from two students.

> I can see that virtually as a picture, and I can review it, and bring in more facts about each part...Looking at a particular part of the diagram sort of triggers off other thoughts. I find schematics, in flow diagrams and the like, very useful because a schematic acts a bit like a

syllabus; it tells you what you should know, without actually telling you what it is. I think the facts are stored separately ... and the schematic is like an index, I suppose.

I got on to this process of constructing a kind of mental map ... as a quick way of putting down the basics ... and making sure I don't leave anything out ... Then (in the exam) I would just image it again, ... and as I wrote it, (add) my own thoughts on what I had picked up from other reading. That's why I have it, because (it holds things together) whilst you're writing, adding in whatever you're thinking ... and extra detail. (Entwistle and Entwistle, 1991, pp. 219, 220)

The first of these comments came from one of our pilot interviews. It alerted us to the use of visualisation, which became one important focus of the interviews which followed. A re-analysis of the data in collaboration with Ference Marton, using phenomenography more directly, concentrated on how students had experienced their understandings. They repeatedly described a feeling that the material being revised had become so tightly integrated that it was experienced almost as an entity with form and structure. Only its general outline could be actually seen as an image, but additional associated knowledge was felt to be readily 'available', whenever needed.

It was this recurring experience among the students which we came to describe as a *knowledge object*. Its defining features involve an awareness of a tightly integrated body of knowledge, visualisation of structure in a 'quasi-sensory' way, an awareness of unfocused aspects of knowledge (Entwistle and Marton, 1994), and a recognition of how the structure can be used to control explanations during examinations (Entwistle, 1995b). This form of awareness, together with the controlling function, can be seen in the following extract, in which the knowledge object seems to be almost a 'felt presence'.

Following that logic through, *it* pulls in pictures and facts as it needs them ... Each time I describe (a particular topic), it's likely to be different ... Well, you start with evolution, say, ... and suddenly you know where you're going next. Then, you might have a choice ... to go in that direction or that direction ... and follow it through various options *it's* offering ... Hopefully, you'll make the right choice, and so this goes to this, goes to this – and you've explained it to the level you've got to. Then, *it* says 'Okay, you can go on to talk about further criticisms in the time you've got left.' (Entwistle, 1995b, p. 50)

This extract also draws attention to the idea that the explanation guided by the knowledge object will differ to some extent from occasion to occasion. Other comments suggest that the structure of the knowledge object offers a generic shape to the explanation, but that the particular answer given will depend on the question set and the dynamics of the evolving explanation. Some students were also very aware of how the examination affected the type of explanation they could provide, and of the expectations of the audience for whom they were writing.

> When you're revising ... you're trying to convince yourself that you can convince the examiner ... You can't use all the information for a particular line of argument, and you don't need to. You only need to use what you think is going to convince the examiner ...
>
> The more I have done exams, the more I'd liken them to a performance – like being on a stage ... having not so much to present the fact that you know a vast amount, but having to perform well with what you do know ... Sort of, playing to the gallery ... I was very conscious of being outside what I was writing. (Entwistle and Entwistle, 1991, pp. 220, 221)

In tackling an examination question, then, the best prepared students sought to relate the specific wording of question set to a pre-existing knowledge object, which is then used to guide the emerging logic of the answer and to pull in evidence and examples as required. The student is monitoring the evolving answer in relation to the wording of the question and to a sense of what will persuade the examiners that a deep level of understanding of the topic has been achieved.

References and further reading

Beaty, E., Gibbs, G. and Morgan, A. (1997) Learning orientations and study contracts, in Marton, F. Hounsell, D. J. and Entwistle, N. J. (Eds.), *The Experience of Learning*, 2nd edn (Edinburgh: Scottish Academic Press).

Bereiter, C. (1990) Aspects of an educational learning theory. *Review of Educational Research*, 60, 603–24.

Biggs, J. B. (1976) Dimensions of study behaviour: Another look at ATI. *British Journal of Educational Psychology*, 46, 68–80.

Biggs, J. B. (1987) *Student approaches to learning and studying* (Melbourne: Australian Council for Educational Research).

Biggs, J. B. (1993) What do inventories of students' learning processes really measure? A theoretical review and clarification. *Educational Psychology*, 63, 3–19.

Bronowski, J. (1965) *The Identity of Man* (London: Heinemann).

Carter, C. F. (1972) Presidential address. Society for Research into Higher Education. Published in *Innovation in Higher Education* (London: SRHE).

Cattell, R. B. and Butcher, H. J. (1968) *The Prediction of Achievement and Creativity* (New York: Bobbs-Merrill).

Choppin, B. H. L. (1973) *The Prediction of Academic Success* (Slough: NFER).

CRLI (1995) *PASS: personalised advice on study skills* [Computer software and supporting materials] (Edinburgh: University of Edinburgh, Centre for Research on Learning and Instruction).

Cronbach, L. J. (1957) On the two disciplines of scientific psychology. *American Psychologist*, 12, 671–84.

Dahllof, U. (1991) Towards a new model for the evaluation of teaching, in Dahllof, U. *et al.* (Eds.) *Discussions of Education in Higher Education* (London: Jessica Kingsley).

Entwistle, N. J. (1987) A model of the teaching – learning process, in Richardson, J. T. E. Eysenck, M. W. and Warren Piper, D. (Eds.) *Student Learning: Research in education and cognitive psychology* (Milton Keynes: Open University Press/SRHE).

Entwistle, N. J. (1988) Motivational factors in students' approaches to learning, in Schmeck, R. R. (Ed.), *Learning Strategies and Learning Styles* (New York: Plenum), pp. 21–52.

Entwistle, N. J. (1995a) The nature of academic understanding, in Kaufmann, G. Helstrup, T. and Teigen, K. H. (Eds) *Problem Solving and Cognitive Processes* (Bergen-Sandviken: Fagbokforlaget).

Entwistle, N. J. (1995b) Frameworks for understanding as experienced in essay writing and in preparing for examinations. *Educational Psychologist*, 30, 47–54.

Entwistle, N. J. (in press). Improving teaching through research on student learning, in Forest, J. J. F. (Ed.) *University Teaching: International perspectives* (New York: Garland Press).

Entwistle, N. J. and Entwistle, A. C. (1991) Contrasting forms of understanding for degree examinations: the student experience and its implications. *Higher Education*, 22, 205–27.

Entwistle, A. C., and Entwistle N. J. (1992) Experiences of understanding in revising for degree examinations. *Learning and Instruction*, 2, 1–22.

Entwistle, N. J. and Entwistle, A. C. (1997) Revision and the experience of understanding, in Marton, F. Hounsell, D. J. and Entwistle, N. J. (Eds), *The Experience of Learning*, 2nd edn, (Edinburgh: Scottish Academic Press).

Entwistle, N. J., and Marton, F. (1994) Knowledge objects: Understandings constituted through intensive academic study. *British Journal of Educational Psychology*, 64, 161–78.

Entwistle, N. J. and Ramsden, P. (1983) *Understanding Student Learning* (London: Croom Helm).

Entwistle, N. J. and Tait, H. (1992) Promoting effective study skills. Module 8, Block A. *Effective learning and teaching in higher education* (Sheffield Universities' and Colleges' Staff Development Unit).

Entwistle, N. J. and Wilson, J. D. (1977) *Degrees of Excellence: The academic achievement game* (London: Hodder and Stoughton).

Entwistle, N. J., Hanley, M. and Ratcliffe, G. (1979) Approaches to learning and levels of understanding. *British Educational Research Journal*, 5, 99–114.

Entwistle, N. J., Thompson, J. B. and Wilson, J. D. (1974) Motivation and study habits. *Higher Education*, 3, 379–96.

Entwistle, N. J., Thompson, S. and Tait, H. (1996) *Guidelines for Promoting Effective Learning in Higher Education*, 2nd edn (Edinburgh: University of Edinburgh, Centre for Research on Learning and Instruction).

Heath, R. (1964) *The Reasonable Adventurer* (Pittsburgh, PA: University of Pittsburgh Press).

Marsh, H. W. (1987) Students' evaluations of university teaching: research findings, methodological issues, and directions for future research. *International Journal of Educational Research*, 11(3) (whole issue).

Marton, F. (1994) Phenomenography, in Husen, T. and Postlethwaite, N. (Eds), *International Encyclopedia of Education* (Oxford: Pergamon), pp. 4424–9.

Marton, F., and Säljö, R. (1976) On qualitative differences in learning. I – outcome and process. *British Journal of Educational Psychology*, 46, 4–11.

Meyer, J. H. F. (1991) Study orchestration: the manifestation, interpretation and consequences of contextualised approaches to learning. *Higher Education*, 22, 297–316.

Meyer, J. H. F., Parsons, P. and Dunne, T. R. (1990) Individual study orchestrations and their association with learning outcome. *Higher Education*, 20, 67–89.

Parlett, M. R. and Hamilton, D. (1972) Evaluation as illumination: a new approach to the study of innovatory programmes. Unpublished report. (Reprinted in Hamilton, D. *et al.* (Eds), *Beyond the numbers game* (Basingstoke: Macmillan).

Perkins, D. N., Jay, E. and Tishman, S. (1993) Beyond abilities: a dispositional theory of thinking. *Merrill-Palmer Quarterly*, 39, 1–21.

Ramsden, P. (1997) The context of learning, in Marton, F. Hounsell, D. J. and Entwistle, N. J. (Eds), *The Experience of Learning*, 2nd edn (Edinburgh: Scottish Academic Press).

Snow, R., Corno, L. and Jackson, D. (1996) Individual differences in affective and conative functions, in Berliner, D. and Calfree, R. (Eds) *Handbook of Educational Psychology* (New York: Macmillan).

Svensson, L. (1977) On qualitative differences in learning, III – Study skill and learning. *British Journal of Educational Psychology*, 47, 233–43.

Tait, H. and Entwistle, N. J. (1996) Identifying students at risk through ineffective study strategies. *Higher Education*, 31, 99–118.

Trigwell, K., Prosser, M. and Taylor, P. (1994) Qualitative differences in approach to teaching first year science. *Higher Education*, 27, 74–84.

Vermunt, J. D. (1996) Metacognitive, cognitive and affective aspects of learning styles and strategies: a phenomenographic analysis. *Higher Education*, 31, 25–51.

Volet, S. E., and Renshaw, P. D. (1995) Cross-cultural differences in university students' goals and perceptions of study settings for achieving their own goals. *Higher Education*, 30, 407–33.

Part II

Teaching

Introduction to Part II

Some researchers have taken the view that if psychology is to have an educational impact then it is at least as important to study teachers and teaching as it is to study learners and learning. Indeed, it has been argued that a psychological understanding of teaching will provide more direct and educationally applicable findings than will studies of learning. This strategic approach is evident in our second section. Wood et al. report their developing work on teaching interactions called tutoring – the aspiration to engage in a meeting of minds.

Rogers surveys work on how the expectations teachers have for learners impact on learners' responses and attainments. Adey and Shayer report work of a slightly different pedigree. They discuss an intervention study in which teachers have been specially trained to design their work on the basis of psychological theory. Edwards and Mercer report their investigations of the complexities of classroom life, showing how knowledge, rather than being transmitted from teacher to pupil, is in fact co-constructed by teachers and pupils. Finally Shepard discusses, at a strategic level, the issue of assessment. It has been well established that assessment systems drive educational systems and Shepard sets out, in terms of psychological theory, some of the major facets of this process.

Again, a very wide range of psychological theory and method is evident in the work reported in this section. And again, it is clear that psychological research has made major contributions to understanding educational activities.

Worldwide, educational systems are under increasing pressure to improve in efficiency and effectiveness. The pace of social change increases relentlessly. If people are to respond to this change productively then they must enhance their most significant human capacity – the capacity to learn. Learning has become the core concept of our time. Psychology continues to make a major social contribution through its scientific programme on learning. This contribution is well illustrated here.

Becoming a Tutor

Introduction

Tutoring is a key process of promoting learning through a form of teaching which involves the direct interaction between teacher and taught. It is an essentially *interactive* process involving, at best, a mutual meeting of minds. Improvements in tutoring skills stand to increase the quality of the student's learning experience and enhance their attainment. Little is known about tutoring practices, about 'what works'.

Tutoring uses a lot of teacher time. In recognition of this it has been suggested that learners' peers could act as tutors. This suggestion has both an economic and a pedagogic rational. Economically, peers might be a large quarry of free teaching resource. Use of peers also frees the teacher and reduces the teacher's opportunity costs involved in tutoring.

Pedagogically it has been argued that the peer tutor stands to profit from the act of tutoring because the intellectual effort involved in a tutoring interaction enriches the tutor's understanding.

The validity of these claims has not been well tested and is unlikely to be properly appraised in advance of a sound theoretical understanding of the tutoring process.

In this paper, David Wood and colleagues report advances on their seminal work in this field. They raise questions about the developmental capacity of very young children to act as tutors. The research explores facets of cognitive development (including the development of children's theory of mind) implicated in Wood's general theory of tutoring and in that sense contributes to our understanding of both general developmental psychology and to a specific theory of tutoring.

Theoretical progress in the field of tutoring has a relatively short history. It could be said to begin with Wood, Bruner and Ross (1976) who first identified the key processes of mutual intellectual adjustment involved in tutoring.

Research in the field has recently shifted focus to pursue human–machine interactions as advances in information and communication technologies (ICT) devices play an increasing role in teaching and learning, with the extensive and increasing presence in schools of desktop and laptop computers extensively interconnected (see Gobet and Wood, 1999 for a review of work in this field).

References

Wood, D., Bruner, J. S. and Ross, G. 1976: The role of tutoring in problem solving. *Journal of Child Psychology and Psychiatry*, 17, 89–100.

Gobet, F. and Wood, D. 1999: in Wood, D. (ed.), *Expertise, models of learning and computer-based tutoring, Computers and Education*, 33, 2/3, 189–208.

SIX

On Becoming a Tutor: toward an Ontogenetic Model

David Wood, Heather Wood, Shaaron
Ainsworth and Claire O'Malley

Reviews and meta-analyses (Rogoff, 1990; Topping, 1992) of the peer-collaboration and peer-tutoring literature leave little doubt that such interactions can support learning and development. In relation to changes in conceptual understanding (Howe, Rodgers, & Tolmie, 1990), skills learning (Azmitia, 1988), self-regulatory or meta-cognitive abilities, communicative competence (G. Brown, Anderson, Shillcock, & Yule, 1984), the development of literacy and aspects of academic achievement (A. L. Brown & Campione, 1990), we can recruit evidence to justify claims that peer interaction can support the learning of both specific and general skills.

Much of the early research effort in this area has gone into establishing the conditions or parameters under which peer tutoring or peer collaboration leads to gains in learning or development (e.g., interindividual differences in ability levels or expertise; the presence or absence of conflict or discussion). This approach has led to several contradictory findings in the literature, with some researchers, for example, finding that pairing a less able with a more able child leads to progress, others finding that equal-ability dyads also lead to progress, and yet others finding no difference (see Tudge & Rogoff, 1989, for a review).

Different predictions concerning these parameters have been derived from Piagetian and Vygotskian frameworks. For researchers from a Piagetian or sociocognitive orientation, the benefit of social interaction derives from a recognition of alternative perspectives, which produces cognitive conflict and motivates the coordination of differing perspectives to arrive at a solution. Piaget, however, believed that the benefits deriving from discussion are only realized in interaction with peers of equivalent intellectual abilities, because, according to him, interaction with peers of higher ability or with adults would lead to the dominance by the more able over the less able partner (Piaget, 1932). In contrast, researchers from a Vygotskian framework emphasize the importance of pairing learners with more expert peers or with adults. As Tudge (1990) noted, however, many studies from a Piagetian perspective have involved pairing (e.g., conservers with nonconservers), and this is more consistent with the Vygotskian position on differences in expertise.

One difficulty faced by anyone attempting to reconcile these findings is deciding on the nature of "differences" between peers: should it be differences in domain expertise, general intellectual abilities, or age? Neither of the two theoretical perspectives nor the numerous empirical studies in this area make this point clear, although there are some examples more recently of research attempting to disentangle these senses of differing abilities more directly. For example, Verba and Winnykamen (1992) found that progress was made both in cases of pairs of unequal general ability and in cases of pairs of unequal domain expertise, but that the nature of the collaboration differed. In pairs where the high-ability child was the domain expert and the low-ability child the novice, the interaction was characterized by tutoring or guidance from the high-ability child. In pairs where the high-ability child was the novice and the low-ability child the expert, the interaction involved more collaboration and joint construction. So the point is not that some types of dyadic or group composition are more effective than others, but that different mixtures of knowledge, experience, and general ability lead to different types of interaction. Rogoff's (1990) comparative review of Piagetian and Vygotskian theory also contains a suggestion for reconciling these apparently contradictory positions. She pointed out that, although Vygotsky focused on acquiring understanding and skills, Piaget emphasized changes in perspectives or restructuring of concepts. Rogoff argued that tutoring or guidance may be necessary for the former, whereas collaboration between peers of equivalent intellectual ability may be better in fostering the latter. So, how dyads or groups should be composed with respect to skills and abilities may also depend on what learning outcomes are being sought (e.g., skill acquisition vs. conceptual change).

Azmitia (1988), for example, looked at domain expertise in pairs of 5-year-olds of equivalent abilities and found that, when novices were paired with experts on a model-building task, they improved significantly during and following the interaction, whereas equal-ability pairs did not. The successful interactions were mediated by observational learning and guidance by the expert rather than discussion produced by conflict. Azmitia argued that, although con-flict has been associated with learning in studies involving older children, preschoolers may lack the skill to sustain discussions of alternative hypotheses. She also noted that, even at 5 years of age, children seem able to identify expertise: both novices and experts spent more time observing experts than novices. As Azmitia noted, learning is mediated not only by experts' guidance but also by novices' own initiative in observing, imitating, and making sugges-tions.

Other investigations have shed some light on age-related changes in the development of tutoring skills. Ellis and Rogoff (1982) found that adult teachers were more effective than 8- to 9-year-olds in helping 6- to 7-year-olds learn classification tasks. The adults used more verbal instruction, provided more group relationship information, and elicited greater participation from learners. The child teachers tended to focus their attention on the immediate actions required to make progress in the activity, at the expense of the overall instructional goal (Ellis & Rogoff, 1986). Similar findings were obtained in a study of errand planning (Radziszewska & Rogoff, 1988). Rogoff (1990) also reported a further version of this study in which 9-year-old tutors were trained to the same level of performance as adults. Although the dyads with a trained peer showed just as sophisticated planning as children working with adults during the collaboration, posttests indicated that collabor-ation with adults led to better performance than either working with a trained peer or working alone. Rogoff attributed these differences to the fact that adult–child dyads involved strategic thinking aloud, for example, which was not evident in peer dyads. Other research has shown, however, that training young tutors can lead to effective peer-tutoring interactions (e.g., the reciprocal-teaching method; A. L. Brown & Palincsar, 1989).

As this field of investigation has matured, attention has been switching away from an almost exclusive interest in the conditions or parameters and the products of peer interaction toward a focus on the analysis of the processes mediating interaction (Howe, 1993; Tudge, 1990; Tudge & Winterhoff, 1993). Several researchers have noted the importance of both tutor and tutee's skills in self- and other regulation, explanation, and intersubjectivity (e.g., Rogoff, 1990; Tudge & Rogoff, 1989; Webb, 1991). The investigation reported in the present article is designed to add to this literature in relation to the development of peer-tutoring skills in children between 3 and 8 years of age and to articulate and explore relations between the development of tutoring and theory of mind.

Study of Peer Tutoring

The task used in the investigation (see Figure 6.1) and the analytic framework employed to analyze tutoring and learning are derived from previous investigations of adult–child tutorial interactions. Some years ago, we coined the scaffolding metaphor to provide an initial framework for conceptualizing the various roles that an adult tutor might undertake in supporting procedural skills learning in children (Wood, Bruner, & Ross, 1976). We attempted to identify those aspects of adult support that enabled children to learn, with help, tasks that they could not master alone. We suggested that the adult facilitated learning with tactics that, for example, served to induct the child learner into task

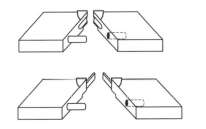
Pegs are inserted into holes to make two pairs which are then put together to make a single square layer

Five layers are piled and a top put on to make a pyramid

Figure 6.1 The Tower of Nottingham

relevant activity or to create recognizable goals for the child, thus making learning tasks manageable and helping the learner to avoid frustration. Or the adult might highlight significant features of the task that the child overlooks. We also suggested that effective instruction involved the progressive transfer of responsibility from tutor to learner as the learner developed task competence.

In subsequent studies, we formulated the principle of *contingent* instruction as a means whereby the transfer of responsibility might be achieved most effectively. Briefly, contingent instruction involves adherence to two rules: when the learner gets into difficulty, immediately offer more help; when a learner manages to execute a task operation with a given level of help, offer less help in any subsequent instruction (Wood, Wood, & Middleton, 1978). Later research provided evidence in support of these principles in other task domains and with different age groups (A. L. Brown & Ferrara, 1985; Pratt, Karig, Cowan, & Cowan, 1988; Rogoff, 1993). We have also demonstrated that the same principles generalize to the design of a computer-based tutoring system (Reichgelt, Shadbolt, Paskiewicz, Wood, & Wood, 1993). To the best of our knowledge, this perspective on contingent instruction has not been extended to investigate the nature of children's skills in peer tutoring. The aim of the investigation reported here is to make this extension. Before doing so, however, we offer a brief review of the development of theory of mind literature to draw out some general hypotheses about possible age-related differences in peer tutoring.

Theory of Mind and Peer Tutoring

Formal analyses of the instructional process implicate three tasks or demands: a performance model of the domain to be taught; a dynamic model of learner knowledge that is updated as the learner learns; and a theory of instruction that specifies what, when, and how to teach (e.g., Anderson, 1987). Using this general framework to analyze research on peer tutoring, we need to consider theory and findings in relation to the effects of a tutor's task competence on their tutoring performance. In this study, we capitalize on our previous investigations that show that the efficiency of learned performance with the current tasks relates to a child's task aptitude for learning. In addition to task competence, we must also consider children's abilities to diagnose and respond to a learner's needs: their aptitude for teaching. In addition, because the study involves children over a wide age range, we also need to consider the tutees' task aptitude for learning.

Tutors' aptitude for learning

In relation to the current task, previous investigations demonstrate that, although it can be taught to children as young as 3 years of age, the nature of learned performance at this age is different from that displayed by children aged 5 and 7 (Reichgelt et al., 1993). The performance of younger children is slower, marked by more trial and error, and, hence, less efficient. Further, children who learned the task more quickly and with less help displayed better postinstruction performance. If the findings of Azmitia (1988) generalize to the current investigation, we predicted that children who exhibit more *task expertise* (defined here as displaying more efficient learning performance) will prove to be more effective tutors than those who are less expert.

Tutors' aptitude for teaching

In relation to age-related differences in children's abilities to analyze and represent the beliefs, knowledge, and instructional needs of a peer, we can draw hypotheses from the extensive research into the development of children's theory of mind. In experimental contexts, 7-year-olds are able to appreciate that others may entertain different beliefs and can reason recursively about those beliefs (i.e., can reason that "You think that I think that...") . Such recursive, or *second-order*, reasoning, is beyond most 5-year-olds (Harris, 1989; Perner, 1988). If such reasoning is implicated in peer tutoring, we would expect to find changes in tutorial abilities occurring between ages 5 and 7. For example, if a child is able to deduce that an attempt to instruct failed because his or her learner misunderstood what he or she had tried to teach (e.g., "X does not know that I meant him to know or do Y") and can then modify his or her subsequent instructions in the light of this deduction, we would expect the emergence of contingent instruction (i.e., modifications of tutorial tactics in response to learner reactions to previous instructions) at around 7 years of age but not at the younger age groups.

Hughes and Russell (1993), arguing against "representational" theories of mind, suggested that age-related changes in theory of mind tasks may result from developments in the child's ability to disengage or, in Piagetian terms, to *de-center* from a dominant response. They appeal to evidence showing correlations between performance on theory of mind tasks and on tasks that demand flexibility in planning, inhibition of dominant responses, and a capacity for autoregulation. These executive demands are seen as constituting the core components of all goal-directed behavior, such as disengaging from strategies and engaging new ones, monitoring the effects of action, inhibiting prepotent but incorrect responses, and retaining task demands in working memory (Russell, Jarrold, & Potel, 1994). It is possible to analyze tutoring strategies in a similar way. For example, effective tutoring demands an ability to disengage from one's own task activity to monitor and evaluate the actions of the learner and to provide verbal instructions in place of task actions. The tutors must inhibit their own actions to provide "space" for the learner to execute the task. Planning what and when to teach next requires retention of task demands in memory. Thus, whether one adopts a representational theory of the theory of mind or one based on assumptions about autoregulation and the development of executive functions, it is possible to make similar age-related predictions about changes in tutorial interactions. We predicted changes between ages 5 and 7 in (a) the ability of tutors to relinquish task construction to the learner and (b) in the capacity to provide contingent instruction.

Tutees' aptitude for learning

Previous investigations using this task have shown that 5-year-olds can learn how to construct the task by observing it being assembled (Murphy & Wood, 1982). Children aged 3 learn almost nothing from such observational learning and require contingent instruction (Wood et al., 1978). Thus, although we predicted that 5-year-old tutors will not be capable of contingent instruction, their peers will learn how to assemble the task through observation. This will not be true of 3-year-old learners who, in order to learn the task, require but will not receive contingent instruction.

Method

Participants

Forty-eight children, 24 boys and 24 girls, participated in the investigation. They comprised eight same-age, same-sex pairs of self-confessed acquaintances at ages 3, 5, and 7 years. Children were drawn from schools in a mainly White, middle-class area. The experimenter who supervised the sessions, which were held in an observation suite at the University, has extensive experience working with these age groups and task setting.

Procedure

Tutors' aptitude for learning

Each of the children selected as tutors was allowed to play with the blocks for a few minutes before being taught how to assemble the task individually. Instructions were delivered by the computer-assisted multimedia tutoring system referred to earlier, which had been programmed to teach contingently. This system had been tested extensively with the age group involved in this study and shown to be as effective as a trained human tutor. The system enabled us to maintain a high level of control over the tutoring process.[1] In addition, it automatically logged all instructions provided to each learner and, at the completion of a teaching session, provided a profile of instructions given and the learner's responses to them. From this, the measures of learning aptitude for the task were derived.

Tutors' aptitude for teaching

After the tutor had been taught how to do the task, the second child, or learner, was brought into the room. The tutor was asked to "help" his or her friend to learn how to do the task (we avoided "show" and "tell"). Parents were asked to sit back from the table while the experimenter sat with the children. The focus here was on the time taken by the pair to complete the task, the numbers of assemblies made by each child, the types and frequencies of instructions given, and the degree of contingency displayed by the tutor. The measures derived to assess these statistics are detailed later.

The experimenter was to say and do nothing substantive unless one of the children persistently insisted that they wanted to leave or seemed to be distressed. At that point, the experimenter would present an operation for assembly to draw the child back to the table. Such occasions are counted as *aided constructions*. We know from previous experience that this task is a very difficult one for 3-year-olds, and we wished to avoid having the children (and their parents) leave with a sense of frustration and failure. How often the experimenter intervened in the collaborative process forms part of our data.

Tutees' aptitude for learning

After the peer-tutoring session, the tutor was asked to leave the room, and the learner was asked to do the task alone. The number of unaided constructions was counted (outcome), and the time per such construction was calculated (efficiency).

The whole procedure was videotaped for subsequent transcription and analysis.

Coding and analyzing tutorial interactions

The coding system that forms the basis for our results concerns the level of control of instructions and contingency. First, we present the basic categories used with adults. Labeled from 1 to 5, they range from least intrusive to most intrusive:

Level 1:   General encouragement: "Carry on!" "You've made a pair!"

Level 2:   Specific verbal information: "Get a bigger one," "Twist them round."

Level 3:   Selection: pointing at or handing over material, as well as verbal cues

Level 4:   Orientation: lining up blocks so they need only a shove for success

Level 5:   Demonstration: successful construction performed by the tutor

Each turn is coded according to the most intrusive level of help reached in that turn. Thus, a demonstration may involve verbal instruction accompanying selection of materials, orientation, and assembly but is only coded as Level 5.

To each code is then added a note of whether such a level of control was contingent (e.g., 4c) or not (4n) in context. If a child has just been successful, the level of control should be lower than in the previous tutor's turn. For example, if two blocks had previously been oriented for him or her (Level 4), a contingent tutor would now do no more than select materials (3c). A learner who is continuously successful soon comes to receive only the odd word of praise (1c). If, on the other hand, a learner continually gets into trouble, it is contingent to offer more and more help. For instance, a young struggler might be able to complete the task only when given materials oriented for him or her (Level 4). A contingent tutor here would keep trying to "back off" by merely selecting after each success (3c) but would be drawn into orientation again by the learner's failure to comply or by requests for help (4c). The performance of the learner drives what a contingent tutor does.

In previous investigations of adult–child interaction, we have found that these categories enable us to encode all the instructional tactics displayed. Some adults attempt to teach the task by demonstrating long sequences of assemblies to children. Others attempt to talk children through the task, seldom selecting pieces for the child to assemble or demonstrating how to comply with verbal instructions. The most successful strategies involve a combination of all these tutorial tactics. With 3-year-old learners, Level 4 instructions, where a child simply has to push blocks together, enable a child to achieve a measure of task success. A contingent tutor then asks the child to make another assembly of the same size and points out the pieces to be put together. If the child then succeeds, the tutor offers a specific verbal instruction without pointing. If the child finds this level of help too hard, the tutor points out material. After successful compliance, the tutor again attempts to "fade" the amount of help offered. Such contingent teaching usually succeeds with 3-year-olds; children discover how to assemble blocks, leaving the adult watching what they are doing or offering the occasional word of encouragement.

Measures

Tutors' task aptitude for learning

This was quantified as the proportion of child successes in assembling the task that does not involve help with selection of material or demonstration. Thus, a child who continually succeeds with only verbal help or no help at all from the system is deemed to have high aptitude for the task in hand. This measure has previously been found to correlate more highly with posttest results than age.

Tutors' aptitude for teaching

The number of correct assemblies (out of 20) completed by the tutoring child was counted to derive a measure of "tutor success." Total time on task during peer tutoring was determined to give an index of how efficiently children assembled the construction. The total incidence of actions and utterances by the tutor was classified according to the five levels of instruction. The rates of verbal instructions (i.e., Levels 1 and 2) and demonstrations (Level 5) were also determined. The percentage of contingent instruction was calculated by counting the total frequency of events in which the tutor offered more help when the learner failed to assemble pieces or made an error of construction, plus the number of times the tutor offered a less intrusive instruction after a learner success. This provided the numerator for a ratio (expressed as a percentage) to which all other instructional events (e.g., more help offered after success, less help after failure, or instructions repeated at the same level) were added to produce the denominator.

Tutees' aptitude for learning

The number of correct assemblies constructed by the learning children in the final posttest were counted, and total time to construct the task was determined. The average time taken to complete an act of assembly was computed.

Assessment of reliability

Six recordings of the tutorial sessions (a boy and a girl pair from each age group) were selected at random and coded by two independent analysts. The reliabilities for each coding category were also assessed by computing the percent agreements divided by the percent agreements plus disagreements over data from all six tapes. These are displayed in Table 6.1.

Table 6.1   Tutoring aptitude: measures and reliabilities

Measure	Reliability (%)
Number of tutor-made assemblies (tutor success)	98
Number of verbal instructions	83
Number of demonstrations	92
% contingent instructions	88

Results and Discussion

Tutors' aptitude for learning

The range of scores on the aptitude measure for 3-year-olds was 20% to 75%, for 5-year-olds was 70% to 92%, and for 7-year-olds was 70% to 100%. Thus, although the middle age group outperformed the youngest one, $U = 4$, $p < 0.001$, and performed less well than the oldest group, $U = 15$, $p < 0.05$, there were exceptional performances by some of the youngest children.

Tutors' aptitude for teaching

As predicted, older pairs took less time to assemble the task together than the younger ones (Table 6.2). The difference between the 3-year-olds and the 5-year-olds was significant, Mann–Whitney U test, $U = 2$, $p < 0.01$, but that between the 5-year-olds and the 7-year-olds was not.

Also shown in Table 6.2 are the means and ranges for the number of assemblies completed by the tutors in each age group. As predicted,

Table 6.2   Analysis of peer tutoring

	Age group					
	3		5		7	
Measures	M	Range	M	Range	M	Range
Tutoring time (min)	18	8–27	5	3–8	4.9	3–5
Tutor success (max 20)	11	1–20	13	5–20	5	0–13
Contingency (%)	28	18–37	24	5–43	68	31–100

7-year-old tutors completed less of the task than the 5-year-olds, $U = 6$, $p < 0.01$, and there was no difference in the performance of the 3-year-olds and the 5-year-olds. By age 7, then, the major responsibility for task construction passed from tutor to learner.

Finally, the incidence of contingent instruction was equally low at ages 3 and 5 but showed a significant increase between ages 5 and 7, $U = 4$, $p < 0.001$.

Levels of instruction by age

Table 6.3 shows the mean frequencies of occurrence at each level of instruction by age, together with the range of scores on each measure. The profile for the 3-year-olds and 5-year-olds is similar. The incidence of demonstration declined significantly between ages 5 and 7, $U = 8$, $p < 0.01$, whereas the frequency of verbal instruction increased, $U = 8$, $p < 0.01$.

Thus, as predicted, most task assembly at ages 3 and 5 was undertaken by the tutoring child, and verbal instruction was infrequent. Indeed, one 3-year-old pair, the least verbal of the 24 dyads, was in the task situation for 16 minutes before any vocalization took place, when the tutor said, "Ooops, it dropped again," as a piece fell down. The lack of explicit tutorial activity did not prevent learning, however. This tutoring session lasted for just under 20 minutes, and the learning child never touched a block. None the less, after the session in the posttest, the learner stayed on task for 23 more minutes and managed to assemble 15 of the 20 task operations in a performance that was one of the best for this age group and one that approached the average levels achieved by contingently taught children (Wood et al., 1978). Here, we suggest, the tutor served as a model for the learning child who, through sustained and careful observation, was able to learn enough to all but complete the task for herself.

By age 7, the most common tactic, at the very beginning of instruction, was to give explicit verbal instructions. For example, six out of eight tutors began the session by saying, variously, "Get the two biggest pieces"; "First, you want all these big ones"; "Well, get the two biggest blocks ... the four biggest blocks." Such attempts at verbal instruction were also observed with only two of the 5-year-old pairs (e.g., "Get the biggest blocks first"), but in each case, the 5-year-old tutors seemed incapable of inhibiting their own activity

Table 6.3 Levels of instruction by age

	Frequencies of Levels of Instruction									
	1		2		3		4		5	
Years	M	Range	M	Range	M	Range	M	Range	M	Range
3	4.0	0–12	2.4	0–8	2.5	0–11	0	—	15.0	4–27
5	2.0	0–9	2.0	0–6	2.0	0–10	0.6	0–5	14.1	6–23
7	13.2	1–20	4.5	0–10	2.3	0–10	0.8	0–3	5.4	0–13

and immediately acted on their own instructions. Conversely, the average profile of instruction found for the 7-year-olds provides strong evidence for the emergence of verbal instruction coupled with self-inhibition. Tutors were able to leave the learning child with time and space to try to act on the instructions given and often simply encouraged their peer as they assembled the task.

In studies of adult tutoring with 3-year-olds, we have found that Level 4 instructions (preparing pieces for assembly) are the most effective in luring a child who has little idea about what to do into relevant task activity. The sight of holes lined up with pegs, for instance, seems naturally to "afford" insertion to young children. Triggering such affordances provides a tutor with a reliable recruitment tactic for this age group. However, no tutoring children in the 3-year-old group seemed able to resist the impulse to put assemblies together themselves. One 5-year-old did manage this feat, and half of the 7-year-old tutors displayed this tactic, albeit infrequently.

Tutees' posttest performance

As predicted, the 3-year-old tutees completed less of the task after instruction than the 5-year-olds. The youngest children completed an average of 8 out of 20 constructions (range 0–16), and the 5-year-olds averaged 19, $U = 0$, $p < 0.001$. The average time to complete an assembly was 1.00 minutes at age 3 and 0.31 minutes at age 5. Again, there was no overlap in scores, with only one 3-year-old (0.60 minutes per assembly) approaching the time taken by the slowest 5-year-old (0.50 minutes).

The 7-year-olds each completed all 20 task assemblies. They assembled the task at a faster rate (0.16 minutes per assembly) than the 5-year-olds, although there was some overlap in scores, $U = 13$, $p < 0.05$.

Aptitude, tutoring, and tutee performance

To test the hypothesis that tutor aptitude exerted effects on tutoring aptitude and tutees' posttest performance, multiple regression analyses were employed.

A model that included tutor age and aptitude predicted 61% of the variance in the measures of time taken to complete the task by tutors and tutees. Dropping age from the model led to a significant decrease in its predictive power to 49%, $p < 0.01$. Thus, as hypothesized, pairs of children, including tutors who had found the task relatively easy to learn, assembled the task together faster than those involving tutors with lower task aptitude measures.

The model including age and aptitude predicted 71% of the variance in the posttest efficiency scores of the learners. Dropping the aptitude measure led to an almost significant decrease in predictive power, $p < 0.053$, two-tailed, offering weak support for the hypothesis that tutees who were taught by higher aptitude tutors (independent of age) learned the task more effectively than those taught by tutors with lower aptitude scores.

In general, the results of this investigation were in line with the hypotheses derived from existing literature on peer tutoring and the theory of mind. The task aptitude of the tutor for task-specific learning, tutoring aptitude, and the learning outcomes of the learning peer followed the age-related patterns predicted and led to the outcomes envisaged. In the following sections, we discuss the preceding results in relation to the hypotheses drawn from the relevant literature and outlined in the introductory paragraphs.

Tutors' aptitude for learning

The predicted age-related differences in learning aptitude derived from previous investigations were obtained. Three-year-old tutors required more frequent and intrusive help in learning to assemble the task than the 5-year-olds. Differences between the 5-year-olds and the 7-year-olds were less marked but still significant. There was, however, some overlap in performance. For example, the 3-year-old tutor with the highest aptitude for that age group outscored the lowest performing 5- and 7-year-old tutors. In line with our predictions, tutors who showed greatest aptitude for learning the task took less time in the peer-tutoring session to complete the task in company with their peers. With age partialed out, the measure of task aptitude predicted tutoring time.

Older tutees, who spent less time overall in the tutoring sessions, also went on to produce better task performances at posttest when they assembled the task alone. Three-year-old tutees assembled less of the task than the 5-year-olds and took longer to complete assemblies.

Five- and 7-year-olds did not differ significantly in how much of the task they could complete; most assembled all of the task alone. However, 7-year-olds were more task efficient, taking less time to complete the construction. There was some support for the prediction that tutors' task aptitude, over and above age, predicted the efficiency of tutee performance at posttest, providing additional evidence, in line with Azmitia's (1988) findings that more task-competent tutors exert a positive influence on the learning outcomes of peers. Our findings extend this conclusion by suggesting that children who learn a task most easily also help to support more effective task-specific learning in peers.

Tutors' aptitude for teaching

The main hypotheses tested in relation to changes in tutor behavior with age were drawn from the theory of mind literature. From Russell et al. (1994), we drew the hypothesis that, by age 7, children are able to inhibit dominant responses, retain task demands in memory, and successfully monitor the effects of task actions: that is, they demonstrate skills in self-regulation. The importance of skill in self- and other-regulation as core abilities in peer tutoring has already been stressed in previous investigations (e.g., Rogoff, 1990; Tudge & Rogoff, 1989; Webb, 1991). These abilities, we suggested, should also enable children, by age 7, to inhibit their own task activity when tutoring in order to provide opportunities for a peer to assemble the task. As predicted, we found major changes in the balance of responsibility for task construction between ages 5 and 7, so that the younger tutors assembled the majority of the task and the older learners did more. Accompanying the transfer of responsibility for task assembly between ages 5 and 7 was an increase in verbal instruction. Seven-year-olds substituted telling for demonstrating as a means of instruction.

The theory of mind literature also indicates that, by age 7, children usually develop a capacity for recursive or *second-order* reasoning about the mental states of others (e.g., Harris, 1989; Perner, 1988). We hypothesized that the ability to instruct contingently (i.e., to modify instructional tactics on the basis of a learner's responses to an instruction) might also draw on the same cognitive abilities. If this is the case, we should find an increase in the incidence of contingent teaching between ages 5 and 7 but not between ages 3 and 5. These predictions were supported by the analyses of results. The most able 7-year-old tutor exhibited perfectly contingent teaching in that she always increased the specificity of her instructions when her tutee got into difficulties but then offered less specific help on the next instruction. By the end of the tutoring session, this tutor had "faded" all help as her tutee made constructions on her own and without error.

The average contingency levels achieved by the 7-year-old tutors were similar to those found in previous investigations of adults teaching 3- to 4-year-olds. If the theoretical connection between second-order theory of mind and tutoring abilities suggested by our results generalize to other investigations, this result will support the hypothesis that second-order reasoning is a necessary condition for contingent instruction and that both abilities are emergent at around age 7.

Tutees' aptitude for learning

Although the 5-year-old learners were less efficient at posttest than the 7-year-olds, they were, as predicted, able to construct the task alone after the tutoring sessions. Previous investigations with this task (Murphy & Wood, 1982) and Azmitia's (1988) study provided evidence that children of this age are able to learn task-specific assembly skills through observations of good task performance by a peer. Thus, although both 3- and 5-year-old tutors displayed few signs of contingent instruction, the finding that 5-year-old pairs assembled the task quickly (averaging 5 minutes compared to the 18 minutes taken by 3-year-olds), coupled with the fact that 5-year-olds, but not 3-year-olds, can learn this task by observation of demonstrations, meant that the conditions needed to support observational learning in the context of peer collaboration were present at age 5 but not at age 3. These results imply that, although contingent tutoring may be established by age 7, the conditions for effective collaborative learning (in learning some procedural skills) are present at age 5.

Note

1 All children were taught according to the same rules, but this did not mean that all children received the same instructions. Help was given only when required and with whatever materials the child happened to be working with. Thus, a child who found the task easy was given less

substantive help than a child who was struggling and would take less time to teach. The struggling child therefore received more exposure to appropriate vocabulary and instructional tactics than the more task-competent child.

References

Anderson, J. R. (1987). Production systems, learning and tutoring. In D. Klahr, P. Langley, & R. Neches (Eds.), *Production system models of learning and development* (pp. 437–458). Cambridge, MA: MIT Press.

Azmitia, M. (1988). Peer interaction and problem solving: When are two heads better than one? *Child Development, 59,* 87–96.

Brown, A. L., & Campione, J. C. (1990). Communities of learning and thinking, or a context by any other name. In D. Kuhn (Ed.), *Developmental perspectives on teaching and learning thinking skills: Contributions to human development* (pp. 108–126). Basel, Switzerland: Karger.

Brown, A. L., & Ferrara, R. A. (1985). Diagnosing zones of proximal development. In J. V. Wertsch (Ed.), *Culture, communication and cognition: Vygotskian perspectives* (pp. 273–305). Cambridge, England: Cambridge University Press.

Brown, A. L., & Palincsar, A. S. (1989). Guided, cooperative learning and individual knowledge acquisition. In L. B. Resnick (Ed.), *Knowing, learning, and instruction: Essays in honor of Robert Glaser* (pp. 393–451). Hillsdale, NJ: Lawrence Erlbaum Associates, Inc.

Brown, G., Anderson, A., Shillcock, R., & Yule, G. (1984). *Teaching talk: Strategies for production and assessment.* Cambridge, England: Cambridge University Press.

Ellis, S., & Rogoff, B. (1982). The strategies and efficacy of child versus adult teachers. *Child Development, 53,* 730–735.

Ellis, S., & Rogoff, B. (1986). Problem solving in children's management of instruction. In E. Mueller & C. Cooper (Eds.), *Process and outcome in peer relationships* (pp. 301–325). Orlando, FL: Academic.

Harris, P. L. (1989). *Children and emotion: The development of psychological understanding.* Oxford, England: Blackwell.

Howe, C. (1993). Editorial for special issue on peer interaction and knowledge acquisition. *Social Development, 2,* iii–vi.

Howe, C., Rodgers, C., & Tolmie, A. (1990). Physics in the primary school: Peer interaction and the understanding of floating and sinking. *European Journal of Psychology of Education, 5,* 459–475.

Hughes, C., & Russell, J. (1993). Autistic children's difficulty with mental disengagement from an object: Its implications for theories of autism. *Developmental Psychology, 29,* 498–510.

Murphy, C. M., & Wood, D. J. (1982). Learning through the media: A comparison of 4–8 year old children's responses to filmed and pictorial instruction. *International Journal of Behavioral Development, 5,* 195–216.

Perner, J. (1988). Higher-order beliefs and intentions in children's understanding of social interaction. In P. Astington, P. L. Harris, & D. Olson (Eds.), *Developing theories of mind* (pp. 141–172). Cambridge, England: Cambridge University Press.

Piaget, J. (1932). *The moral judgment of the child.* London: Routledge & Kegan Paul.

Pratt, M., Karig, P., Cowan, P., & Cowan, C. (1988). Mothers and fathers teaching three-year-olds: Authoritative parenting and adults' scaffolding of young children's learning. *Developmental Psychology, 24,* 732–739.

Radziszewska, B., & Rogoff, B. (1988). Influence of adult and peer collaborators on children's planning skills. *Developmental Psychology, 24,* 840–848.

Reichgelt, H., Shadbolt, N., Paskiewicz, T., Wood, D., & Wood, H. (1993). EXPLAIN: On implementing more effective tutoring systems. In A. Sloman (Ed.), *Prospects for artificial intelligence* (pp. 239–249). Brighton, England: University of Sussex, Society for the Study of Artificial Intelligence and Simulation of Behaviour.

Rogoff, B. (1990). *Apprenticeship in thinking: Cognitive development in social context.* New York: Oxford University Press.

Rogoff, B. (1993). Analysis of developmental processes in sociocultural activity. In L. Martin, K. Nelson, & E. Tobach (Eds.), *Cultural psychology and activity theory* (pp. 122–140). Cambridge, England: Cambridge University Press.

Russell, J., Jarrold, C., & Potel, D. (1994). What makes strategic deception difficult for children – The deception or the strategy? *British Journal of Developmental Psychology, 12,* 301–314.

Topping, K. (1992). Cooperative learning and peer tutoring: An overview. *The Psychologist, 5,* 151–157.

Tudge, J. (1990). Vygotsky, the zone of proximal development, and peer collaboration: Implications for classroom practice. In L. C. Moll (Ed.), *Vygotsky and education: Instructional implications and applications of sociohistorical psychology* (pp. 155–172). Cambridge, England: Cambridge University Press.

Tudge, J., & Rogoff, B. (1989). Peer influences on cognitive development: Piagetian and Vygotskian perspectives. In M. H. Bornstein & J. S. Bruner (Eds.), *Interaction in human development* (pp. 17–40). Hillsdale, NJ: Lawrence Erlbaum Associates, Inc.

Tudge, J., & Winterhoff, P. (1993). Can young children benefit from collaborative problem solving? Tracing the effects of partner competence and feedback. *Social Development, 2,* 242–259.

Verba, M., & Winnykamen, F. (1992). Expert–novice interactions: Influence of partner status. *European Journal of Psychology of Education, 7*, 61–71.

Webb, N. (1991). Task-related verbal interaction and mathematics learning in small groups. *Journal for Research in Mathematics Education, 22*, 366–389.

Wood, D., Bruner, J. S., & Ross, G. (1976). The role of tutoring in problem solving. *Journal of Child Psychology and Psychiatry, 17*, 89–100.

Wood, D., Wood, H., & Middleton, D. (1978). An experimental evaluation of four face-to-face teaching strategies. *International Journal of Behavioural Development, 1*, 131–147.

Teacher Expectations

Introduction

The review reported here had its origins in the findings of 'experimenter effects' in laboratory studies of animal learning. Rats, whose experimenters had been led to believe were superior at learning, performed better on learning tasks than equally able animals whose experimenters had not been so misled. Those findings were replicated in a study of young children whose teachers had been fed misinformation about their potential attainment (Rosenthal and Jacobsen, 1966). Modest information leading to discriminant expectancies on the part of teachers was associated in this study with significant differences in children's attainment.

This original study was technically flawed in many respects and subject to widespread criticism (Rogers, 1982). It did lead, however, to the development of extensive research on teacher expectations, and to development in research on classroom processes (how teachers appraise, design, present and evaluate work for students based on the teachers' estimations of students abilities) and attribution theory (how pupils explain the links between how we think of ourselves as learners and how we engage with the business of learning). Cognitive theories of motivation may be contrasted with more traditional theories which have been couched in terms of rewards and punishments.

This field of research has considerable significance in discussions of how to enhance learners' attainments. This question and related issues are discussed in the present review.

SEVEN

Teacher Expectations: Implications for School Improvement

Colin Rogers

For some 30 years the social psychology of education has given a central role to the operation of teacher expectations. The highly influential and equally controversial research of Rosenthal and Jacobson (1968) is still cited as the origin of this work. A steady stream of studies has testified to the enduring interest of researchers in the processes involved together with the complexity and significance of the educational issues concerned. Some of the developments in this field can be traced through reviews and key collections of work including Rosenthal and Rubin (1978), Rogers (1982), Dusek (1985), Miller and Turnbull (1986), Jussim (1989), Goldenberg (1992), and Blanck (1993). A glance through these sources will reveal a variety of models put forward to explain the process of expectation effects with a variety of views expressed concerning what is central.

In recent years this whole enterprise has been given a new emphasis by the search for the key to effective education. The school effectiveness researchers and members of the school improvement movement see expectations as a key to effective schooling. Two recent examples serve to make the point.

Stoll and Fink (1996) set out a detailed review of work into school effectiveness and school improvement. I shall return to explore this in greater detail later in this chapter. For the moment, let it be noted that the expectations of teachers soon appear in this work as an important component of effective schooling. Drawing on the Halton Effective Schools project, Stoll and Fink indicate three broad categories of factors associated with effective schools. One of these is an 'emphasis on learning'. Amongst other things this includes 'high expectations' held by the school for its students. They also draw on a review by Sammons, Hillman and Mortimore (1995) which concludes with a list of 11 factors for effective schools. Again, one of these is 'high expectations'.

A rather different work also indicates the perceived importance of expectations for effective schooling (National Commission on Education, 1996). Entitled *Success against the Odds*, this work presents a number of accounts of schools that are judged to be effective even though they operate 'against the odds' in disadvantaged areas. The claimed importance of positive expectations runs consistently through the accounts, each produced by a panel of people external to the school in question. The book's small index contains a number of references to expectations and indeed the indexers thought it necessary to include a separate entry for high expectations, also one of the longest. (Given that this book focuses on successful schools there is no index entry for low expectations.) The report on one of the schools says:

> We have been struck forcibly by how frequently we heard high expectations being expressed of other people in this school. (p. 161)

In talking about the staff of another school the team of reporters said:

> They subscribe to the view that it is necessary to have high and consistent expectations of all students ... (p. 76)

The concluding chapter states that:

> The powerful relationship between high expectations and effective learning has long been recognised. (p. 325)

The authors go on to discuss the pivotal role of the school's leadership or management in promoting high expectations and the concomitant success.

High Expectations

How do we describe expectations? The examples from the effective schooling literature generally cite high expectations and then go on to add that these are or ought to be consistent. Is this an entirely adequate basis for a typology of teacher expectations?

Almost certainly not. The high–low dimension is of obvious importance. High expectations refer, for example, to the school grades to be achieved, the number of days of attendance children will manage over the coming school year or the standards of behaviour to be displayed in the school. These and other examples can all be measured and assessed in some way. As grade scores are the simplest to deal with, and form the cornerstone of much of the effective schooling research, let us take them as an instance.

Two teachers express their expectations for the grades students will achieve by the end of compulsory secondary schooling. One indicates a range of Cs to A*s with a definite skew to the top end, the other a range that indicates only a handful of A and B grades with C grades being the best that most of the students are expected to achieve. Who has the high expectations? In one sense the answer is obvious, but also somewhat trivial. High expectations, like effective schooling, need to be understood in a value-added manner. If the teacher expressing higher expectations works in a highly selective school then the value-added component of those expectations might be relatively low or even non-existent. In other words, as the student enters the school these high standards are what the regression equations of the school effectiveness researcher would have predicted. The teacher's expectations are a simple reflection of what she or he has experienced in the past and therefore has come to expect for the future. The second teacher, who has the lower absolute expectations, might be expressing greater optimism in that their predictions are higher than might be expected on the basis of student intake characteristics.

Prescriptive and Probabilistic Expectations

Rogers (1982) drew a distinction between expectations that were prescriptive and those which were probabilistic. Probabilistic expectations

represent what we think is most likely to happen. Prescriptive expectations, on the other hand, tend to be expressed by the use of the word
'ought'. People are not just thought likely to perform at a particular
level; they ought to. To put it another way, teachers take steps to try to
ensure that they will. Prescriptive expectations are more than a passive
response to the accumulation of experience; they are more than an
individual's own estimate of regression curves. They are an expression
of what they think ought to happen, what they want to happen and
what they think they might be able to make happen.

Prescriptive expectations are at the centre of the concerns of the
school effectiveness researcher. Prescriptive expectations are based on
reality. We are discussing expectations here, not fantasies. However,
prescriptive expectations can be more than just realistic predictions;
they may also represent optimistic views of the future. At the end of the
last paragraph I claimed that prescriptive expectations are what
people think *ought* to happen, what they would *like* to happen and
what they think they can *make* happen. The emphasis in this chapter
will be on the third of these three conditions. What are the factors that
determine the extent to which people believe themselves to be able to
make the desirable happen?

Expectations then vary not only in terms of how high or low they
may be, they vary too in terms of the extent to which they are
prescriptive or probabilistic.

Individual and Shared Expectations

Blease (1983) drew a distinction between expectations held by one
individual teacher and those shared throughout the school (or a
department or any other section of the school that would be meaningful from the point of view of the student). We need therefore to consider
ways in which networks of expectations might have different effects
from those held by individual teachers. *School* effectiveness implies that
effects will take place across the school. In as much as schools make a
difference to the progress made by students, and in as much as the
expectations held by teachers are part of that effect, then these expectations will be common across the school. School effectiveness researchers have recognised that the school might not always be the most
appropriate level of analysis (e.g. Sammons *et al.*, 1994) and that

school effectiveness might be a matter of departmental effectiveness. Either way, the recognition of shared expectations requires us to consider a number of further points. Blease (1983) argued that shared expectations would be more powerful in terms of producing self-fulfilling prophecies. Whatever impact the expectations of a single teacher might have will be magnified if repeated from one year to the next, or, in the secondary context, from one lesson to the next. If everybody seems to see us in the same way it must be harder to deny the validity of those perceptions than if some perceptions are contradicted, or at least not supported by others.

However, there is another issue here that this chapter will wish to address. Models of the teacher expectancy process (e.g. Rogers, 1982) have attended to the ways in which individual teachers build up their initial expectations of individual students. Teachers can draw on a variety of information, and use a variety of processes and sub-processes in the task of generating specific expectations. Shared expectations across a system (school, department, etc.) suggest some commonality of process. There are a variety of ways in which this can take place. For example, the system itself can influence the information available and therefore the formation of expectations. The point to be made here is that system-wide expectations, the consistent expectations referred to above, suggest the operation of school culture. The ways in which the culture of the school may influence the expectations held by teachers is another aspect of the process. This will have to be considered in order to achieve a full understanding of the role of expectations in effective schooling.

The Functions of Expectations

So far, however, we are only beginning to describe expectations in terms of what they might look like, not yet in terms of what they might do. Expectations will also need to be considered in terms of their functions.

Snyder (1992) has considered the functions served by the process of behavioural confirmation (or self-fulfilling prophecies). Although his discussion does not touch directly upon teacher expectations and their effects it does contain some important implications for our present concerns.

Snyder's own analysis concerns the work of social psychologists who have examined behavioural confirmation (and disconfirmation) as a part of the acquaintance process. Such situations, where individuals are beginning a relationship, offer a number of advantages for the social psychologist's research agenda. These situations enable the manipulation of potentially relevant factors in ways that would often be impossible, or unethical, in educational settings. It is important to acknowledge the need for caution in using the ideas emerging from this particular literature here. However, there does seem to be some general applicability to present concerns of the ideas discussed by Snyder.

Teachers will presumably have a concern with the learning of their students and, related to this, the behaviour of their students. The perceptions of students generated by teachers will be rich in terms related to these objectives with students being characterised as fast or slow learners, well or poorly behaved, and so on. A self-fulfilling prophecy occurs when a student who is perceived incorrectly as being of, say, a low level of ability comes to match those assumptions. A functional approach to this process requires us to ask not only how this might happen but also why. Why should a teacher persist with underestimations of a student's potential to the extent of 'forcing' that student to conform to the expectation? Perhaps more tellingly, we also need to ask why students would come to change their behaviour so as to match an expectation that would appear to offer them little. Social psychology, in education and elsewhere, has too often ignored these 'why' questions in favour of 'how' questions. A number of models of the teacher expectancy process exist which set out the various steps involved in the formation, transmission, perception and acceptance of expectations. To the extent that these models are correct they tell us how expectations may be formed, how they may be transmitted, how they may be perceived and how those perceptions may be acted upon. None of this tells us why any of this should happen, or in whose interests it might be.

A functional analysis of expectations requires us to think in almost Darwinian terms about the nature of the process. If self-fulfilling prophecies have been taking place in classrooms, often to the disadvantage of students and teachers alike, then we must ask why this has continued. In evolutionary terms forms of behaviour that have no adaptive function would wither and eventually disappear. The converse of this suggests that continuing processes do have some significant purpose that in some way benefits the participants. The challenge of a functional analysis of teacher expectations and their effects is to attempt to say what these benefits might be.

Snyder (1992) first draws attention to the function of control. It is useful to conceptualise interpersonal perception as a control system. It is assumed that people construct understandings of others that enable them to predict and control the interactions they have with them (see also Zebrowitz, 1990). The reasons people may have for wanting control over their interactions with others will themselves be varied and will relate to the broad patterns of purposes lying behind the interactional sequence in the first place. The general assumption is that in most instances where we interact with others a sense of control is necessary for us to be able to anticipate a smooth interaction with the other. Social interaction with people we do not know well is always more difficult than with those with whom we are more familiar. We are not likely to be able to anticipate their reactions to our own remarks and moves. When the sensibilities of others are not understood the risk of causing unintentional offence is always greater.

Snyder's (1992) second relevant function concerns processes of ego-defence. Behavioural confirmation takes place when one or more of the participants in the relevant interaction are seeking to protect some facet of a self-image that some aspects of the interaction might challenge. As Snyder puts it, some expectations may serve the 'function of protecting people from accepting unpleasant truths about themselves' (p. 95). From the point of view of the teacher, it is not difficult to see how ego-defensive functions might operate. A failing student suggests a failing teacher. Low expectations help to reduce the sense of failure in a number of ways. Failure can be seen as the shortfall between outcome and expectation. Lower initial expectations clearly reduce the probability of failure so defined. (The deliberate lowering of expectations regarding economic well-being is a tried and trusted trick of politicians eager to encourage positive perceptions of themselves by the electorate.) Expectations can also help to direct the apportionment of responsibility (or blame) for failings seen to have occurred. It is clearly helpful to the teacher's ego to 'set things up' so that blame for failure will tend to attach to the student rather than to the teacher.

The Dimensions of Expectations

I asserted above that a unidimensional model of expectations was unlikely to provide a sufficient descriptive or analytical framework for the consideration of effective schooling. I have suggested that the degree to which teachers share expectations and the functions served by these expectations also need to be considered. However, this still leaves us with the single dimension of height (are the expectations high or low?). This unidimensional description is still likely to be inadequate to the task of explaining some of the variance between more and less effective schools. It is necessary to add a further dimension of breadth.

A high expectation sets a standard of performance in relation to particular criteria. A low expectation does just the same, simply setting a different standard. I stated above that prescriptive expectations concern the things that people think they will be able to make happen. It is in relation to this aspect that a multidimensional approach is needed.

An example will illustrate the point. A teacher expects low grade scores for a particular student. This expectation is currently probabilistic. We are looking at an early stage in the student's school career and the expectation is a prediction based on performance to date. The teacher's prescriptive expectation, however, is higher. This student ought to do better and it ought to be possible to make this happen. How can the prescriptive and the probabilistic expectations be reconciled?

The answer would seem to lie in the breadth of the expectation. In other words, we need to consider the other assumptions that a teacher makes alongside an appraisal of where the student will get to if current performance continues. At issue here is the belief system of the teacher regarding the elements seen to determine student success. This will clearly involve assumptions made by the teacher about the levels of ability and motivation characteristic of that student. However, in adding breadth to this we are also going to have to consider the beliefs the teacher has concerning the nature of that ability and motivation. In particular, what does the teacher believe that he or she can do about changing ability and motivational levels? When the teacher sees these characteristics of the student as fixed, or at least not amenable to teacher influence, then a low probabilistic expectation begins to develop into a prescriptive one. However, if the teacher sees ability and/ or motivation as student characteristics subject to influence by teacher action, then he or she may yet see a low probabilistic expectation take on a higher prescriptive tone.

The discussion so far has drawn attention to a number of claims.

- High expectations are frequently and regularly associated with effective schooling.
- There is an implication following from this that raising expectations will have the effect of enhancing the effectiveness of a school.
- Expectations are not merely actuarial predictions of future performance based on the past, they can contain prescriptive elements relating to what people think ought to happen.
- We need to consider the extent to which teachers might believe themselves capable of changing the outcomes expected on a probabilistic basis to those desired on a prescriptive basis.
- In doing this, teachers are drawing on a multidimensional conception of expectations, considering expectations in terms of breadth as well as height.
- Expectations, in common with other aspects of interpersonal perception, are considered to have a functional basis. An understanding of these functions is necessary if any change programmes are likely to be at all effective.
- Effective schools or school departments will presumably have expectations that are common to many if not all of the members of the staff of that school or department. Shared expectations are likely to be more powerful than idiosyncratic ones in influencing the attainments of students and are therefore likely to be a particularly important aspect of effective schools. However, there is a need to understand the development of school- or department-wide expectations.

In other words, we need to examine the impact of school culture upon teacher expectations, with expectations understood in terms of breadth and height.

The Normative Basis of Expectations

Waterhouse (1991) discusses some of the processes involved when teachers form impressions of students. He makes a number of points including the important observation that the process of building up an impression of a student may well vary from one school to another. However, the main point to draw on here is that teachers will base their perceptions on the idea of the average or 'normal' student. It is, suggests Waterhouse, the normal student who provides the rather indeterminate bedrock upon which teachers build other, more idiosyncratic or consociate relationships, with other students. In an historical context this has some significance. It presents a different light on the conclusions of other researchers such as Sharp and Green (1975). They have claimed that it is the ideal student who provides the core and with whom teachers form closer, more consociate relationships. Students who deviate from this ideal are to some extent rejected and excluded from closer and developing consociate relationships. Waterhouse (1991) reports that teachers often find it difficult to say very much about the normal, average student. It is when a student deviates from this average image that the teacher is likely to begin to consider them in relation to the particular needs of each individual.

It seems reasonable to take this argument a step further and suggest that normative variations across schools will have important implications for the setting of expectations. Further, it will often be those who fall below the norm that teachers single out for special attention.

Accounts of expectancy effects have often assumed that teachers form expectations against the yardstick of the ideal student. It would be the ideal that determined what teachers thought ought to be happening. On the assumption that a considerable proportion of the teaching profession shares a view of the ideal, it is possible to suggest that the basis for expectations across the system also have a common foundation. However, if Waterhouse is correct in assuming that it is the normal that determines the basis of perceptions, then expectations will be more likely to vary across schools in line with the prevailing norms. Thus we would expect to find that teachers working in geographical areas with historically low levels of attainment will form lower expectations than those held by teachers working in more favoured areas. Thus the student from such an area might be doubly disadvantaged.

Second, Waterhouse's analysis suggests that teachers are likely to form particularly strong and well-formed expectations for those students who deviate from the norm. This may well advantage those who perform significantly above the normal level, but would again serve to disadvantage those whose careers start with below norm performance.

Good Intentions, Low Expectations

The work on teacher expectations of Cooper and his colleagues (Cooper and Good, 1983) provides an example of some of the implications of this. Cooper's work is important for present purposes as it touches upon a number of the aspects of expectations alluded to above. In particular, Cooper's work emphasises the function of expectations and aspects of the breadth of expectations.

Reflecting the concerns of Snyder (1992) Cooper (1983) places a considerable emphasis on the control function. He reminds us that we need to consider why teachers would act to apparently disadvantage certain students. Cooper suggests that teachers single out lower attaining students for particular attention as a consequence of teachers' wishes to help their development. The lower attaining student falls into Waterhouse's (1991) category of those the teacher perceives in terms both richer and more fully and personally developed than the 'normal' student. These fuller, more consociate perceptions, suggest to the teacher a need for special attention in order to maximise that student's learning. In order to provide this attention the teacher believes that they need to exercise greater control over interactions with these students than with others. This in turn reflects the belief of the teacher that lower attaining (and lower ability) students will gain most benefit from interactions with a teacher where the teacher can direct what happens. Such control is most likely obtained when the interactions take place in relatively private one-to-one settings, and where the teacher is able to initiate the various steps taken. Consequentially, these students find teachers appearing unwilling to accept contributions made to classroom discussions (relatively public settings). Teachers also seem resistant to their contributions even when offered in the private setting of a one-to-one discussion. Cooper completes his analysis by arguing that the impact of this on student attributions is detrimental to the development of positive motivational forms.

This very sketchy outline of Cooper's (1983) work serves to illustrate how the road to lowering student motivation and standards of achievement is paved with good teacher intentions. While Cooper's analysis suggests a clear and fairly direct link between teacher expectations and worsening student performance, it is also clear that teachers are seen to be acting with the best of intentions. The problem, of course, is that the action which to the teacher logically follows from these initial expectations has a depressing rather than an elevating effect on the student. The final sting, the core of all self-fulfilling prophecies, is that the subsequent failure on the part of the student to improve simply serves to confirm the teacher's initial expectations. The damaging cycle of events runs on.

The critical point here is not that the teachers in Cooper's studies held low expectations for their students. When teachers set expectations against a normative background then low expectations are unavoidable for some students. It is the other aspects of the expectations, referred to here as the breadth dimension, that is important. Essentially these further aspects concern the beliefs a teacher has about critical student characteristics, and the consequential beliefs concerning appropriate courses of teacher action.

Models of Ability and Motivation

The suggestion here is that these teacher beliefs concerning student characteristics will centre upon notions of the nature of ability and motivation. Essentially it is not the teacher's judgement of the level of ability and motivation that it is critical. It is the teacher's view of the nature of these constructs that matters most.

Research in motivation has emphasised the importance of an individual's belief concerning not only the level of their ability but also the nature of that ability. Dweck (1991) presents a particularly clear account of this. Students who perceive themselves as having a low level of ability are clearly likely to experience motivational problems. Life is simply easier in many respects if we see ourselves as being relatively able (in relation to others and to the tasks at hand). However, Dweck argues that low perceived ability does not necessarily lead to poor motivation unless the individual in question also believes that there is little or nothing they can do to improve the situation. Dweck and others (e.g. Nicholls, 1989) have provided evidence to show that people see ability either as a fixed entity or as an incremental facet of a person. As an entity, ability is seen as fixed (perhaps due to genetic factors or the impact of early experience) and as setting a ceiling on the ultimate level of performance possible. Low ability is therefore debilitating because it naturally suggests that one's personal ceiling may be lower than is needed to gain success within the school system or elsewhere. Given this scenario, most of us give up. The incremental view, however, holds that ability ought to be understood as a skill, or collection of skills, and is therefore capable of enhancement. Current low levels of ability make life more difficult but do not preclude the possibility of ultimate success. One's focus therefore shifts to ways of enhancing ability, and, in so doing, one maintains motivation. Work by Nicholls (Nicholls and Miller, 1984) has suggested that young children will be unlikely to hold the entity view of ability and are therefore also unlikely to suffer the same motivational difficulties as their older counterparts. More recent work by Dweck (e.g. Cain and Dweck, 1995) suggests that even pre-school children may hold beliefs of an entity kind (although not directed at ability as such) which have a similar debilitating motivational impact.

Other researchers have shown potentially important links between teacher self-efficacy and teacher beliefs. For example, Marshall and Weinstein (1984) show that teachers who see themselves as higher on self-efficacy are more likely to see student ability as incremental. Importantly, of course, these ability beliefs refer to the teachers' views of the students. However, there is no available data concerning the nature of any causal relationships that might be involved here. It is quite possible that a heightened sense of teacher efficacy is a result of the prior belief that student ability is incremental. It is also possible that teacher efficacy beliefs will influence beliefs concerning ability. The nature of these relationships are of obvious importance when considering the implications for school improvement. I will return to the relationship between school culture and teacher efficacy beliefs below. Woolfolk and Hoy (1990) have further demonstrated relationships between general teacher efficacy and a custodial approach to teaching.

While there is some limited evidence to suggest a link between teacher efficacy beliefs and teacher views on the nature of ability, far less is known concerning the nature of the relationship between teacher efficacy beliefs and teacher's attitudes towards student motivation. Indeed, teachers' beliefs concerning the nature of motivation are a sadly neglected area of research. As with ability beliefs, at issue here is not simply the views teachers have about the level of their students' motivation. Of equal, if not greater, significance are the beliefs held by teachers regarding the nature of this motivation.

Rogers (1992) has suggested a number of different models of motivation which could act as guides to teachers' thinking. All of these
models have been subjected to extensive research as models of motivation itself. What is unclear is the extent to which they are adopted
by teachers and the range of factors that might determine the use that
teachers make of them. Each of the models will be reviewed briefly here
before their implications are discussed.

The first model owes most to the research and theorising of Atkinson
(e.g. Atkinson and Raynor, 1977). Atkinson was concerned to set out
the relationship between key aspects of personality and situational
variables in the determination of an individual's motivational response
to success and failure. The essence of this work, for present purposes, is
to see motivation as being essentially a *function of personality*. Although
the precise response of a person to any one experience of success or
failure is determined by aspects of the situation, it is the relatively
stable and enduring characteristics of personality that determine the
broad brush of their response. Consistency over time and place is
therefore to be expected.

The second model was derived from the work of Weiner (e.g. Weiner,
1986, 1992) who has applied attribution theory to an analysis of
motivational dynamics. Weiner's essential claim is that motivational
patterns are determined by the patterns of attributions people make for
their successes and failures. Attribution theory has assumed that people
are concerned to identify credible causes of significant events. Important
instances of success and failure, therefore, are likely to be understood by
reference to what was believed to have made them happen. Weiner has
demonstrated that these inferred causes of success and failure can be
located on a number of dimensions and that the dimensional characteristics of particular causes determine further consequential beliefs, attitudes and emotions. For example, a cause of success or failure can be
seen to be either stable or unstable. Stable causes are not likely to change
in terms of how they operate or the level at which they operate, while
unstable causes are. Effort is commonly given as an example of an
unstable cause of success and failure while ability is frequently cited as
a stable cause. (It will be noted that an entity view of ability is being
invoked here. If an incremental view was to apply then ability, like effort,
would be seen as an unstable cause.) Weiner (1986) then goes on to
suggest that variations in attribution along the stability dimension will
have an impact on future expectations. If events are attributed to stable

causes, then more of the same is to be expected. This is essentially a recognition of logic. If the cause of an event continues to operate in a stable manner then it is difficult to resist the idea that the event is likely to be repeated. If the cause is unstable then it must follow that the repetition of the event itself must be less certain. Weiner goes on to develop similar ideas concerning other dimensions such as internal–external and controllable–uncontrollable.

There is a core simplicity to Weiner's ideas that has doubtless helped to develop the substantial level of interest and research effort they have provoked. As always this work has added a number of complicating factors that lie well beyond this present discussion. However, from Weiner's work arises a model of motivation as a *function of information processing*. One interpretation of attribution theory as applied to motivation has it that the rules of cognition which determine the attributions to be made are held in common (at least by those sharing key aspects of a culture) and that individual variation is therefore dependent upon the nature of the information to be processed. In the case of motivation this information will concern the frequency and nature of instances of success and failure. As people begin to develop different histories so their motivational dynamics also begin to diverge.

The third model identified by Rogers draws on subsequent work emphasising the importance of goals and related beliefs. Much of this has been alluded to above and the work of Dweck (Dweck and Leggett, 1988; Dweck, 1991) figures prominently. A goal-based approach to motivation emphasises the individual's current goal state and other key beliefs that will determine the nature of their response to the vicissitudes of task engagement. A key distinction is that between learning and ego goals. Under a learning goal an individual focuses on the extent to which they personally have obtained task mastery, their focus is on individual progress. Under ego (or performance) goals the individual is more likely to be concerned with how they might appear to others. Have they presented themselves as capable or incapable? Have they maintained their position relative to other members of the pack? Learning goals also tend to encourage incremental views of the nature of ability. The distinction between the two goal states is most critical for those who are of lower levels of ability because performance goals, and the associated entity views of ability, are particularly debilitating when the task appears to be particularly difficult or when social comparisons tend to be negative. More importantly, it is now clear that changes in the operation of a classroom can have a strong impact on the goals adopted by students (Jagacinski, 1992). Jagacinski's review provides clear evidence for the importance of classroom context in determining the goals adopted by students, but also reveals the clear need for further research in order for the precise impact of the teacher to be laid bare. The third model of motivation then is one conceptualising motivation as a *function of learning goals*.

The three models, stressing the functions of personality, information processing and learning goals, may serve as a potted history of the development of motivation theory itself. However, it is also the case that as theory development has moved from an emphasis on the relatively stable and enduring aspects of personality through to an emphasis on the less stable function of learning goals, there has been an increase in the recognition of the potential for teacher influence. Motivation as personality allows for little in the way of teacher intervention. Teachers subscribing to this view are unlikely to regard personality change as falling within their remit (and the older the students the more likely this is to be the case). The information processing model allows for increased teacher intervention, but again suggests that as time passes, and the weight of the student's history of success and failure grows, the influence of a teacher on student motivation will decrease. However, the information processing model does recognise that information patterns can develop differently across different areas of experience. The student with a history of relative failure in maths, but of success in English, for example, might be expected to have different motivational patterns in these two domains. The most recent goal-based approach offers the greatest role for the impact of the teacher. If learning goals can be influenced by teacher action (the manner of presentation of tasks, the feedback given, the assessment procedures used) then there is always hope that student motivation can be improved. Furthermore, student motivation is increasingly recognised as a joint function of the interactions between teacher and student, rather than as a relatively fixed student characteristic.

In relation to teacher expectations and their bearing on the effectiveness of schooling it is the beliefs of teachers rather than researchers that matter. Whatever research evidence might say, if teachers perceive motivation as a stable function of personality then they will make their judgements on that basis. If motivation is seen as fixed, and it is seen as inadequate, then the prognosis is poor. Just as there is limited evidence to show that teachers with greater belief in their own efficacy see student ability as something that can be developed, so it is suggested that higher teacher self-efficacy will also relate to perceptions of motivation as something that teachers can enhance.

References

Atkinson, J. and Raynor, J. (Eds.) (1977) Personality, Motivation and Achievement (Washington, DC: Hemisphere).

Blanck, P. D. (Ed.) (1993) Interpersonal Expectations: Theory, research and applications (Paris: Cambridge University Press).

Blease, D. (1983) Teacher expectations and the self-fulfilling prophecy. Educational Studies, 9, 123–30.

Cain, K. M. and Dweck, C. S. (1995) The relation between motivational patterns and achievement cognitions through the elementary-school years. *Merrill-Palmer Quarterly*, 41(1), 25–52.

Cooper, H. and Good, T. (1983) Pygmalion Grows Up: Studies in the expectation communication process (New York: Longman).

Covington, M. V. (1992) Making The Grade: A self-worth perspective on motivation and school reform (Cambridge: Cambridge University Press).

Cuttance, P. (1992) Evaluating the effectiveness of schools. In Reynolds, D. and Cuttance, P. (Eds.), *School Effectiveness: Research, policy and practice* (London: Cassell).

DeCharms, R. (1976) Enhancing Motivation: Change in the classroom (New York: Irvington).

Deci, E. L. and Ryan, R. M. (1985) Intrinsic Motivation and Self-determination in Human Behavior (New York: Plenum).

Dusek, J. B. (Ed.) (1985) Teacher Expectancies (London: Lawrence Erlbaum).

Dweck, C. S. (1991) Self-theories and goals: their role in motivation, personality and development. Nebraska Symposium on Motivation, 1990, 38, 199–235.

Dweck, C. S. and Leggett, E. L. (1988) A social-cognitive approach to motivation and personality. *Psychological Review*, 95, 256–73.

Eden, D. (1990) Pygmalion without interpersonal contrast effects – whole groups gain from raising manager expectations. *Journal of Applied Psychology*, 75, 394–8.

Eden, D. (1993) Interpersonal expectations in organisations in Blanck, P. D. (Ed.), *Interpersonal Expectations: Theory, research and applications* (Paris: Cambridge University Press).

Goldenberg, C. (1992) The limits of expectations: A case for case knowledge about teacher expectancy effects. *American Educational Research Journal*, 29, 517–44.

Hargreaves, D. (1995) School culture, school effectiveness and school improvement. *School Effectiveness and School Improvement*, 6, 23–46.

Jagacinski, C. M. (1992) The effects of task involvement and ego involvement on achievement related cognitions and behaviours. In Schunk, D. H. and Meece, J. (Eds.), *Student Perceptions In The Classroom* (Hillsdale, NJ: LEA).

Jussim, L. (1989) Teacher expectations: Self-fulfilling prophecies, perceptual biases and accuracy. *Journal of Personality and Social Psychology*, 57, 469–80.

Maehr, M. L. (1987) Managing organisational culture to enhance motivation. In Maehr, M. L. and Kleiber, D. A. (Eds.) *Advances in motivation and achievement, Volume 5, Enhancing motivation* (Greenwich, CT: JAI Press).

Maehr, M. L. and Fyans, L. J.Jr. (1989) School culture, motivation and achievement. In Maehr, M. L. and Ames, C. (Eds.), *Advances In Motivation and Achievement: Motivation enhancing environments, Volume 6* (Greenwich, CT: JAI).

Marshall, H. and Weinstein, R. (1984) Classroom factors affecting students' self-evaluations: an interactional model. *Review of Educational Research*, 54, 301–25.

Miller, D. T. and Turnbull, W. (1986) Expectancies and interpersonal processes. *Annual Review of Psychology*, 37, 233–56.

Mortimore, P., Sammons, P., Stoll, L., Lewis, D. and Ecob, R. (1988) *School Matters: The Junior Years* (Wells: Open Books).

National Commission on Education (1996) *Success Against The Odds: Effective schools in disadvantaged areas* (London: Routledge).

Nicholls, J. G. and Miller, A. T. (1984) Development and its discontents: the differentiation of the concept of ability. In Nicholls, J. G. (Ed.), *Advances in Motivation and Achievement, Volume 3. The Development of Achievement Motivation* (London: JAI Press).

Oz, S. and Eden, D. (1994) Restraining the golem – boosting performance by changing the interpretation of low scores. *Journal of Applied Psychology*, 79, 744–54.

Rogers, C. (1984) *Freedom to Learn in the Eighties* (Columbus, OH: Merrill).

Rogers, C. G. (1982) *A Social Psychology of Schooling* (London: Routledge and Kegan Paul).

Rogers, C. G., (1992) The enhancement of motivation: Some core concerns. Conference paper. British Psychological Society, Education Section Conference. November, Berkhamstead.

Rosenthal, R., and Jacobsen, L. (1966) Teachers' expectancies: determinants of pupils' IQ gains. *Psychological Reports*, 19, 115–18.

Rosenthal, R. and Jacobsen, L. (1968) Pygmalion in the Classroom (New York: Holt, Rinehart and Winston).

Rosenthal, R. and Rubin, D. (1978) Interpersonal expectancy effects: the first 345 studies. *Behavioural and Brain Sciences*, 3, 377–86.

Sammons, P., Thomas, S., Mortimore, P., Cairns, R. and Bausor, J. (1994) Understanding the process of school and departmental effectiveness. Conference Paper, BERA, Oxford.

Sammons, P., Hillman, J. and Mortimore, P. (1995) *Key Characteristics of Effective Schools: A review of school effectiveness research* (London: Office for Standards in Education).

Sharp, R. and Green, A. (1975) *Education and Social Control* (London: Routledge and Kegan Paul).

Snyder M (1992) Motivational foundations of behavioral confirmation. *Advances In Experimental Social Psychology*, 25, 67–114.

Stoll, L. and Fink, D. (1996) *Changing Our Schools: Linking school effectiveness and school improvement* (Buckingham: Open University Press).

Waterhouse, S. (1991) Person formulation in the process of schooling. *British Journal of Sociology of Education*, 12, 45–60.

Weiner, B. (1986) *An Attributional Theory of Motivation and Emotion* (New York: Springer-Verlag).

Weiner, B. (1992) *Human Motivation: Metaphors, theories and research* (London: Sage).

Woolfolk, A. E. and Hoy, W. K. (1990) Prospective teachers' sense of efficacy and beliefs about control. *Journal of Educational Psychology*, 82, 81–91.

Zebrowitz, L. (1990) *Social Perception* (Milton Keynes, Open University Press).

Accelerating Development
Introduction

The Cognitive Acceleration in Science Foundation project (CASE) is an intervention which set out to raise standards of pupils' learning, in this instance of high-school aged pupils' knowledge of science. It is unusual in several ways. First, although there have been a number of attempts to produce cognitive acceleration in various forms of thinking (Nickerson, Perkins and Smith, 1985; Resnick, 1987) it has not proved easy to produce successful results which generalize beyond the immediate context of training. Adey and Shayer, however, show gains in English and maths, as well as the more expected gains in science, appearing several years after the initial intervention. Second, these authors have worked with a Piagetian analysis of cognitive development and of the demands of the school science curriculum. In doing this they have gone against the mainstream course of opinion in developmental and educational psychology, which had largely discarded Piaget's theory by the 1980s. Third, they have succeeded in integrating their project within the normal school and back-up support to teachers in order to bring about lasting changes in those teachers' practices.

Intervention programmes, in which psychological theory is successfully used to generate a programme of teaching which is then carefully evaluated, using control groups, are not very common in educational research, probably because they are so difficult. Another fine example is reported by Palincsar and Brown (1984).

The concept of 'formal operations' or 'formal operational thinking', which Adey and Shayer wanted to promote, derives directly from Piaget, who considered such thinking to define the final stage of his series of four main stages of cognitive development. It is typical of formal operations that they go beyond simple perceptual features of the world (for example, the size, shape and weight of a series of jars) and deal with more abstract general relationships (for example, the ratio of mass to volume for the same jars). To give another example, a simple fraction, such as a half, can be easily represented in a diagram or demonstrated by cutting an apple in half. However, the operation of multiplying one fraction by another (for example, 'multiply a quarter by a quarter') is less easily represented visually, although it becomes important in arithmetic. Thinking in formal operations thus involves thinking about general patterns of possible relationships, often using some form of symbolic notation, and this is typical of much thinking in mathematics and the sciences.

After this paper was written, the project continued and its progress is reported more fully in Adey and Shayer (1994). The original paper has been shortened, in this version, by leaving out most of a section concerning further detailed analysis of the results obtained by different groups within the study.

References

Adey, P. and Shayer, M. 1994: *Really Raising Standards*. London: Routledge.
Nickerson, R., Perkins, R. and Smith, E. 1985: *The Teaching of Thinking*. Hillsdale NJ: L. Erlbaum Associates.
Resnick, L. B. 1987: *Education and Learning to Think*. Washington DC: National Academy Press.

Further reading

Palinscar, A. S. and Brown, A. L. 1984: Reciprocal Teaching of Comprehension-Fostering and Comprehension-Monitoring Activities. *Cognition and Instruction*, 1, 2; 117–75.

EIGHT

An Exploration of Long-term Far-transfer Effects Following an Extended Intervention Program in the High School Science Curriculum

Philip Adey and Michael Shayer

During the late 1960s and 1970s, there was considerable interest in the Piagetian model of stepwise cognitive development. Educationalists used it both to seek explanations for the difficulties encountered by students in learning and as a basis for the design of more effective instruction (e.g., Karplus, 1978; Lawson, Blake, and Nordland, 1975; Renner et al., 1976; Shayer, 1978). At the same time, academic psychologists were questioning the mechanisms of cognitive development and both the construct and the empirical validity of domain-general stages proposed by the Genevan school (Brainerd, 1978; Brown and Desforges, 1979). This is not the place to review whether the change in fashion against the Genevan model was justified. We merely note our opinion that the British version of the critical position (Brown and Desforges, 1979) was shown to be selective in its use of the literature and empirically unjustified (see Shayer, 1979, and the reply by Desforges and Brown, 1979). Whatever one's position is in this debate, it is relevant to recognize that the work reported here grew out of results obtained at Chelsea College, London in the 1970s based on a broadly Piagetian paradigm.

At that time, we conducted a national survey to determine levels of cognitive development using a large representative sample of the adolescent population (Shayer, Küchemann, and Wylam, 1976; Shayer and Wylam, 1978). At the same time, we developed an instrument for the analysis of curricula in terms of the cognitive demands made on learners (the "Curriculum Analysis Taxonomy" in Shayer and Adey, 1981) and applied it to curricula then in use. The coordination of these two pieces of evidence provided some explanation for what had been the empirical experience of many science teachers – that the demands made by much of the material then used in schools was beyond the reach of most pupils.

We thus came to the question that had been bothering American instructors theoretically for some years: can cognitive development be accelerated? In 1975, Neimark wrote:

> One of the more surprising gaps in the reported research concerns what Piaget has called "The American Question": the possibility of accelerating cognitive development through specific training... When more is known about the course of normal development and the variables which affect it, it is quite likely that sophisticated training research will begin in earnest. Piaget's prediction would be that all such attempts are doomed to failure. (pp. 584–585)

In 1980, following discussion with the Clarkes, who had earlier surveyed the whole field of intervention studies (Clarke and Clarke, 1976), Shayer worked with a number of studies using different intervention models, summarized in Shayer (1987). One of these was a small-scale replication of Feuerstein's Instrumental Enrichment program (Feuerstein, Rand, Hoffman, and Miller, 1980). The reported effect sizes in relation to controls were large, including a figure of 1.2 SD on a battery of individual interview Piagetian tasks and 1.1 SD on Raven's Matrices (Shayer and Beasley, 1987). With this intervention model, however, teachers found it difficult to relate the improved thinking skills of the students, achieved in the context of subject-free intervention lessons, to the specifics of the school curriculum. No effects on school achievement were found at immediate posttest.

At the same time, there was something of a rush of cognitive acceleration studies reported from North America and Australia (e.g., Case, 1974; Kuhn and Angelev, 1976; Lawson and Snitgen, 1982;

Rosenthal, 1979), reviewed in Adey (1988) and Goossens (1989). Now, when the Piagetian star has waned somewhat and the majority of cognitive psychologists are emphasizing domain-specific skills rather than a general underlying cognitive structure, the question of cognitive acceleration may seem meaningless or at best irrelevant. Nevertheless, some continue to dig for the possibility of general thinking skills that are amenable to influence and enhanced development. Nickerson, Perkins, and Smith (1985) expressed the search in a form of Pascal's wager:

> If (teaching thinking) cannot be done, and we try to do it, we may waste some time and effort. If it can be done, and we fail to try, the inestimable cost will be generations of students whose ability to think effectively will be less than it could have been. So we are better advised to adopt the attitude that thinking can be taught, try hard to teach it, and let experience prove us wrong if it must. (p. 324)

We started from both this viewpoint that the possibility of teaching general thinking skills was worth pursuing and the viewpoint that what has recently been referred to as "higher order thinking skills" (Resnick, 1987) is well characterized by Inhelder and Piaget's descriptions of formal operations. Again, this is not the place to reopen debates on the validity of the Inhelder–Piaget account of formal operations, but it is worth noting that the characteristic performance of children on the Inhelder tasks has always replicated the original findings and can be regarded as a fact requiring explanation.[1] Although Piaget's propositional calculus can be handled in a general form, his use of it as an explanatory model is invariably contextualized. This may infuriate logicians (Parsons, 1960), but it does lead to a consistent descriptive model of thought, as Papert (1961) demonstrated. If further justification for pursuing the Piaget model is required, it may be found in a challenge given to Shayer by Alan Clarke. "If you want to go on using the Piagetian model," he said, "bear in mind that one of the best ways of studying a phenomenon is to try to change it." If the intervention model is incoherent, no successful change can come from it. Thus, by acting on the belief that the Piagetian account of formal operations is a satisfactory description of general higher order thinking skills, the best test is to look for evidence that, both in terms of the model (Piagetian tests) and inferred consequences if the model is true (school achievement in science and other subjects), the results are in accord with the prediction.

Funding was obtained in 1980 from the Social Science Research Council (SSRC) to investigate the possibility of promoting formal operational thinking in 11- to 14-year-olds. A pilot study conducted in one school led to further SSRC funding to involve teachers in a sample of ordinary state high schools in Britain. The Cognitive Acceleration Through Science Education (CASE) projects were based at the (then) Chelsea College Centre for Science and Mathematics Education, University of London.

The results of the experiment, especially as they relate to science education, have been reported piecemeal as they occurred (Adey and Shayer, 1990; Shayer and Adey, 1992a, 1992b, 1993). Here we provide more detail of the instructional strategies employed, summarize these results in a uniform manner, try to fill in the overall picture that emerges, and (by looking especially at the language development) draw implications for models of the mind.

Context

In approaching a high school principal with a proposal to introduce a set of activities that might or might not help pupils to develop higher-order thinking skills, there are (at least in Britain) two negative answers: (a) "It will interfere with preparation for external examinations" and (b) "I am not going to rewrite the timetable to provide a new space for thinking lessons." The riposte to Answer (a) is to offer to work with the younger pupils, before they get near the end-of-school examination, and that to Answer (b) is to embed the new activities in an existing subject. In any case, if an intervention model can be interpolated within the context of an existing body of widely used teaching skills and content, both students and teachers are helped immediately to apply new thinking skills to that context. Given successful application within such a context, accompanied by an emphasis on the generalizable skills, chances should be much increased of the students' improved cognition subsequently affecting performance in other contexts. Although it has been shown that the Piagetian account of concrete and formal operations can usefully be applied to the context of history (e.g., Hallam, 1967; Jurd, 1973) and English comprehension and social studies (Fusco, 1983), the field of science learning was chosen for micropolitical reasons. These include our own familiarity with the foundations of science teaching and because in the United Kingdom the science teaching fraternity has shown the greatest interest in the application of learning theories to the curriculum. It also seemed that, whether or not Piaget and Inhelder (1958) intended the schemata of formal operations to be free of domain constraints, they do look very scientific and are initially easier to "sell" to science teachers than, say, to language teachers.

The Bases of the Intervention Activities

We thus set about designing a set of activities, set in a scientific context and using the schemata of formal operations as a guiding framework. We considered that the chances of achieving domain-general improvements in higher order thinking skills would be maximized by addressing all 10 of Piaget's schemata. Reviews of the literature (Adey, 1988; Goossens, 1989) on cognitive acceleration suggested certain features that should maximize an intervention program's chances of bringing about long-term effects on the general ability of learners, including:

- The introduction, through concrete activities, of the terminology of relationships and the context in which a problem is presented. Goossens (1989) called this *perceptual readiness*, but we now prefer the term *concrete preparation*.
- The presentation of problems that induce *cognitive conflict*.
- The encouragement of *metacognition*.
- The *bridging* of thinking strategies developed within the context of the special lessons to other areas.

We may say that concrete preparation is the "setup," cognitive conflict the "sting," metacognition makes the thinking process conscious in the learner, and bridging provides a wide range of applications. The set of activities developed is called *Thinking Science* (Adey, Shayer, and Yates, 1989).

Concrete preparation

Formal operations operate only on a situation that has first been described by the subject in terms of descriptive concrete models.

Thus, concrete preparation involves establishing that students are familiar with the technical vocabulary, apparatus, and framework in which a problem situation is set. The first few activities concentrate on the key ideas of *variables* and *relationships between variables*. The terms are introduced in a way that requires only concrete operational processing. For example, the teacher displays a selection of books on the table. "In what ways are these different from one another?" she asks. Answers typically include "color," "size," "hard- or soft-back." "These are ways in which the books *vary* from each other. We call color, size, et cetera, *variables*." Pupils are then shown a collection of shapes (Figure 8.1). "What are the variables here?" Typically 11-year-olds have no difficulty in establishing that shape, color, and size are variables. Now we move on. "Can you see any way in which any of these variables go together?" Some more probing questions and verbal or nonverbal prompting lead pupils from specific statements ("the triangles are red; the squares are blue") to the more general recognition that "color goes with shape." After further similar examples, the term *relationship* is introduced. There is a relationship between the variables color and shape. Cartoon examples give practice in recognizing relationships between variables in terms such as, "as the number of sausages goes up, their size goes down" (see Figure 8.2). Within the same sequence, it is also important to recognize when there is no relationship. For example, with a set of loaded but opaque colored jars, there is a relationship between color and size (big ones are blue; small ones are red), but pupils find that the weight of the jars bears no relationship to either color or size.

Where there is a relationship, pupils can be encouraged to use the relationship to make predictions. In the squares and triangles activity, the teacher may ask, "Now, if I produce another triangle that follows the same pattern, what color will it be?" Where there is no relationship, no prediction can be made. Knowing the color of the jar does not help you to decide what its weight is.

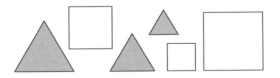

Figure 8.1   What are the variables here?

Figure 8.2   What are the variables? What relationship is there among them?

Other terms introduced early in the scheme, *input variable* and *outcome variable*, are used instead of the more formal terms *independent* and *dependent* variables, respectively.

The examples given illustrate some CASE activities that provide concrete preparation for the whole. *Thinking Science* scheme. In addition, almost every activity starts with a conceptual readiness phase for that particular activity, as will be shown. Note that the strategy here is to give the student confidence in the use of the technical vocabulary in a situation requiring only concrete modeling before he or she needs to apply it in a context requiring formal modeling.

Cognitive conflict

This term is used to describe an event or observation that the student finds puzzling and discordant with previous experience or understanding. All perceptions are interpreted through the subjects' present conceptual framework. When current conceptualization fails to make sense of an experience, constructive mental work by students may lead to accommodation and a change in their conceptual framework. Kuhn, Amsel, and O'Loughlin's (1988) investigation of the coordination of new evidence with existing cognitive schemata confirms that instances of cognitive conflict do not automatically produce a "Road to Damascus" conversion to a new conceptualization. Younger and less able pupils often appear unaware of a conflict or at least are not bothered by it. But if there is no conflict, there is no chance of accommodation. In Vygotsky's (1978) words:

> Learning which is oriented toward developmental levels that have already been reached is ineffective from the viewpoint of a child's overall development. It does not aim for a new stage of the developmental process but rather lags behind this process... The only "good learning" is that which is in advance of development. (p. 82)

The following two examples illustrate activities designed to induce conflict.

Floating and sinking jars

Two sets of jars are prepared (see Figure 8.3). Five jars, A through E, are all the same size but are loaded to have different masses. Six jars, 1 through 6, are each successively smaller than the one before, but they all have the same mass. Jar 6/A is common to both sets. The jars

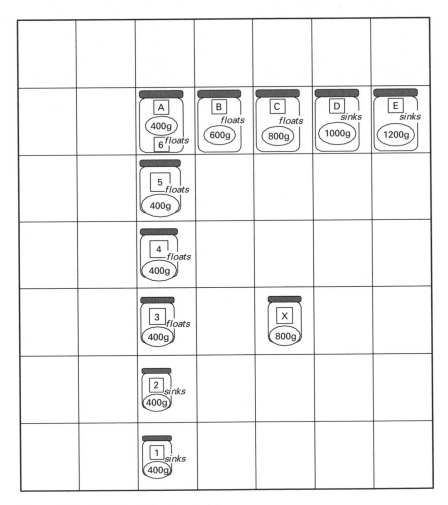

Figure 8.3   Will Jar X float or sink?

are opaque and labeled only with their number or letter. Pupils have worksheets showing the jars arranged in a matrix. They are invited to weigh each jar and then drop it into a large bowl of water. On the worksheets, they record each jar's weight and whether it floats or sinks. The discussion centers first on Jars A through E. What conclusions can be drawn? Only two variables, weight and buoyancy, are involved, so students can develop a simple concrete model relating the two: "Heavy things sink; light things float." Similarly, a focus on Jars 1 through 6 leads to another concrete model: "Small things sink; big things float" (they know that pins sink and ships float, so this accords with experience, albeit rather selected experience). Next, Jar X is produced. It is established that it is the same size as Jar 3 (a floater) and the same weight as Jar C (also a floater). Students must predict what they think will happen when Jar X is put in water. Application of the two concrete models already developed leads to the prediction that Jar X will float. When put into the water, it sinks. Thus, there is conflict between perceptual experience and the concrete operations used so far. Concrete operations do not provide an explanation for the sinking of Jar X. A three-variable, formal model is required, employing the notion of "weight for a certain size."

Wheelbarrow

Introductory discussion and demonstration (the conceptual readiness phase) establishes the parallel between a notched stick and the wheelbarrow as lever systems (Figure 8.4). Students record and tabulate the

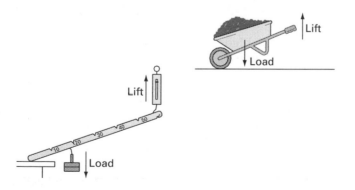

Figure 8.4   The wheelbarrow as a lever system

force at the "handle" as successive loads are added. With about six pairs of values completed, they draw the straight line graph relating the two on a given grid. From this, they are asked to make predictions about what the force would be with extra loads, which are not available. The first predictions can be read off by simple extrapolation of the graph, but then the graph paper runs out. A concrete strategy is no longer available. This is the point of conflict, requiring the invention of a more sophisticated view of the relationship – that involving the constant ratio of load to effort. They have to go beyond the conceptual support of the graph and construct a more general mathematical model through which they can extrapolate. Cognitive operations on the data must become formalized to achieve a successful solution to the problem.

We aimed to maximize the permanent effect on subjects of conflict situations by (a) effective concrete preparation and (b) repeated, sometimes small, doses of conflict over an extended period. Note that these small doses were given in many different contexts with the underlying implication that such treatment would lead to accelerated development of a general cognitive structure. This contrasts with the conflict situations presented by curriculum materials founded in the Alternative Conceptions Movement (ACM; see, e.g., Children's Learning in Science Project, 1987). An ACM-style teaching sequence devotes considerable time to setting up and, it is hoped, to resolving cognitive conflict about one concept. The ACM aim is the development of that concept rather than the development of general thinking skills. The CASE aim was less specific and potentially more widely generalizable. Our expectation was not that after the floating and sinking activity pupils would have a grasp of density (some did; some did not), but that they would develop their repertoire of general ideas – in this case that of compound variables – that provide explanatory power. Such higher-order thinking skills are developed so that new problems in completely different contexts can be treated effectively.

Metacognition

It is now widely accepted (Nickerson et al., 1985; Perkins and Salomon, 1989) that students are more likely to develop wide-ranging thinking skills if they are encouraged to think about their own thinking, to become aware of the strategies of their own thinking and actions. This is what is meant by *metacognition*. In a *Thinking Science* lesson, the teacher asks pupils to talk both with the teacher and with each other about difficulties and successes they have with problems, not just saying "that was difficult," but also explaining "what was difficult about it, and how did I overcome the difficulty?" Students become accustomed to reflecting on the sort of thinking they have been engaged in, to bringing it to the front of their consciousness, and to making of it an explicit tool that may then be available for use in a new context. Using words to describe reasoning patterns is another aspect of metacognition. The aim is for CASE students not only to be better equipped to recognize a proportionality problem, for example, when they see one but also to be able to say, "That's a proportionality problem!", and so open the door to a particular set of solution strategies. This is a special application of what Vygotsky (1978) described as the use of language as a mediator of learning. The language of reasoning mediates meta-learning.

It is not easy to illustrate this metacognitive element from *Thinking Science* activities, because it is more a feature of the teacher's strategy introduced through staff development programs than of the printed materials. One example illustrates how a worksheet can act as a starting point for metacognitive speculation, although, in prosecuting the activity, the teacher plays an essential role in building on this starting point:

> *Classification:* Students go through a set of simple exercises such as putting animals into groups (according to their own criteria), arranging a variety of foodstuffs on the shelves of a larder, and sorting chemicals by color and by solubility.

Finally (see Box 8.1), students are asked to consider the classifications that they have done and to reflect on which was the most difficult for them and why, and on which was the easiest and why. They compare their feelings with other groups and discuss why some groups found some activities difficult and others found the same ones easy.

Bridging

The explicit bridging to other contexts is the final link in this chain of developing, abstracting, and generalizing reasoning. During inservice introductions to *Thinking Science*, teachers engaged in exercises to develop their own links between the *Thinking Science* activities and their regular science curriculum and pupils' experiences in everyday

Thinking back

Put a tick by the classification activity you found easiest.
Put a cross by the one you found most difficult.

Why was the one you ticked the easiest?
Why was the one you crossed the most difficult?

Has everyone ticked and crossed the same ones as you?

Write a sentence about a friend, using the word "characteristic."

Why do you think that it is useful to be able to classify things?

Note: The British English "tick" is equivalent to the US English "check".

Box 8.1   The last of a series of classification activities

life. During visits by members of the project team to schools, further opportunities for bridging were explored in the context of each school's curriculum and environment. This can be illustrated with one activity concerned with probability:

Tea tasting

Some people think that tea tastes different if you put the milk in before or after the tea. One student volunteer leaves the room while five cups of tea are prepared, some with milk first, others with tea first. She or he returns and tastes each cup, reporting "tea first" or "milk first" on each. The problem before the class is, how many out of five must she or he get right before the students believe that she or he really can tell the difference? (American readers may wish to substitute Coke® vs. Pepsi®, although that is much easier.) Typically, 11- and 12-year-olds may consider that three out of five or four out of five would be convincing. Next, everyone spins five coins many times, producing a large number of spins. In a concrete way, the children discover the percentage of times all five coins show heads, just by chance. The conflict arises as they realize that there is no simple answer to the question "How many rights is convincing?" Even 100 out of 100 could occur by chance. There is no deterministic answer, only a probabilistic one. The bridging occurs through discussion of, for example, the relationship between smoking and lung cancer. Not everyone who smokes will get lung cancer. Not everyone who does not smoke will avoid it. The idea of a probabilistic relationship between a cause and effect is given meaning.

Development of the Intervention, Experiment, and Tests

Activities were drafted and taught by the research team (the authors and Carolyn Yates) to two classes of 12-year-olds in an ordinary London comprehensive secondary school. A total of 30 such activities, each designed to last about 60 to 70 minutes, were thus devised, pretested, revised, and duplicated.

Nine schools representing a variety of environments in England were chosen in consultation with local education authorities' science advisers who were asked to recommend what they considered to be ordinary mixed comprehensive schools typical of their locality. In some cases, advisers directed us to schools that they felt would "do a good job" for us and in others to schools that they felt needed some help. A total of 24 classes of pupils of average ability[2] in these schools was selected and randomly assigned to experimental and control conditions, with experimental and control classes in each school. Some control classes were taught by the same teacher as the experimental classes; others were taught by different teachers. Four classes were of the 11+ age group (UK Year 7, U.S. Grade 6), eight of 12+ (UK Year 8, U.S. Grade 7). These separate cohorts are referred to simply as the "11+" and "12+" groups.

In 1985, the 12 experimental classes started to receive a *Thinking Science* lesson in place of a regular science lesson about once every two weeks. Classes in this age group typically receive two or three science lessons per week, so the *Thinking Science* lessons could have taken as much as 25% of the normally allotted science time. The *Thinking Science* activities were introduced to teachers through a series of one-day workshops and followed up by visits to the schools during which lessons were observed and discussed with the teacher. We did not expect the psychological foundation of the proposed teaching strategies to become readily accessible to teachers through the printed material alone.

One school withdrew after two terms, and another, working under especially difficult circumstances, failed to deliver the intervention even approximately as planned. We report results here for the 10 experimental classes (four 11+ and six 12+) in seven schools that continued with the program, more or less as intended, for two years. After the two-year intervention program, students were no longer maintained in identifiable experimental and control groups but were mixed together as they chose options for the subjects they continued to study. In the case of three of the 11+ classes, the end of the intervention coincided with the end of the middle school period, and pupils were dispersed to a number of different high schools. The experimental design and testing program is illustrated in Figure 8.5.

Testing occasions were *pretest*, before the intervention began; *posttest*, immediately after the two-year intervention; *delayed posttest*, one year after the end of the intervention; and the *General Certificate of Secondary Education (GCSE)* taken two (for those who started at 12+) or three (for those who started at 11+) years after the end of the intervention. We have no reason to suppose that those who moved from the schools in which we were able to trace them for testing, or who missed particular tests, did so because they had been experimental or control pupils.

To test cognitive development, we used demonstrated group Piagetian Reasoning Tasks (PRTs). These tasks were developed as Science Reasoning Tasks (Shayer, Wylam, Küchemann, and Adey, 1978) in

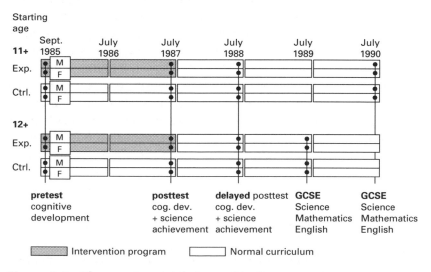

Figure 8.5 The experimental design and testing program

the 1970s for the Concepts in Secondary Science and Mathematics project's large-scale survey of the school population and have been widely used since. Information on the validity and reliability of PRTs is available in Shayer, Adey, and Wylam (1981). There were originally six PRTs that yielded scores within a common scale ranging from *preoperational* (1) to *mature formal operational* (3B). Since their development and before the analyses reported here, PRT data were reanalyzed using Rasch scaling to give a finer estimate of person level. Now the total number of items correct on a given PRT can be converted directly into a decimal score on the scale ranging from *early preoperational* (1) to *mature formal operational* (10), with a standard error of about 0.4. Table 8.1 shows some PRT titles, including those used in this experiment and the ranges within which each operates. When two PRTs were used, the mean was taken.

Science achievement was assessed at posttest by a common achievement test that the teachers agreed fairly reflected the objectives of their science curricula for the previous year. At the delayed test, each school's end-of-year science test or mean of module tests was used. By definition, these tests, thus, covered the objectives of each school's curriculum. They were converted to percentages before further treatment.

The GCSE is now the examination taken in England and Wales by most 16-year-olds as a school-leaving examination and/or as a selection test for further education. There are four different regional examining boards and, within each board, a number of syllabus options. Schools may choose the regional board they wish to use for each subject. For instance, a school may decide to enter some pupils for one, two, or occasionally three out of chemistry, physics, or biology, others for double certificate general science, others again for single general science, and these examinations may be set by the same or by different regional boards. Norm-referenced grades are awarded

Table 8.1 Some Piagetian Reasoning Tasks

Name of task	Range	Use in CASE experiment
1. Spatial relations	1 to 5	Not used in CASE
2. Volume and heaviness	2 to 7	Pretest
3. Pendulum	5 to 10	Pretest and posttest
4. Probability	3 to 10	Posttest and delayed posttest

in all GCSE examinations on a scale ranging from A through G and unclassified, eight grades in all, moderated across boards to ensure equivalence of standards. For the purpose of treatment here, they were mapped onto an equal-interval scale with values 7 down to 0.

Treatment and Presentation of Results

Post and delayed cognitive development scores could be reported simply as raw gains over pretest scores, comparing control and experimental groups. The common science achievement test could be reported as a comparison between experimental and control means, although this ignores any difference between starting ability levels as assessed by the pretest. However, the variety of tests used among different schools for the delayed achievement measures and for the GCSE made it impossible to make such simple comparisons. For these measures, the method of *residualized gain scores* was used (Cronbach and Furby, 1970).

The method depends on the fact that PRT scores are fair predictors of subsequent academic success. For each particular achievement test or GCSE exam, we compute the predictive relationship between pre-PRT score and achievement (regression of achievement test score on pre-PRT) for the control group that took that particular test. Then, for each corresponding experimental subject, we use the same regression equation to predict from their pre-PRT score what achievement test score they would obtain, if there were no difference between the experimental and control groups. Finally, we compare the experimental subjects' scores predicted on this assumption with the actual scores they obtained. The difference is the residualized gain score (rg score). For any group of students, the mean rg score is a measure of the extent to which their development or learning has been different from the initially matched control group.

For convenience of comparisons, all results are reported in terms of rg scores. Note that rg scores build in comparison with controls and that, by definition, the mean rg score of a control group must be zero.

Results are presented separately for the two groups, 11+ and 12+ (as explained earlier, these represent the ages at which pupils started the intervention program). Results are broken down further by gender. For each experimental group, the number of subjects (*n*), their mean rg score (*M*), the standard deviation of the rg score (σ), and the probability that the mean score is significantly different from that of the corresponding control group (*p* <) are shown. For significant differences, the effect size (e) is also shown in units of standard deviation of the control group (σ$_c$). The distribution of the rg scores for the experimental group is shown as a histogram.

In many of the distributions, we claim evidence of bimodality. This is based on computing the cumulative χ^2 values for the numbers occurring at each interval compared with those expected on the basis of normal distribution. A sharp rise in the significance of the χ^2 value indicates that a second peak in the distribution is significant.

Results

1985 pretests

Pretest scores for each group are shown in Table 8.2. There are no significant differences between any of the subgroups within an age range, but the 11 + group was generally more able than the 12 + group, because the mean scores of the two age groups are similar despite their age difference.

Table 8.2   Pretest Scores

	Boys		Girls	
Age group	Experimental	Control	Experimental	Control
11 +				
N	39	55	31	35
M	6.04	5.94	6.26	6.00
σ	0.88	1.06	0.69	0.57
12 +				
N	65	76	59	64
M	6.09	6.20	6.01	6.10
σ	0.75	1.06	0.89	0.93

1987 immediate posttests

PRT posttests

These are the tests of cognitive development given immediately after the end of the two-year intervention program. The results are summarized in Figure 8.6.

Clearly, the 12 + boys made highly significant gains in levels of cognitive development compared with controls. Further analysis reveals that, for this 12 + boys group, the distribution of gain scores is bimodal. That is, one group made little or no better gain than the controls, and another group had gains far greater than the controls. The distribution of scores for the 11 + girls is also bimodal, although overall their gain was not significantly greater than that of the corresponding control group.

Science achievement posttest

This was the common science achievement test given in many of the schools immediately after the intervention. At this point, no significant differences emerged between any of the experimental and control

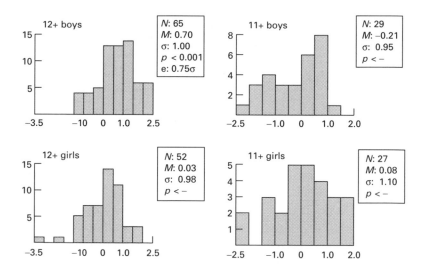

Figure 8.6 Post-PRT residualized gain scores for experimental groups: means, distribution, etc.

groups, although it should be noted that the experimental group lost about 25% of its science curriculum time to the *Thinking Science* intervention lessons, so it may be considered a virtue that this group's achievement remained at the same level as that of the controls. It is not reasonable to expect an intervention program that addresses under-lying cognitive functioning to show an immediate effect on academic achievement, because only after completing the intervention do the subjects have an opportunity to apply their newly acquired thinking skills to new learning. Thus, measures of achievement should not be expected to show improvement until some time after the end of the intervention.

1988 delayed posttests

PRT delayed posttest

This was the measure of cognitive development given one year after the end of the intervention program. Data from this test are summar-ized in Figure 8.7. One year after the end of the intervention, none of the experimental groups showed any overall difference from the con-trol groups in these measures of cognitive development. The gains that

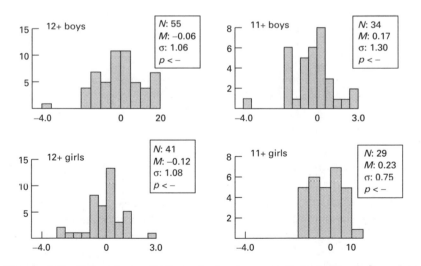

Figure 8.7 Delayed post-PRT residual gain scores for experimental groups: means, distribution, etc.

were present immediately after the intervention apparently dissipated. There is, however, some evidence of bimodality in the distributions of the 12 + boys and the 11 + girls that is very marked in the former group. As shown later, this particular result seems to be anomalous in the whole pattern of data that emerges.

Delayed science achievement

These were the schools' own tests, very different in nature from the Piagetian measures already reported. At this point, the CASE intervention was over, and the schools were asked to provide end-of-year examination results that tested the students on the science they learned during the year following the intervention. In most cases, the students were no longer in classes that could be identified with previous experimental and control groups but were mixed and taught by different teachers. Pupils in most of the 11 + groups had actually moved from middle school to high school and so were in a completely different environment. Figure 8.8 provides a direct comparison between ex-CASE and control students of their ability to benefit from the same instruction. The 12 + boys again showed a very strong effect and the bimodality noted previously. The 11 + girls also showed a

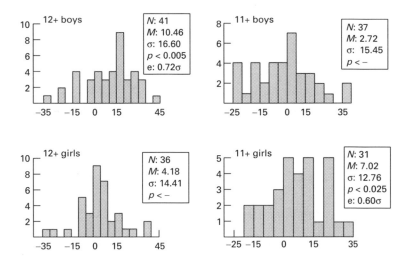

Figure 8.8 Delayed postscience residualized gain scores for experimental groups: means, distribution, etc.

significant effect, confirming the suspicion raised already about an effect with this group. Note that all groups showed positive effects, although they did not reach statistical significance for 12 + girls or 11 + boys.

1989–1990: GCSE examinations

The six 12 + classes completed their Year 11 (U.S. Grade 10) at secondary school and took the GCSE examinations in June 1989, two years after the end of the CASE intervention program. The three 11 + classes took their GCSE in 1990, three years after the end of the intervention program. We analyzed GCSE results for science (amalgamated results for whichever combination of chemistry, physics, biology, and integrated science an individual took), mathematics, and English. Results for science are shown in Figure 8.9. The effect on the 12 + boys group was even stronger than in the delayed test results just reported. This group averaged one grade higher than controls, after individual pretest differences are taken into account. This represents an effect size of 1 *SD*, achieved two years after the end of the CASE intervention program. The 11 + boys and the 12 + girls showed no significant effects, although the girls who started the experiment aged 11+ showed a significant effect. Their science grades

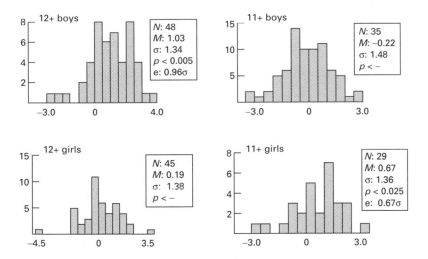

Figure 8.9 Residualized gain in grades of experimental group on General Certificate of Secondary Science Education: science

improved, compared with controls, by two-thirds *SD*. Thus, the hints from data reported earlier that there was some effect with the 11 + girls finally showed up strongly in externally set and marked national examinations of science achievement, three years after the end of the intervention. By any standard, this must be counted as a long-term effect. In both of the groups that showed significant effects, bimodality of distribution appeared again, indicating that some benefited far more than others from the *Thinking Science* experience.

So far, the data provide evidence consistent with the hypothesis that the strategies incorporated into the teaching and materials of *Thinking Science* promote the long-term development of general thinking ability within the domain of science, which can be applied to a wide variety of new learning within that domain. Even allowing for the inconsistency of the effect across different individuals, this already provides substantial support for a particular approach to the long-term improvement of learning in science through the development of general science thinking ability. We discuss the age and gender differences after results for other subjects are presented.

Results from the other domains throw more light on the underlying psychological model. Figure 8.10 shows the results for GCSE mathematics. The results follow a similar pattern to those in science, with

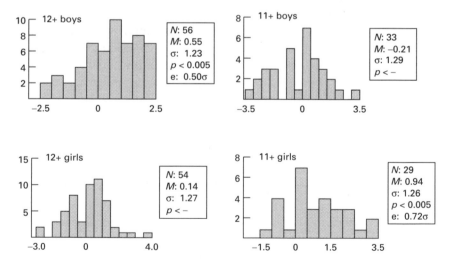

Figure 8.10 Residualized gain in grades of experimental group on General Certificate of Secondary Education: mathematics

significant effects achieved in the 12 + boys' and 11 + girls' groups. The former result is weaker than that for science but is consistent with a possible "knock-on" effect of the mathematical nature of many of the *Thinking Science* activities on achievement in mathematics itself, although the longevity is again remarkable. For the 11 + girls, the effect was stronger than for science (over 0.7 *SD*) and was longer lasting even than for the 12 + group. This could be taken as evidence for the effect of the intervention on general underlying cognition. We return to this discussion later. For both groups, there was again evidence of bimodality of distribution of gains.

For a completely different domain, we turn to the GCSE English data. Before presenting results, it is worth looking at some tasks typical of a GCSE English examination:

- A tape recording of some dialogue is played twice, and a transcript is provided. Students are given 50 minutes to write assessments of some of the characters portrayed, to describe the views of one of them on a particular issue discussed in the dialogue, and to write their own response to these views.
- Three excerpts from guidebooks describing the same place but written in very different styles are presented. The student is given 45 minutes to write two pieces: one describing the place from a historical perspective and one providing technical information useful for a group making a school visit to the place.
- Students are given an hour to write a free composition of about 600 words based on the students' choice of one out of five topics. Each topic is stimulated by a title, an opening sentence, a picture, or the topic of one of the earlier questions.

The skills required in these tasks include analysis and comprehension, as well as imagination, creativity, and style. Enhanced achievement in such an English test following an intervention set in a science context must be described as *far transfer* of an effect from one domain to another very different domain.

Now, consider the experimental groups' residualized gain in grades on GCSE English shown in Figure 8.11. These results show significant effects in three out of the four groups. As before, there were effects in the 12 + boys and the 11 + girls, although they were rather weak in the former. Additionally, there was an effect in the 12 + girls' group.

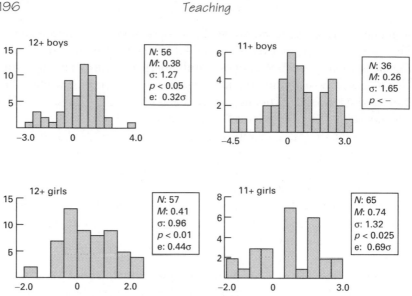

Figure 8.11   Residualized gain in grades of experimental group on General Certificate of Education: English

Even the one group that showed no overall effect, the 11 + boys, showed very marked bimodality of distribution and would have shown a significant effect if just one of two very low-scoring individuals had scored at the average for the group.

Possible explanations

Evidence of long-term far transfer has potential importance for models of cognition; therefore, it is necessary to explore in more detail possible explanations for these results.

Confidence?

The suggestion is sometimes made that the intervention boosts the confidence of students in their own abilities and that this, in turn, improves learning across domains. It seems unlikely, however, that confidence developed within science would affect performance in other domains (see the gender-difference work in physical and biological sciences; e.g., Hadden and Johnstone, 1983; Kelly, 1981; Ormerod and Duckworth, 1975). In any case, a global notion of "confidence" is vacuous as a causal explanation for improved learning without a mechanism by which confidence influences learning, which brings us back to some sort of cognitive model. At the risk of sounding like behaviorists rejecting mentalistic concepts, we will not consider this line further.

Language training?

An apparently simple explanation of how pupils who followed the *Thinking Science* program subsequently performed better in English is that of a direct training effect. This supposes that, although the program was set in a science context, it encouraged reasoned discussion among pupils exploring the meaning of new vocabulary in the search for explanations of physical events. This enrichment of language use is then supposed to persist (in memory?) and show up in enhanced performance in general English tests two and three years later. We find it implausible that a language-development effect that is almost incidental to the aims of the program and is set in a science context could be so long lived and become generalized. A more deep-rooted explanation seems to be necessary.

Language develops language?

Perhaps the intervention enhances linguistic development so that the new linguistic skills open the way for improved subsequent learning in language. Such a self-promoting system or "virtuous circle" would be characteristic of development, as contrasted with learning, and as such would be consistent with the hoped-for outcomes of the experiment. This explanation still relates particularly to the development of a domain-specific function, as something parallel to but not integral with the development of scientific and mathematical proficiencies.

General cognitive development?

Results from the English GCSE are also consistent with the possibility that the CASE intervention, by directly addressing the promotion of the development of underlying cognitive structures, raises students' general intellectual processing power and thus enables them to make better use of all of the learning experiences provided by their schooling. This is the most general level of cognitive explanation and the one for which long-term far transfer is cited as necessary evidence.

In summary, we seriously consider two hypotheses at different levels of generality: (a) parallel development in linguistic and mathematical–scientific domains and (b) general intellectual development. We use differences in effects on different age and gender groups in trying to construct possible explanations but admit to some hesitation in this: 11 + and 12 + groups were not different only with respect to starting age. Those in the 11 + group were somewhat more able generally, and many of them were in middle schools that provide a rather different learning milieu from secondary schools. There are thus at least two potentially confounding factors militating against simple 11 + versus 12 + comparisons.

With this proviso in mind, it is consistent with either hypothesis (a) or (b) that the girls make the predominant contribution to the overall gains in language learning. In the first hypothesis (a), it is claimed that girls have a greater propensity for language and make the most of the linguistic opportunities within the intervention program. If the general cognitive development hypothesis (b) is favored, the claim is that students apply their enhanced intellectual power in learning domains that are of greatest interest to them and that the domains of interest tend toward science and mathematics for boys and language for girls.

The difference in effects with 11 + and 12 + groups is not readily explained by hypothesis (a). Why should 11- to 13-year-old boys be less susceptible to the development of domain-specific scientific thinking strategies than 12- to 14-year-old-boys? Why should 11- to 13-year-old girls be more susceptible to the development of domain-specific scientific thinking strategies than 12- to 14-year-old girls? We suggest that only if one uses hypothesis (b) (based on general intellectual enhancement), includes a maturational factor, and adds the long-established evidence on the faster intellectual development of girls over boys at this age can an adequate explanation be provided. Using hypothesis (b), we can say that at 11, the intervention struck a chord with the girls' earlier emerging higher-level cognitive processing system but failed to resonate with the boys, who were still mostly limited to concrete operational reasoning. Just a year later, the boys had reached the emergent phase that the girls were in previously and so were ready to make the most of the intervention experiences. Why the 12-year-old girls seemed to have passed the period of most effective intervention is another question, and we can only speculate that the answer may be found in the evidence on girls' affective disillusion with things that appear scientific when they reach Years 8 and 9 (Grades 7 and 8).

Further analyses

To explore the suggested possibilities further, our analyses focus on the immediate posttest of cognitive development, because this is the best measure we have of underlying cognitive structure and the development in that structure that took place during the intervention. Any explanation based on the idea of cognitive structure should refer back to this measure.

First, we must answer two technical questions.

1 How widely distributed among the experimental classes were pupils who made the greatest gains?

We consider as "high gainers" the 19 11 + pupils and the 31 12 + pupils who showed the highest residualized gains on the PRT posttest, who formed the top three bars of the distribution histograms of those scores (see Figure 8.7). Table 8.3 shows the percentage of each of the experimental classes that were high gainers. The percentage of high gainers in any one class ranges fairly evenly from 15.4 to 45.5, with no outstandingly good or poor results. This argues in favor of the effect being due to the general CASE strategy rather than to its particular expression through one or two exceptional teachers.

2 Were the high gainers those who started either with a low score (and, therefore, had much to make up) or with a high score (who might be thought to be "ready" for the CASE-type activities)?

The answer is shown in Figure 8.12. The high gainers highlighted in the distribution of PRT posttest gains are also highlighted in the distribution of PRT pretest scores. Clearly, high gainers come from a wide range of starting levels, which is supported by the absence of any correlation between starting level and gain.

Table 8.3 Distribution of high gainers among experimental classes

	Age group									
	11 +						12 +			
Class identity	51	52	61	91	31	32	71	81	92	111
% high gainers	15.4	42.9	33.3	40.0	18.8	20.0	28.6	19.0	45.5	22.7

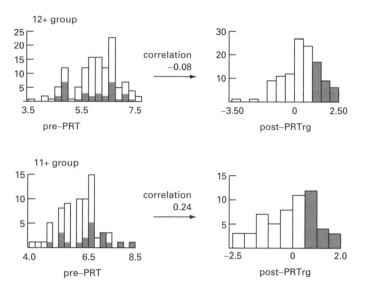

Figure 8.12 Pretest levels of cognitive development of those who made the greatest gains to posttest PRT

Now, we must consider three additional questions, which cannot be answered so simply.

1 Do gains in cognitive development predict gains in academic achievement?

Table 8.4 shows the correlations between post-PRT rg scores and the various measures of academic achievement. If the *Thinking Science* intervention program enhances cognitive development, and if enhanced cognitive development facilitates learning in all academic subjects, one would expect pupils making the greatest gains during the intervention program to be the same as those who subsequently show the greatest gains in measures of academic achievement. In other words, there should be significant correlations between post-PRT gains and gains in academic achievement. Table 8.4 shows that this is generally the case: Immediate gains in the posttest measure of cognitive development successfully predict all GCSE gains achieved by boys two and three years after the intervention, and they also predict gains made by girls in science and mathematics. However,

Table 8.4 Correlations between rg scores of PRT posttest, science-delayed posttest, and GCSE

	Delayed science rg	Science	Math	English
		\multicolumn{3}{c}{GCSE rg score}		
Post-PRT rg				
11 + boys	0.52	0.47	0.41	0.45
11 + girls	0.62	0.73	0.61	0.22[a]
12 + boys	0.39	0.33	0.67	0.38
12 + girls	0.32	0.28	0.30	0.24[a]

[a]Number does not reach a significance of < 0.05.

there appear to be only weak nonsignificant correlations between girls' immediate gains in cognitive development and their subsequent gains in English GCSE. That this occurs in both 11 + and 12 + groups independently suggests that it is not a chance effect.

A possible explanation is that both boys and girls must approach learning and examinations in science and mathematics in an analytical way, and the PRT tests of cognitive development are good measures of analytical thinking. But boys and girls approach language tasks in different way. Boys still rely mainly on analytical methods, whereas girls predominantly use a different cognitive function that is not well tapped by the PRTs. Whatever this different function may be, it seems to be positively affected by the intervention, because girls who have experienced *Thinking Science* do, in fact, make gains in English scores. Our cognitive instruments, however, are less useful for detecting growth of this function.

2   What happened to the gains in cognitive development during the year following the intervention?

If we use the word *development* to indicate a nonreversible change that provides the potential to improve further learning, the hypothesis of enhanced underlying cognitive development is not served by data indicating that gains are not maintained (Figure 8.8). Table 8.5 shows the correlations between delayed PRT rg scores, immediate post-PRT rg scores, and the measures of academic achievement. There is little unusual about the data for the 12 + boys or girls.

Table 8.5 Correlations between rg scores of delayed PRT posttest, PRT posttext, science delayed posttest, and GCSE

	Post-PRT rg	Delayed science rg	GCSE rg Score		
			Science	Math	English
Delayed PRT rg					
11 + boys	0.49	0.36	0.44	0.46	0.45
11 + girls	0.27[a]	0.34	0.28[a]	0.25[a]	0.24[a]
12 + boys	0.65	0.63	0.40	0.64	0.45
12 + girls	0.40	0.29[a]	0.53	0.47	0.29

[a]Number does not reach a significance of < 0.05.

Correlation coefficients are generally higher than the corresponding values for the immediate post-PRT gains, as one would expect for tests taken one year nearer to the academic achievement measures. Correlations with English GCSE are low, as we found with the post-PRT gains and for which we have already offered a possible explanation. In the 12 + groups, only the low correlation with the delayed science gains differs from expectation.

For the 11 + groups, the data are distinctly odd. Correlation values for delayed PRT gains are not higher than they were for post-PRT gains; and, in the girls' case, there are no significant correlations between delayed PRT gains and GCSE gains. In reviewing this element in the whole story some years after these delayed PRTs were administered, it is worth noting that three out of four 11 + classes were in middle schools. This meant that the *Thinking Science* intervention program was completed at the end of the pupils' stay in those schools and that the delayed tests were given after the pupils had spent one year in new (to them) high schools. The school change and becoming accustomed to new friends, new teachers, and new working methods may have caused a hiatus in the normal progress of cognitive development. If so, for the 11 + group, we can set aside the apparently aberrant delayed PRT gain scores and point to the ultimate long-term success in GCSE gains as the most important evidence for the eventual real effect of the intervention program on academic achievement.

For the 12 + group, this explanation is not available, but here, except for the absence of difference between the experimental and control groups' delayed PRT gain scores, the pattern of correlations is inconsistent with the view that (a) the intervention has caused an enhanced development of cognitive operations and (b) this enhanced development has improved academic achievement in a range of domains. We believe that explaining the aberrant result would require a further longitudinal study in which the same measures of cognitive development were administered each year for at least three years and related with academic achievement.

3 How can we explain the bimodality in many of the distributions?

It seems clear from the distributions of gain scores that some pupils from the 11 + and 12 + groups, boys and girls, have made great gains in achievement compared with controls, whereas others have made little or no gain. Even regarding tests on which the greatest mean gains were achieved, only two subgroups can be interpreted: Subgroup 1, consisting of perhaps one-third of the group, made gains of 2 *SD* or more; Subgroup 2, the remainder, made little or no greater gain than the controls.

  We strongly suggest that this effect can be explained in terms of learning styles: The whole *Thinking Science* approach suited some students better than it did others. Unfortunately, the design of the experiment, including limitations of time and money, did not allow us to carry out the in-depth classroom observations and interviews with pupils that might have elucidated this suggestion further. We recognize this as a limitation of the study.

Conclusion

Evidence has been presented of substantial and long-lasting effects on general academic achievement of a cognitive acceleration program that concentrates on cognitive conflict, metacognition, and bridging, and that uses the schemata of formal operations as a framework for the development of activities. In particular, boys starting at 12 + and girls starting at 11 + showed strong and actually increasing effects over the period following the intervention program. The gender differences observed may be due to the different conjunction of the intervention program with critical periods for girls' and boys' cognitive development.

Two hypotheses rooted, respectively, in domain-specific and in general models of cognition have been explored: (1) that the intervention program influenced one underlying general cognitive structure, the enhanced development of which permitted improved learning in all academic domains, and (2) that the intervention acted independently on two intellectual structures (e.g., a spatial–numerical one and a linguistic one), each of which in turn led to improved performance in its own domain. The evidence does not allow one to choose with a high degree of confidence between these two hypotheses, and the apparent loss of cognitive advantage by the experimental group one year after the intervention is a puzzling feature. Nevertheless, the gains in English remain a reality in need of explanation, and to science-teachers-turned-psychologists, who in this project worked through science teachers and the science curriculum, it seems unlikely that our intervention directly influenced language behavior more effectively than language teachers and language curricula did.

Which of the results presented do we expect to be replicable? New work in Korea and in England, currently in preparation for publication, provides replication of the immediate gains in cognitive development following a CASE intervention. In addition, we are confident that CASE or similar work in ordinary public high schools can bring about a long-term gain in academic achievement across a range of subject areas. We are less confident about the apparent age and gender differences and the point at which the intervention is most effective. This and a careful longitudinal tracking of cognitive development using measures consistent from year to year remain areas in need of further investigation.

We believe that we have responded to Alan Clarke's challenge. An intervention heavily dependent on Piaget's account of operational thinking has produced large effects on theory-independent national school examinations. We believe that the strongest contender for an explanation of these results is that of a general cognitive processor that has been positively influenced by the CASE intervention. If we have succeeded in raising the head of such a contender an inch above the parapet without it being blown off, we hope that will be sufficient encouragement for others to investigate its viability further. Come back, Piaget. Much (but not all) is forgiven.

Notes

1 Although Kuhn, Amsel, and O'Loughlin (1988) criticized Piaget's logical explanation of formal operations, they accepted that (a) there is a developmental aspect in the growth of scientific thinking and (b) the Inhelder–Piaget schemata have provided a rich source for a broadly consistent body of empirical studies into the development of thinking.

2 A typical but by no means universal pattern for a six- or seven-form entry comprehensive high school in Britain is to assign children with learning difficulties to a remedial group, and sometimes to select especially able children for a second group, and to form four or five equivalent mixed-ability groups from the remainder.

References

Adey, P. S. (1988). Cognitive acceleration – Review and prospects. *International Journal of Science Education, 10*, 121–134.

Adey, P. S., and Shayer, M. (1990). Accelerating the development of formal thinking in middle and high school students. *Journal of Research in Science Teaching, 27*, 267–285.

Adey, P. S., and Shayer, M. (in press). *Really raising standards: Cognitive intervention and academic achievement*. London: Routledge.

Adey, P. S., Shayer, M., and Yates, C. (1989). *Thinking science: The curriculum materials of the CASE project*. London: Thomas Nelson and Sons.

Brainerd, C. J. (1978). *Piaget's theory of intelligence*. New York: Prentice-Hall.

Brown, G., and Desforges, C. (1979). *Piaget's theory: A psychological critique*. London: Routledge and Kegan Paul.

Case, R. (1974). Structures and strictures: Some functional limits to cognitive growth. *Cognitive Psychology, 6*, 544–574.

Children's Learning in Science Project (1987). *CLIS in the classroom*. Leeds, England: University of Leeds Centre for Studies in Science and Maths Education.

Clarke, A. M., and Clarke, A. D. B. (1976). *Early experience: Myth and evidence*. London: Open Books.

Cronbach, L., and Furby, L. (1970). How should we measure change, or should we? *Psychological Bulletin, 74*, 68–80.

Desforges, C., and Brown, G. (1979). The educational utility of Piaget: A reply to Shayer [with final comment by Shayer]. *British Journal of Educational Psychology, 49*, 277–281.

Feuerstein, R., Rand, Y., Hoffman, M., and Miller, M. (1980). *Instrumental enrichment: An intervention program for cognitive modifiability.* Baltimore: University Park Press.

Fusco, E. T. (1983). *The relationship between children's cognitive level of development and their responses to literature.* Unpublished PhD thesis, Hofstra University, Hempstead, NY.

Goossens, L. (1989). *Training scientific reasoning in children and adolescents: A critical review and quantitative integration.* Paper presented at the Third European Conference for Research on Learning and Instruction, Madrid (September).

Hadden, R. A., and Johnstone, A. H. (1983). Secondary school pupils' attitudes to science: The year of erosion. *European Journal of Science Education, 5,* 309–318.

Hallam, R. N. (1967). Logical thinking in history. *Educational Review, 119,* 182–202.

Inhelder, B., and Piaget, J. (1958). *The growth of logical thinking from childhood to adolescence.* London: Routledge and Kegan Paul.

Jurd, M. (1973). Adolescent thinking in history-type material. *Australian Journal of Education, 17,* 2–17.

Karplus, R. (1978). *Teaching for the development of reasoning.* Unpublished manuscript.

Kelly, A. (1981). Science achievement as an aspect of sex roles. In A. Kelly (Ed.), *The missing half: Girls and science education* (pp. 73–84). Manchester, England: Manchester University Press.

Kuhn, D., Amsel, E., and O'Loughlin, M. (1988). *The development of scientific thinking skills.* San Diego: Academic.

Kuhn, D., and Angelev, J. (1976). An experimental study of the development of formal operational thought. *Child Development, 47,* 697–706.

Lawson, A. E., Blake, A. J. D., and Nordland, F. (1975). Training effects and generalization of the ability to control variables in high school biology students. *Science Education, 59,* 387–396.

Lawson, A. E., and Snitgen, D. A. (1982). Teaching formal reasoning in a college biology course for preservice teachers. *Journal of Research in Science Teaching, 19,* 233–248.

Neimark, E. (1975). Intellectual development during adolescence. In F. D. Horowitz (Ed.), *Review of child development research* (Vol. 4, pp. 541–594). Chicago: University of Chicago Press.

Nickerson, R. S., Perkins, D. N., and Smith, E. E. (1985). *The teaching of thinking.* Hillsdale, NJ: Lawrence Erlbaum Associates, Inc.

Ormerod, M. B., and Duckworth, D. (1975). *Pupils' attitudes to science: A review of research.* Slough, England: National Foundation for Educational Research in England and Wales.

Papert, S. (1961). *The growth of logical thinking: A Piagetian viewpoint.* Unpublished manuscript, Archives Jean Piaget, Geneva.

Parsons, C. (1960). Critical notice. *British Journal of Psychology, 51,* 75–84.

Perkins, D. N., and Salomon, G. (1989). Are cognitive skills context-bound? *Educational Researcher, 18,* 16–25.

Renner, J. W., Stafford, D. E., Lawson, A. E., McKinnon, J. W., Friot, F. E., and Kellogg, D. H. (1976). *Research, teaching, and learning with the Piaget model.* Norman: University of Oklahoma Press.

Resnick, L. B. (1987). *Education and learning to think.* Washington, DC: National Academy Press.

Rosenthal, D. A. (1979). The acquisition of formal operations: The effect of two training procedures. *Journal of Genetic Psychology, 134,* 125–140.

Shayer, M. (1978). Nuffield combined science: Do the pupils understand it? *School Science Review, 211,* 210–223.

Shayer, M. (1979). Has Piaget's construct of formal operational thinking any utility? *British Journal of Educational Psychology, 49,* 265–267.

Shayer, M. (1987). Neo-Piagetian theories and educational practice. *International Journal of Psychology, 22,* 751–777.

Shayer, M., and Adey, P. S. (1981). *Towards a science of science teaching.* London: Heinemann Educational.

Shayer, M., and Adey, P. S. (1992a). Accelerating the development of formal thinking in middle and high school students II: Post-project effects on science achievement. *Journal of Research in Science Teaching, 29,* 81–92.

Shayer, M., and Adey, P. S. (1992b). Accelerating the development of formal operational thinking in high school pupils, III: Testing the permanency of the effects. *Journal of Research in Science Teaching, 29,* 1101–1115.

Shayer, M., and Adey, P. S. (1993). Accelerating the development of formal operational thinking in high school pupils, IV: Three years on after a two year intervention. *Journal of Research in Science Teaching, 30,* 351–366.

Shayer, M., Adey, P. S., and Wylam, H. (1981). Group tests of cognitive development – Ideals and a realization. *Journal of Research in Science Teaching, 18,* 157–168.

Shayer, M., and Beasley, F. (1987). Does instrumental enrichment work? *British Educational Research Journal, 13*(2), 101–119.

Shayer, M., Küchemann, D. E., and Wylam, H. (1976). The distribution of Piagetian stages of thinking in British middle and secondary school children. *British Journal of Educational Psychology, 46,* 164–173.

Shayer, M., and Wylam, H. (1978). The distribution of Piagetian stages of thinking in British middle and secondary school children. II – 14- to 16-year olds and sex differentials. *British Journal of Educational Psychology, 48,* 62–70.

Shayer, M., Wylam, H., Küchemann, D. E., and Adey, P. S. (1978). *Science reasoning tasks*. Slough, England: National Foundation for Educational Research. (Now available from Science Reasoning, 16 Fen End, Over, Cambs., CB4 5NE, UK)

Vygotsky, L. S. (1978). *Mind in society*. Cambridge, MA: Harvard University Press.

Classroom Knowledge
Introduction

When psychologists tried to come to grips with the complexities of classroom life, they soon discovered in the language of the classroom a rich topic for research (see Edwards and Westgate, 1987). The authors of the following paper go beyond the analysis of the typical patterns of interaction, the distinctive discourse of teaching and learning, to look at the way that language shapes what counts as 'knowledge' in the context of schooling. The process of learning is often thought of as one that goes on inside an individual person's head. But any learning that involves another person generally relies on some sort of conversation and joint activity between them. Language is thus a social mode of thinking and the authors of this paper build on Vygotsky's idea that much of what children come to know they learn first of all in the context of social interaction, by taking part in dialogues with more knowledgeable others. Such 'shared knowledge', Vygotsky argued, would later be internalized by children to form part of their own internal mental repertoire.

In this context, teachers are viewed as mediators of an existing culture of educated thought. But in the process of mediation, the children's own experiences in the classroom may be selected, reconstructed, reshaped and reinterpreted so as to fit the teacher's notion of what is right and what is important. The idea of the 'context' of learning is here developed beyond the details of the physical setting and the identities of the participants to refer to a shared mental context which is built up over time in classroom dialogues between teacher and taught. Knowledge itself is no longer seen in terms of independently existing facts, concepts and theories, but is conceptualized as the emerging product of various forms of social construction and interaction. This is referred to as a 'socio-cultural' approach to teaching and learning.

Reference

Edwards, A. and Westgate, D. 1987: *Investigating Classroom Talk*. London: Falmer.

Further reading

The same approach is followed up in greater detail in the following two books:

Edwards, D. and Mercer, N. 1987: *Common Knowledge: The Development of Understanding in the Classroom*. London: Methuen/Routledge.

Mercer, N. 1995: *The Guided Construction of Knowledge*. Clevedon: Multilingual Matters.

NINE

Reconstructing Context: the Conventionalization of Classroom Knowledge

Derek Edwards and Neil Mercer

> Ultimately, social contexts consist of mutually shared and ratified defin-
> itions of situation and in the social actions persons take on the basis of
> these definitions. (Erickson & Schultz, 1981, p. 148)

The "context" of any utterance or stretch of discourse is more complex
and more interesting than it first appears to be. At the simplest
level, context can be defined as the surrounding speech, or text.
And perhaps to this definition can be added the surrounding circumstances of persons, time, and place in which the discourse is created.
But the implication remains that context is something finite and
observable, available for scrutiny in the transcript or the video
recording.

Things are not so convenient. Although the investigators might
have the luxury of access to recordings and transcripts, the participants themselves, like the referees whose decisions are examined in
television's slow-motion replays, must rely on what they perceive,
understand, and remember at the time. It is a commonplace of
cognitive psychology that perception, remembering, and understanding are not processes that have a straightforward, veridical relationship to the world. But, the fact that the investigator's recourse to
context was only, in the first place, made in an effort to understand

the communications of the participants leads to the conclusion that this apparent luxury of a privileged vantage point could be illusory. Context is not concrete for the observer, but intersubjective for the participants.

In Vygotsky's (1978; cf. Wertsch, 1985) terms, context is "intermental," a function of the joint actions and understandings of the communicators. Vygotsky was not much concerned with the context and continuity of discourse but, rather, with the social, intermental origins of individual thought. He strove to develop a cultural–historical account of the nature of thinking and knowledge, of the "higher mental processes." This concern with the cultural basis of knowledge, and more specifically with its linguistic and semiotic basis, was an important feature of Vygotsky's psychology, which, though neglected by subsequent generations of cognitive psychologists, he shared with one of the founders of that discipline, Sir Frederick Bartlett (1932). Much of Bartlett's work was devoted to exploration of the cultural basis of thinking and remembering, especially with the process of "conventionalization," through which cultural symbols, signs, and texts, and the mental schemata that used them, took on their recognized properties. In an extended discussion of this and other aspects of Bartlett's work, Edwards and Middleton (1987) show that it was the sociohistorical process through which symbolic materials become conventionalized, not merely some version of schematic information processing, that Bartlett was trying to reproduce in his well-known studies of serial remembering in individuals.

> The method of serial reproduction, famous as a paradigm for the study of memory, was essentially designed to capture the process of conventionalization. Remembering was for Barlett not simply the recalling of experience, but rather a fundamentally symbolic process both rooted in and constitutive of culture, forming and formed by symbols and meanings transmitted in texts and pictures. (p. 79)

So, the Vygotskian approach encourages an examination of the process of classroom education as a joint enterprise involving teacher and learner in the establishment of a common understanding. Bartlett's psychology offers the notion that what develops between teacher and pupil might be conceived of as a collective memory, a joint version of things encoded symbolically, in which shared understandings become established through the development of a common language and a common discursive context. The study of classroom discourse therefore offers an appropriate basis for looking at how classroom understandings are constituted socially.

Studies of classroom discourse have concentrated, for the large part, upon the structured nature and sequencing of talk (e.g., Sinclair & Coulthard, 1975), and on the role of this talk in the social organization of classrooms (e.g., Edwards & Furlong, 1978; Mehan, 1979). They offer a version of classroom talk in which what occurs is revealed as a cooperative negotiation of meanings from moment to moment as the interaction proceeds. But as Griffin and Mehan (1981) have stressed, "interlocutors have a history" (p. 191). This paper concerns the development of shared knowledge rather than the micro social order. It is a matter of emphasis, the psychologist's concern rather than the sociologist's. Not that these disciplines can or should sustain their usual distance. In fact, the authors agree with Griffin and Mehan (1981) that

> There is no evidence, as far as we know, that the process or structures proposed as acceptable analyses of the cognitive, academic or content aspects of lessons would be any different from the processes or structures involved in the social aspects...The increments to a child's skills, concepts or information base that a lesson is designed to facilitate are not available for the teacher to offer, or for the child to grasp, or for the analyst to locate except as they are instantiated in the social negotiations of the speech event. (p. 191)

For pupils in school, the only knowledge that counts is that which is, or can be, communicated (cf. Mercer & Edwards, 1981).

Transcripts of classroom dialogue shall be examined, looking for some features of how the participants establish a shared understanding of the curriculum, what has been called a "common knowledge" (Edwards & Mercer, 1987). The specific features of concern here are those that might have interested Bartlett, the *reconstructive rememberings*. As the discourse proceeds, it carries and builds with it a basis of shared understandings in terms of which the participants are able to make joint sense of what they are saying and doing, of how these things should be understood and talked about, and of what constructions to put upon experience. This *intermental context* is precisely that – intermental, defined, created, and assumed by the participants, rather than simply available to the investigators through flipping back through the pages of transcript. The aim of this study is to demonstrate a conception of educational knowledge (and by implication, other sorts of knowledge too), as socially constructed and reconstructed, conventionalized and historical, socialized and socializing. The historical and socializing aspects derive from two further, and related, facts about our school classroom data.

1 The preexistence of the curriculum and of the great historical accumulation of fact and method, procedure and assumption from which this is drawn.
2 The teacher's role in controlling and guiding the learning process, as authoritative representative of the educated culture.

These two aspects are considered to have been neglected in discourse-analytic and ethnomethodological studies of classroom talk.

Context as Common Knowledge

The video recordings of classroom lessons derive from a larger study in state schools in the Midlands of England, with teachers and groups of 9-to 10-year-olds. They were made in sequences of three lessons that successively developed some particular topic (e.g., how to do computer graphics using LOGO, or experiments on the science of pendulums). This facilitated the gain of some information about how collective knowledge was built from lesson to lesson, as well as within lessons.

This building process was most apparent at the beginnings of lessons. Sequence 1 is the opening talk from the first of three lessons on computer graphics. In this and subsequent sequences of dialogue, diagonal slashes represent pauses (one for pauses less than 2 sec, two for longer ones). Notes on situational features, actions, and gestures are in the right-hand column.

Sequence 1:   *Introducing the lesson*

T: Right/this is our new computer/the four   (An RML 480Z micro)
eighty zed, You haven't seen this one before.
Erm when you've used computer programs
before/what's happened is that the words
have come up on the screen/or the instruc-   Teacher gestures with
tions/ for you/have come up on the screen/   arm toward screen.
and you've just answered the questions/ and/
typed in/ what the/ computer wanted you to
do. This program is different. In this program
the computer doesn't know what to do.
You've got to tell it what to do/ so you have
got to instruct the computer.

The teacher began the lesson by introducing the pupils to their new
computer and immediately established a context for it in terms of their
previous experience with computers in the classroom. Lessons typically
began in this manner, with introductions to the work to be done and
continuity links established with what had been done previously. Thus
Lesson 2, recorded a week later, began with a back reference to where
the previous computer lesson had left off.

Sequence 2:   *Building upon the previous lesson.*

T: Now you've got your programs from last
week have you/ to show me what you're

Pupils: Yes.   T reminding pupils of

T: (continuing) going to do/ with angles not   instructions she gave
ninety degrees./ We had to try something   last week.
else didn't we. What did you find most difficult Susan? What's yours?

Besides these opening links, explicit references were also made during
lessons to what had been done and said earlier. Sequence 3 lists the
teacher's back references from the last of three lessons on making clay
pottery. (This is a different teacher, pupils, and school.)

Sequence 3:   *Back references to shared experience and talk*

– What did I tell you about thin bits? What happens when they dry?
– What did I tell you about eyes?
– Can you remember what you forgot to do Patricia/ when you put that little
belt thing round?

– Look when you put its eyes in./ I did tell you this before Lorraine.
– John/ you seem to have forgotten everything you've learned don't you?
– Don't forget/if it's too wide chop it off.

In Sequence 3, the teacher's remarks to John and Lorraine reflect the fact that constructing a continuity of shared knowledge can be a problematic process. Indeed, all of the cases listed in Sequence 3 occurred in the context of some difficulty arising with regard to the understanding that teacher and pupils had established up to that point in the lesson. That is, the teacher was most likely to point out that knowledge was, in her opinion, shared when pupils were acting as though it were not. When the pupils seemed not to have grasped some significant principle, procedure, or instruction, the teacher would remind them that this matter had, in fact, been dealt with previously.

It has been suggested that this association of explicit references to past shared experience, including previous discourse, with occasions on which the commonality of knowledge appears to be in doubt, is a general feature of conversation, not something peculiar to school classrooms. It has been observed in adult conversation in educational and noneducational settings (Edwards & Middleton, 1986; Mercer & Edwards, 1987) and in parent–child conversation during early language learning (Edwards & Goodwin, 1986). In the classroom, however, such explicit appeals to significant aspects of past shared experience might have an important pedagogical function. As transactions between child and adult, they occur in Vygotsky's "zone of proximal development," at precisely the points at which common knowledge is being created. It is the teacher's role to draw children's attention to such matters, and so establish knowledge that is both common and communicable. The next sequence illustrates this very clearly.

Sequence 4: *Continuity: What have you been doing all along?*
T: Now/ how are you fixing them on Katie?
Katie: Putting them/ well its (. . .)
T: Now/ what do you think you should do what   Katie mutters
have you been doing all along every time   hesitantly.
you've joined anything?
Katie: Putting grooves in it.
T: Putting grooves in it/ haven't you and water/
grooves and water/the water to fill up the
grooves/on both bits of clay./ You must do

it/otherwise it will dry/ and when it's dry like
those are dry/those ears will just be lying on
the floor/or on the table. Take them off/ other-   Katie refits the ears.
wise you'll be very sad./You've got to do
things the right way round with clay or they
just don't work.

Sequence 4 is taken from the second of three pottery lessons. The
teacher noticed that Katie was having problems and so intervened and
appealed explicitly to a continuity of shared experience: "What have
you been doing all along?" The exchange succeeded in focusing Katie's
awareness on what the teacher perceived to be the salient part of her
actions, this, then, becoming the necessary shared mental context for
the teacher's explanation of why those actions were important – "You
must do it/ otherwise it will dry." One might argue that this is an
essential element of good teaching: explanation is built upon an appeal
to shared experience, or rather to selected aspects of joint experience
and activity, made explicit through the discourse.

It would seem, then, that the teachers' use of explicit recaps was to
ensure that pupils had developed a joint understanding, with the
teachers, of the significant aspects of what had been said and done.
The establishment of this *legitimized* version of shared past experience
could then become the basis of further teaching, a shared mental
context for what was to follow. This is a process particularly well
illustrated in the next sequence, taken from the second of a series of
lessons on solvents (in this case, on the effects of different household
washing products on stained fabrics). It is an abbreviated part of a
lesson introduction that went on for about 10 min. Omitted discourse
has been indicated thus: (...). In it, the teacher is attempting to
establish continuity among what has happened in the previous
lesson, the present situation, and what the children will go on to do
next.

Sequence 5:   *Past, present, and future*
T: Now the other day we were talking about
         which washing powder was going to wash
         best. And when we began talking about it
         you gave me some positive firm answers. /
         What made you say what you did say?   To Tom
Tom: Well// we used a popular television things

T: Yes erm// well you were thinking about the ones that were advertized on television./ Yes/ What did you say first of all? Which washing powder did you think was going to wash best?

Tom: Persil.

T: What did you think?   To Ellie

Ellie: Persil.

T: Persil. Somebody said Daz./ Who was that? (...) And you were thinking *then* about what your mothers said.

Pupils: Yeh.

T: And what your mothers used.

Pupils: Yeh.

T: Weren't you? (...) Then we went on and we looked at what the manufacturers said on the packets about their products and you then thought that which washing powder was going to wash best?

Mary: Ariel.

T: Ariel. And what made you say that Ariel

Mary: It digests dirt and stains (...)   Mary interrupts T.

T: Yes it digests dirt and stains (...) *Now when   *T turns to equipment
you're staining your fabrics you've got your   laid out on table.
stains out here.// How much stain are you
going to use?

Ellie: Two blobs// two blobs of five on the cloth.

T: You're going to make two separate areas of five drops not squirts. And then (...)

Reconstructing a Collective Memory

It should not be thought that the establishment of collective classroom memories was a process dominated merely by communicative necessity, nor the pursuit of an accurate record of events. It was also an arena in which what might actually have happened could be creatively reinterpreted in the light of what ought to have happened, a process guided in turn by the teacher's privileged position as one who knew in advance what truths were there to be discovered. The teachers studied made use of a variety of powerful discursive devices (for an account of these, see Edwards & Mercer, 1987), through which, despite an overtly child-oriented, invitational, and eliciting style of talking to pupils, a tight reign could nevertheless be kept upon what was collectively done, thought, and understood. These devices ranged from the obvious, such as controlling pupils' contributions; sanctioning who should speak, when, and about what; ignoring unwelcome contributions and selectively encouraging others, to the very subtle, such as introducing understandings or versions of events via presupposition and implication, effectively defining them as "given," to be taken as understood, as not open to question.

Through another such device, that of "reconstructive paraphrasing," the teacher was able to impose a preferred vocabulary, or conventional description, merely by paraphrasing her repetition of what a pupil had just said. But the most extensive reconstructions were those that occurred typically at the beginnings and ends of lessons, when teacher and pupils were establishing what was to count as common knowledge, how the context of shared experience, upon which subsequent teaching and learning would proceed, should be defined. The concentration here will be on these latter sorts of events, in which the process of creating a joint version of events, a joint understanding, can be seen as one of symbolic conventionalization of knowledge, controlled by the teacher.

Sequence 6 occurred in Lesson 2 on the pendulum, when the teacher was recapping, via the familiar sorts of IRF elicitations (see Mehan, 1979; Sinclair & Coulthard, 1975), Lesson 1. Both teacher and pupils took advantage of the opportunity to offer a more acceptable version of events. The teacher was in the process of asking each pair of pupils to recount what they had discovered in their respective experiments.

Sequence 6: *Recapping the main empirical findings*
T: Jonathan/ you and Lucy.
Jonathan: Well we tried different weights/ on
    the end of the*/ on the end of the pen thing   *Pauses, points to pen-
    whatever you call it.   dulum.
T: And how did you change the weight? What
    did you use?
Jonathan: Erm/ washers.   Points with pencil at
    pendulum.

T: That's right yes.

Jonathan: And did them at the same height
each time/ and then/ they all came out/ the
same.
T: Which surprised you didn't it?
Jonathan: Yeh.   Jonathan nods.

It had been Jonathan and Lucy's task to vary the weight of the pendulum
bob, using different numbers of metal washers, and to measure the effect
this had on its period of swing (the time taken to swing to and fro). As
the teacher knew, but the pupils did not, the weight variable ought to
have no effect on the period of swing. After some negotiation with the
teacher in Lesson 1, this had been agreed upon as what had indeed been
"found." The most notable reconstruction in Sequence 6 is Jonathan's
declaration that he and his partner had varied weight alone, that they
had changed the number of washers "and done them at the same height
(angle) each time." What had actually happened was that angle of
swing, as well as weight of the bob, had been varied, a fact that the
teacher had clearly witnessed but chose at the time (in Lesson 1) to
ignore. This was important for scientific reasons. It had never been
established whether or not the proper experimental controls had
been observed when altering the two variables. By Lesson 2, the experimental principle of altering variables one at a time had been grasped
(though its rationale remained unexplained), and pupils and teacher
were now prepared to collude in a blatant revision of what had actually
occurred in Lesson 1.

In the same vein, Jonathan's claim that the results surprised him
was a direct contradiction of his declaration in Lesson 1 that the results
were precisely as he had predicted. Indeed, his reconstruction in Lesson 2
of what he had done and thought in Lesson 1 now incorporated the
subsequently confirmed hypothesis: "I thought it might go faster because it has a different weight." These discrepancies are not treated as
mere errors of recall or, for that matter, of honesty. Indeed, surrounded
as he was by witnesses and video-recording paraphernalia, there
would seem little point in such motives. Here is the collective establishment of a common version of events, the construction of a small piece
of conventional wisdom.

Also in Lesson 2, Sharon and Karen were called upon to recount
their experiment, the one that varied angle of swing.

Sequence 7:   *Reconstructing a principle of equal intervals*

T: Right we started off at/ what was this one?	T indicates leftmost position on x-axis of graph displayed on OHP.
Sharon: Forty degrees	
T: Forty?	T pointing to next position (55 degrees).
Sharon: Fifty five degrees.	
T: Yes	T pointing to 70 degrees, then to 85 degrees marks on x-axis of graph.
Sharon: Seventy degrees and eighty five degrees.	
T: Yes/ erm/ did you follow any particular pattern? Is there any reason why you chose those angles or did you just sort of chalk/	
Sharon: Fifteen degrees difference.	
T: Good girl fifteen degrees difference between the two. That's valuable when you're doing an experiment/ to try and establish some sort of a pattern/ in the numbers/ or the erm timing or/ whatever it is that you're using. Try and keep the pattern the same/ the interval* the same/ for example between the degrees.	T looking around group, using upturned hand with finger tips joined (precision gesture). *T holds palms of hand a fixed interval apart and moves them sideways through the air.

The clear impression to be gained from Sequence 7 is that Sharon and Karen chose angles that were equal distances apart, 15°, as a matter of proper scientific procedure. This time the text of Lesson 1 (Sequence 8) shall be examined to see what actually happened. In fact, the four angles had first been marked without measurement on the top of the pendulum, and then, only after the experiment was completed, were estimated, under the teacher's guidance, to be equidistant at intervals of 15°. The girls had in fact determined their various angles of swing earlier in the lesson by uncalibrated trial and error, constrained, not by any principle of scientific measurement, but by the angles at which the string was found to snag on the pendulum upright.

Sequence 8: *How the equal intervals were measured.*
Sharon: We're stuck.
T: You're stuck Sharon?

> T gets up & moves round table to Sharon & Karen.

Sharon: We're going to find (...)
T: What love?

> T moving into position in front of Sharon & Karen's pendulum.

Sharon: I'm going to find the angles/ and/
T: The angles that you've used
Karen: We can't get the protractor on there.

> Karen pointing to top plate of pendulum where lines are marked at different angles.

T: Well what I always do in cases like that I usually guess.

> Sharon turns away laughing.

Karen: I know that that one's roughtly ninety degrees.

> Karen pointing to the uppermost line.

T: What one would that one be Karen?
Karen: That's roughly ninety degrees.

> Karen still pointing.

T: Roughly/ is it quite ninety or would it be more/ less?

> (Square brackets mark simultaneous speech).

Karen: Not quite/ just less I think.
T: So what then?
Karen: Just/
Sharon: Eighty five?

> Sharon to Karen.

Karen: Yeh.
T: Come on then/ eighty five/ Now what

> Sharon, T & Karen bend forward, watching as Sharon writes on her notepad.

about this one at the bottom then? That's ninety.

> T points in turn to bottom line & then to top (90 degrees) line.

Karen: That one's ninety. That one's roughly forty five.

> Karen points appropriately to top and bottom lines in turn.

T: More or less than forty five?

Karen: Less.
T: Less than forty five so/
Karen: Forty.
T: Forty.//   Rising intonation; all
                                          bend forward and
                                          watch again as Sharon
                                          writes on the pad.

And what about the ones in between?   T & Karen look up at
                                          top plate.

Karen: Well/ that's going to be/   Karen points to 3rd line
                                          down.

Sharon: That one will be seventy then//   Sharon points up
                                          towards 2nd line down
                                          then writes on pad.

Karen: So that one must be about/   T walks over to Antony
                                          & David as Karen &
                                          Sharon work out the re-
                                          maining angle, between
                                          70 & 40.

Sharon: Thirty.
Karen: Thirty five?   (Note that 30 and 35
                                          are both less than 40°;
                                          these impossible esti-
                                          mates were later sur-
                                          reptitiously replaced by
                                          "55°")

The conventionalization of classroom knowledge can be seen in the way that what began as a casual positioning of marks on the pendulum was constructed in Lesson 1, and further refined in Lesson 2, into the guiding scientific principle of using equidistant measurement intervals. Clearly, notwithstanding the edifice of Piagetian developmental psychology, it would be inadvisable to place too much emphasis on the importance of what pupils learn simply from their own activity and experience. At least as important is the conventional sense put upon that experience, the words that define and communicate it, the principles encapsulated in the words, and the reworking of events that those words carry. Furthermore, the social basis of what pupils come to understand is founded not only upon the intrinsically social nature of discourse, but also upon the nature of the relationship between teacher and pupil. In the various lessons that have been observed, it was largely the teacher who provided the criteria of conventionality, the terms and versions to be adopted, while eliminating others from the common vocabulary and all the time governing the discursive process in which particular descriptions and versions of events were established. The establishment of a conventional wisdom was contingent upon an exercise of power.

Conclusion: Intermental Contexts and Collective Memory

In agreeing on a reconstructed version of classroom knowledge and experience, pupils are indeed active participants in the process. But their role is not the same as the teacher's. The eventual conventionalizations of remembered experience are those that the teacher knew in advance, or could at least judge when they arose, to be "right." In his account of the creation of conventions, David Lewis (1969) shows how social rituals, the conventionalized and implicit bases of social encounters, are initially explicated and later become implicit, or "understood," through reiteration. This is the sense of "ritual" invoked by Goffman (1971) and by Griffin and Mehan (1981). Although there are intriguing similarities, it is Bartlett's (1932) notion of conventionalization that is closer to the one pursued here, being concerned more explicitly with the cultural-historical dimension of psychological representations and depictions of events. From the cultural perspective, much of the knowledge that children must acquire is older than they are, originates from outside of the classroom and beyond their discourse with the teacher, and operates as a constraint and guide, through the teacher's mediating agency, to the significance of classroom discoveries and experiences.

The role of memory, or remembering, in school has a long and controversial pedigree. It is associated most strongly with what has become known as the "traditional," or "transmissional" sort of education, in which children were required to rehearse verbatim their multiplication tables, pages of classical poetry, conjugations and declensions, dates of battles and kings and treaties, mathematical formulae and derivations, the number of pounds in a ton or yards in a furlong. With the advent of the more "child-centered," "progressive" sorts of pedagogy, the importance of brute memory has been diminished. According to this more modern educational philosophy, children are to be guided along a more personal path of development, and it is as much a process of growth from within as of learning what is given. Knowledge is created, constructed by the learner, not merely passively acquired from textbooks and teacher talk, nor written upon some *tabula rasa*. But it is not rote learning that has been examined here. The study of educational discourse as the development and shaping of collective accounts and understandings has much to offer our conception of schooling. Indeed, it is the key to reconciling the active, exploratory conception of learning with the one strength that the older, traditional sort of pedagogy possessed: a recognition of culture, of the preexistence of knowledge. Children do not just happen to reinvent the knowledge of centuries.

The notion of memory, or remembering, as the rote learning of materials has little relevance to modern educational practice. The notion of a developing consensus of shared knowledge is much more interesting. The idea that education involves collective remembering, discourse-based construction, and conventionalization of experience, has two complementary foundations. One is that educational knowledge has the properties of a ready-made culture that precedes the coming together of teacher and pupils. The other is the process of collective remembering itself, the building of a context and continuity of shared knowledge as joint activity and discourse proceed. In developing a shared vocabulary for experience and understanding, and a jointly held version of events in the classroom, teacher and pupils construct together a framework of educational knowledge that reflects both sides of the process, that is, pupils' experiences in the classroom and the principles and categories of understanding that the curriculum, or the teacher's preconceptions, have set as the agenda to be learned.

References

Bartlett, F. C. (1932). *Remembering: a study in experimental and social psychology*. Cambridge: Cambridge University Press.

Edwards, A. D., & Furlong, V. J. (1978). *The language of teaching*. London: Heinemann.

Edwards, D., & Goodwin, R. Q. (1986). The language of shared attention and visual experience: A functional study of early nomination. *Journal of Pragmatics, 9*, 475–493.

Edwards, D., & Mercer, N. M. (1987). *Common knowledge: The growth of understanding in the classroom.* London: Methuen.

Edwards, D., & Middleton, D. J. (1986). Conversation and remembering: Constructing an account of shared experience through conversational discourse. *Discourse Processes, 9,* 423–459.

Edwards, D., & Middleton, D. J. (1987). Conversation and remembering: Bartlett revisited. *Applied Cognitive Psychology, 1,* 77–92.

Erickson, F., & Schultz, J. (1981). When is a context? Some issues and methods in the analysis of social competence. In J. L. Green & C. Wallat (Eds.), *Ethnography and language in educational settings.* Norwood, NJ: Ablex.

Goffman, E. (1971). *Relations in public: Microstudies of the public order.* Harmondsworth, England: Penguin Books.

Griffin, P., & Mehan, H. (1981). Sense and ritual in classroom discourse. In F. Coulmas (Ed.), *Conversational routine: explorations in standardized communication situations and prepatterned speech.* The Hague: Mouton.

Lewis, D. K. (1969). *Convention: A philosophical study.* London: Oxford University Press.

Mehan, H. (1979). *Learning lessons: Social organization in the classroom.* Cambridge, MA: Harvard University Press.

Mereer, N. M., & Edwards, D. (1981). Ground rules for mutual understanding: Towards a social psychological approach to classroom knowledge. In N. M. Mercer (Ed.), *Language in school and community.* London: Edward Arnold.

Mercer, N. M., & Edwards, D. (1987). Knowledge development in adult learning groups. *Open Learning, 2,* 22–28.

Sinclair, J. McH., & Coulthard, R. M. (1975). *Towards an analysis of discourse: The English used by teachers and pupils.* London: Oxford University Press.

Wertsch, J. V. (1985). *Vygotsky and the social formation of mind.* London: Harvard University Press.

Vygotsky, L. S. (1978). *Mind in society: The development of higher psychological processes.* London: Harvard University Press.

Assessment and Learning

Introduction

Assessment plays a very salient role in modern educational systems. It has been argued that assessment systems drive educational systems in the sense that tests and examinations focus the attention of teachers, students and policy makers. One function of assessment, it is argued, is that it provides information to both teachers and students which can take the form of feedback. Assessment information can, in principle, help inform the next step in teaching or learning. 'Feedback' is a significant factor in every theory of learning.

Whatever the theoretical attractions of assessment, the processes in practice are little understood. There is very little empirical research on assessment. What there is tends to suggest that assessment is at least as likely to distract from, or even damage, learning processes as it is to enhance them (Desforges, 1989).

In this paper Shepard reviews various models of assessment and their relationship to school learning. Shepard exposes how different conceptual frameworks for learning are implicated in different approaches to assessment and to teaching. She discusses the necessity of aligning educational goals, teaching programmes (curriculum) and assessment models if school experience is to lead to culturally desired outcomes.

There is massive literature on assessment, most of which is rhetorical. For a review of empirical work in the field of assessment and classroom learning see Black and William (1998).

Further reading

Black, P. and William, D. 1998: Assessment and classroom learning. *Assessment in education: principles, policy and practice*, 5, 1, 7–25.
Desforges, C. 1989: *Testing and Assessment*. London: Cassells.

TEN

The Role of Assessment in a Learning Culture

Lorrie A. Shepard

This article is about classroom assessment – not the kind of assessments used to give grades or to satisfy the accountability demands of an external authority, but rather the kind of assessment that can be used as a part of instruction to support and enhance learning.

The article is organized in three parts. I present, first, an historical framework highlighting the key tenets of social efficiency curricula, behaviorist learning theories, and "scientific measurement." Next, I offer a contrasting social-constructivist conceptual framework that blends key ideas from cognitive, constructivist, and sociocultural theories. In the third part, I elaborate on the ways that assessment practices should change to be consistent with and support social-constructivist pedagogy.

The impetus for my development of an historical framework was the observation by Beth Graue (1993) that "assessment and instruction are often conceived as *curiously separate* in both time and purpose" (p. 291, emphasis added). As Graue notes, the measurement approach to classroom assessment, "exemplified by standardized tests and teacher-made emulations of those tests," presents a barrier to the implementation of more constructivist approaches to instruction.

To understand the origins of Graue's picture of separation and to help explain its continuing power over present-day practice, I drew the chronology in Figure 10.1. A longer-term span of history helps us see that those measurement perspectives, now felt to be incompatible with

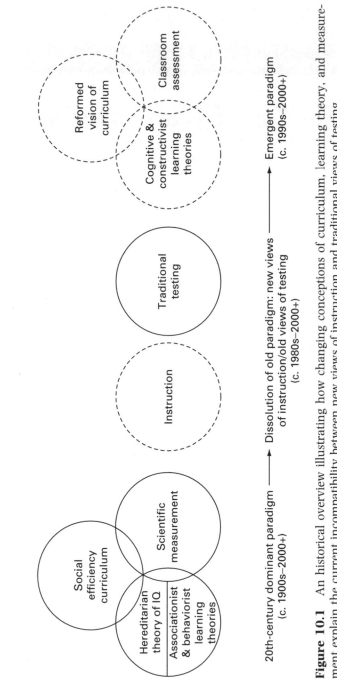

Figure 10.1 An historical overview illustrating how changing conceptions of curriculum, learning theory, and measurement explain the current incompatibility between new views of instruction and traditional views of testing

instruction, came from an earlier, highly consistent theoretical framework (on the left) in which conceptions of "scientific measurement" were closely aligned with traditional curricula and beliefs about learning. To the right is an emergent, constructivist paradigm in which teachers' close assessment of students' understandings, feedback from peers, and student self-assessments would be a central part of the social processes that mediate the development of intellectual abilities, construction of knowledge, and formation of students' identities. The best way to understand dissonant current practices, shown in the middle of the figure, is to realize that instruction (at least in its ideal form) is drawn from the emergent paradigm, while testing is held over from the past.

Historical Perspectives: Curriculum, Psychology, and Measurement

It is important to remind ourselves where traditional views of testing came from and to appreciate how tightly entwined these views of testing are with past models of curriculum and instruction – because dominant theories of the past continue to operate as the default framework affecting and driving current practices and perspectives. Belief systems of teachers, parents, and policymakers derive from these old theories.

A more elaborated version of the paradigm that has predominated throughout the 20th century can be shown as a set of interlocking circles (Figure 10.2). The central ideas of social efficiency and scientific management in the curriculum circle were closely linked, respectively, to hereditarian theories of individual differences and to associationist and behaviorist learning theories. These psychological theories were, in turn, served by scientific measurement of ability and achievement.

In the early 1900s, the social efficiency movement grew out of the belief that science could be used to solve the problems of industrialization and urbanization. According to social efficiency theory, modern principles of scientific management, intended to maximize the efficiency of factories, could be applied with equal success to schools. This meant taking F. W. Taylor's example of a detailed analysis of the movements performed by expert bricklayers and applying similar analyses to every vocation for which students were being prepared

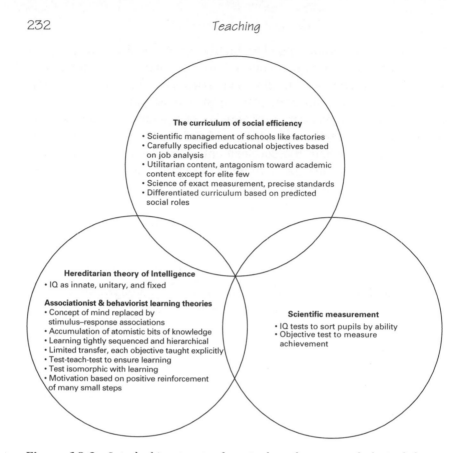

Figure 10.2 Interlocking tenets of curriculum theory, psychological theories, and measurement theory characterizing the dominant 20th-century paradigm

(Kleibard, 1995). Then, given the new associationist or connectionist psychology with its emphasis on fundamental building blocks, every step would have to be taught specifically. Precise standards of measurement were required to ensure that each skill was mastered at the desired level. And because it was not possible to teach every student the skills of every vocation, scientific measures of ability were also needed to predict one's future role in life and thereby determine who was best suited for each endeavor. For John Franklin Bobbitt (1912), a leader in the social efficiency movement, a primary goal of curriculum design was the elimination of waste, and it was wasteful to teach people things they would never use. Bobbitt's most telling principle was that each individual should be educated "according to his capabilities." These views led to a highly differentiated curriculum and a largely utilitarian one that disdained academic subjects for any but college preparatory students.

Alongside these curriculum theories, Edward Thorndike's (1922) associationism and the behaviorism of Hull (1943), Skinner (1938, 1954) and Gagne (1965) conceived of learning as the accumulation of stimulus–response associations. The following quotation from B. F. Skinner (1954) is illustrative:

> The whole process of becoming competent in any field must be divided into a very large number of very small steps, and reinforcement must be contingent upon the accomplishment of each step. This solution to the problem of creating a complex repertoire of behavior also solves the problem of maintaining the behavior in strength...By making each successive step as small as possible, the frequency of reinforcement can be raised to a maximum, while the possibly aversive consequences of being wrong are reduced to a minimum. (p. 94)

Note that this viewpoint promotes a theory of motivation as well as one of cognitive development.

Several key assumptions of the behavioristic model had consequences for ensuing conceptualizations of teaching and testing:

1 Learning occurs by accumulating atomized bits of knowledge.
2 Learning is tightly sequenced and hierarchical.
3 Transfer is limited, so each objective must be explicitly taught.
4 Tests should be used frequently to ensure mastery before proceeding to the next objective.
5 Tests are isomorphic with learning (tests = learning).
6 Motivation is external and based on positive reinforcement of many small steps.

It is no coincidence that Thorndike was both the originator of associationist learning theory and the "father" of "scientific measurement," a name given him by Ayers in 1918. Thorndike and his students fostered the development and dominance of the "objective" test, which has been the single most striking feature of achievement testing in the United States from the beginning of the century to the present day. Recognizing the common paternity of behaviorist learning theory and objective testing helps us to understand the continued intellectual kinship between one-skill-at-a-time test items and instructional practices aimed at mastery of constituent elements.

Looking at any collection of tests from early in the century, as shown in Box 10.1, one is immediately struck by how much the questions emphasized rote recall. To be fair, at the time, this was not a distortion of subject matter caused by the adoption of object-ive-item formats. One hundred years ago, various recall, comple-tion, matching, and multiple-choice test types, along with some essay questions, fit closely with what was deemed important to learn. However, once curriculum became encapsulated and repre-sented by these types of items, it is reasonable to say that these formats locked in a particular and outdated conception of subject matter.

New Stone Reasoning Tests in Arithmetic (1908)
1. James had 5 cents. He earned 13 cents more and then bought a top for 10 cents. How much money did he have left?

*Answer:*_____

Sones-Harry High School Achievement Test, Part II (1929)
1. Write "25% of" as "a decimal times."............. (_____)
2. Write in figures: one thousand seven and four hundredths
   .... (_____)

The Modern School Achievement Tests, Language Usage

	a. off	
1. I borrowed a pen	b. off of	my brother. _____
	c. from	

The Barrett-Ryan Literature Test: Silas Marner
1. Dolly Winthrop is:
   a. an ambitious society woman.   c. a haughty lady.
   b. a frivolous girl.   d. a kind, helpful neighbor.

Examples of True–False Objective Test (Ruch, 1929)
1. Tetanus (lockjaw) germs usually enter the body through open wounds.   *True   False*

American History Examination, East High School

1. Below is a list of statements. Indicate by a cross (X) after it, each statement that expresses a social heritage of the present-day American nation.

   Place a (0) after each statement that is not a present-day social heritage of the American nation.

   1. Americans believe in the ideal of religious toleration.   —
   2. Property in land should be inherited by a man's eldest son.—
   3. Citizens should have the right to say what taxes should be put upon them.   —

II. To test your ability to see how an intelligent knowledge of past events helps us to understand present-day situations and tendencies.

   (Note: Write your answer in essay form on a separate sheet of paper.)

   State your reasons for every position assumed.

   4. Take some *economic* fact or group of facts in American History about which we have studied and briefly show what seems to you to be the actual significance of this fact in the past, present and future of America.
   5. Show this same *three-fold relationship* using some *political* fact or facts.
   6. Show this same *three-fold relationship* using a *religious* fact or facts.

Note: The first four examples are borrowed from Ross (1941); the last two, including the Everett-Riley American History Examination, appeared in Ruch (1929)

Box 10.1 Examples from some of the earliest 20th century "standard" tests and objective-type classroom tests

The dominance of objective tests in classroom practice has affected more than the form of subject-matter knowledge. It has also shaped beliefs about the nature of evidence and principles of fairness. In a recent assessment project, for example, both teachers and researchers were surprised to find that despite our shared enthusiasm for developing alternatives to standardized tests we none the less operated from different assumptions about how "standardized" assessments needed to be in classrooms. More surprising still, it was teachers who held

beliefs more consistent with traditional principles of scientific measurement. From the perspective of our teacher colleagues, assessmentneeded
to be an official event, separate from instruction (Bliem & Davinroy,
1997). To ensure fairness, teachers believed that assessments had to be
uniformly administered, so they were reluctant to conduct more intensive individualized assessments with only below-grade-level readers.
Because of the belief that assessments had to be targeted to a specific
instructional goal, teachers felt more comfortable using two separate
assessments for separate goals, "running records" to assess fluency and
written summaries to assess comprehension rather than, say, asking
students to retell the gist of a story in conjuction with running records.
Most significantly, teachers wanted their assessments to be "objective,"
and this was the word they used. They worried often about the subject-
ivity involved in making more holistic evaluations of student work and
preferred formula-based methods, such as counting miscues, because
these techniques were more "impartial."

Any attempt to change the form and purpose of classroom assessment to make it more fundamentally a part of the learning process must acknowledge the power of these enduring and hidden beliefs.

Conceptual Framework: New Theories of Curriculum, Learning, and Assessment

To consider how classroom assessment practices might be reconceptua-
lized to be more effective in moving forward the teaching and learning
process, I elaborated the principles of a "social-constructivist" conceptual framework, borrowing from cognitive, constructivist, and sociocultural theories.[1] (Though these camps are sometimes warring with each
other, I predict that it will be something like this merged, middle-ground
theory that will eventually be accepted as common wisdom and carried
into practice.) The three-part figure (Figure 10.3) was developed in
parallel to the three-part historical paradigm to highlight, respectively,
changes in curriculum, learning theory, and assessment. In some cases,
principles in the new paradigm are the direct antitheses of principles in
the old. The interlocking circles again are intended to show the coherence and inter-relatedness of these ideas taken together.

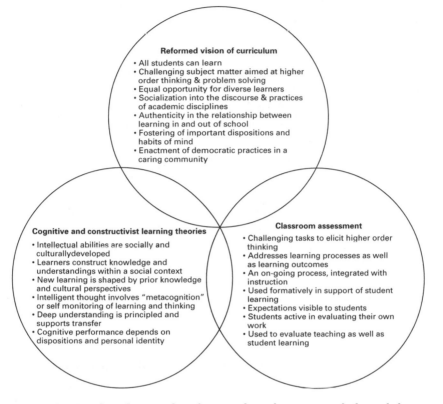

Reformed vision of curriculum

- All students can learn
- Challenging subject matter aimed at higher order thinking & problem solving
- Equal opportunity for diverse learners
- Socialization into the discourse & practices of academic disciplines
- Authenticity in the relationship between learning in and out of school
- Fostering of important dispositions and habits of mind
- Enactment of democratic practices in a caring community

Cognitive and constructivist learning theories

- Intellectual abilities are socially and culturallydeveloped
- Learners construct knowledge and understandings within a social context
- New learning is shaped by prior knowledge and cultural perspectives
- Intelligent thought involves "metacognition" or self monitoring of learning and thinking
- Deep understanding is principled and supports transfer
- Cognitive performance depends on dispositions and personal identity

Classroom assessment

- Challenging tasks to elicit higher order thinking
- Addresses learning processes as well as learning outcomes
- An on-going process, integrated with instruction
- Used formatively in support of student learning
- Expectations visible to students
- Students active in evaluating their own work
- Used to evaluate teaching as well as student learning

Figure 10.3   Shared principles of curriculum theories, psychological theories and assessment theory characterizing an emergent, constuctivist paradigm

The cognitive revolution reintroduced the concept of mind. In contrast to past, mechanistic theories of knowledge acquisition, we now understand that learning is an active process of mental construction and sense making. From cognitive theory we have also learned that existing knowledge structures and beliefs work to enable or impede new learning, that intelligent thought involves self-monitoring and awareness about when and how to use skills, and that "expertise" develops in a field of study as a principled and coherent way of thinking and representing problems, not just as an accumulation of information.

At the same time, rediscovery of Vygotsky (1978) and the work of other Soviet psychologists led to the realization that what is taken into the mind is socially and culturally determined. Fixed, largely hereditarian theories of intelligence have been replaced with a new understanding that cognitive abilities are "developed" through socially supported interactions. Although Vygotsky was initially interested in how children learn to think, over time the ideas of social mediation have been applied equally to the development of intelligence, expertise in academic disciplines, and metacognitive skills, and to the formation of identity. Indeed, a singularly important idea in this new paradigm is that both development and learning are primarily social processes.

These insights from learning theory then lead to a set of principles for curriculum reform. The slogan that "all students can learn" is intended to refute past beliefs that only an elite group of students could master challenging subject matter. A commitment to equal opportunity for diverse learners means providing genuine opportunities for high-quality instruction and "ways into" academic curricula that are consistent with language and interaction patterns of home and community (Au & Jordan, 1981; Brown, 1994; Heath, 1983; Tharp & Gallimore, 1988). Classroom routines and the ways that teachers and students talk with each other should help students gain experience with the ways of thinking and speaking in academic disciplines. School learning should be authentic and connected to the world outside of school not only to make learning more interesting and motivating to students but also to develop the ability to use knowledge in real-world settings. In addition to the development of cognitive abilities, classroom expectations and social norms should foster the development of important dispositions, such as students' willingness to persist in trying to solve difficult problems.

To be compatible with and to support this social-constructivist model of teaching and learning, classroom assessment must change in two fundamentally important ways. First, its form and content must be changed to better represent important thinking and problem solving skills in each of the disciplines. Second, the way that assessment is used in classrooms and how it is regarded by teachers and students must change. Furthermore, to enable this latter set of changes within classrooms, I argue that teachers need help in fending off the distorting and de-motivating effects of external assessments.

Improving the Content and Form of Assessments

The content of assessments should match challenging subject matter standards and serve to instantiate what it means to know and learn in each of the disciplines. Therefore, a broader range of assessment tools is needed to capture important learning goals and processes and to more directly connect assessment to ongoing instruction. The most obvious reform has been to devise more open-ended performance tasks to ensure that students are able to reason critically, to solve complex problems, and to apply their knowledge in real-world contexts. In addition, if instructional goals include developing students' metacognitive abilities, fostering important dispositions, and socializing students into the discourse and practices of academic disciplines, then it is essential that classroom routines and corresponding assessments reflect these goals as well. This means expanding the armamentarium for data gathering to include observations, clinical interviews, reflective journals, projects, demonstrations, collections of student work, and students' self-evaluations, and it means that teachers must engage in systematic analysis of the available evidence.

In this article, I do not elaborate further on needed changes in the content and form of assessment primarily because this aspect of reform has received the most attention to date. Although I cannot claim that common practice has moved significantly beyond the end-of-chapter test, there are none the less already promising models being developed and used in literacy, mathematics, science, history, and so forth. For example, Pat Thompson (1995) provided the set of questions in Box 10.2 to illustrate how non-algorithmic problems can help students "see" a mathematical idea. Two additional open-ended tasks are shown in Box 10.3 and serve to illustrate the point that good assessment tasks are interchangeable with good instructional tasks.

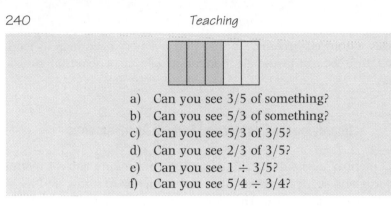

a) Can you see 3/5 of something?
b) Can you see 5/3 of something?
c) Can you see 5/3 of 3/5?
d) Can you see 2/3 of 3/5?
e) Can you see 1 ÷ 3/5?
f) Can you see 5/4 ÷ 3/4?

Box 10.2   An example of a set of questions designed to help students visualize part-whole relationships as a way to understand fractions (Thompson, 1995)

Grade 4 Mathematics Problem Set
(Mathematical Sciences Education Board, 1993)

All of the bridges in this part are built with yellow rods for spans and red rods for supports, like the one shown here. This is a 2-span bridge like the one you just built. Note that the yellow rods are 5 cm long.

Yellow

red

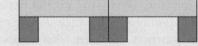

1. Now, build a 3-span bridge.
    a. How many yellow rods did you use?_____
    b. How long is your bridge?_____
    c. How many red rods did you use?_____
    d. How many rods did you use altogether?_____

2. Try to answer these questions without building a 5-span bridge. If you want, build a 5-span bridge to check your answers.
    a. How many yellow rods would you need for a 5-span bridge?_____
    b. How long would your bridge be?_____
    c. How many red rods would you need?_____
    d. How many rods would you need altogether?_____

3. Write a rule for figuring out the total number of rods you would need to build a bridge if you knew how many spans the bridge had.

Grade 5 Science Tasks
(California Learning Assessment System, 1994)

Fossils

You are a paleontologist (a scientist who studies past life forms).

You were digging and just discovered a large group of fossils.

Directions:

Open BAG A and spread the fossils on the table.

Use the hand lens to carefully observe each fossil.

Sort your fossils into groups. You may make as many groups as you like.

Write answers to these questions in your journal.

1. Draw your groups. Circle and number each group.
2. How many groups do you have?
3. List the number of each group and tell why you sorted your fossils into these groups.

BAG B has a fossil that was found in the area near where you were digging.

Directions:

Open BAG B.

Take out the new fossil and compare it with the other fossils on the table.

4. Does this new fossil fit into one of your groups? If YES, how are they alike?
5. If the new fossil does not fit into any of your groups, describe a new group in which this fossil would fit.
6. Choose one of the fossils and draw a picture of it.
7. In what kind of habitat (environment) do you think this fossil might have once lived? Why?

Box 10.3 Examples of open-ended assessment tasks intended to engage students in thinking and reasoning about important content

Protecting Classroom Assessment from the Negative Effects of High-stakes Accountability Testing

The arguments advanced thus far – in support of social-constructivist learning theory, challenging curriculum for all students, and imaginative new forms of assessment – follow closely the rhetoric of standards-based reform. I have avoided using that term, however, because, from the beginning, standards-based reform has additionally placed great faith in externally imposed standards and "tests worth teaching to." More recently, the standards movement has been corrupted, in many instances, into a heavy-handed system of rewards and punishments without the capacity building and professional development originally proposed as part of the vision (McLaughlin & Shepard, 1995). Although both large-scale, system-monitoring assessments and classroom assessments could benefit from the same kinds of substantive reform and alignment of content with important learning goals, there is more at stake here than reform of assessment format. If we wish to pursue seriously the use of assessment *for* learning, which I consider in the next section, it is important to recognize the pervasive negative effects of accountability tests and the extent to which externally imposed testing programs prevent and drive out thoughtful classroom practices. In presenting these ideas to an audience of educational researchers and teacher educators, I used the image of Darth Vader and the Death Star to convey the overshadowing effects of accountability testing.

The negative effects of high-stakes testing on teaching and learning are well known (e.g., Madaus, West, Harmon, Lomax, & Viator, 1992). Under intense political pressure, test scores are likely to go up without a corresponding improvement in student learning. In fact, distortions in what and how students are taught may actually decrease students' conceptual understanding. While some had imagined that teaching to good tests would be an improvement over low-level basic-skills curricula, more recent experiences remind us that all tests can be corrupted. And all can have a corrupting influence on teaching (Whitford & Jones, 2000).

Moreover, as Darling-Hammond (1988), McNeil (1988), and others have pointed out, external accountability testing leads to the de-skilling and de-professionalization of teachers, even – in my own state recently – to the denigration of teaching. High-stakes accountability teaches students that effort in school should be in response to externally administered rewards and punishment rather than the excitement of ideas. And accountability-testing mandates warn teachers to comply or get out (or move, if they can, to schools with higher scoring students).

Again, these ideas are not new. It is likely that teacher educators say something about this litany of complaints in teacher preparation courses. But, what do diatribes against testing teach candidates about more meaningful forms of assessment? Given their own personal histories, our students are able to hate standardized testing and at the same time reproduce it faithfully in their own pre-post testing routines, if they are not given the opportunity to develop and try out other meaningful forms of assessment situated in practice. So we must teach them how to do assessment well.

Also, teacher candidates need to find support and a way of protecting their own developing understandings of constructivist assessment practices from the onslaught of test-driven curricula. I have in mind here something like the double-entry teaching that teachers had invented in Linda McNeil's (1988) study of the *Contradictions of Control*. In contrast to teachers who trivialized content and taught defensively as a means to control and win compliance from students, McNeil found that excited and engaging teachers in the magnet schools she studied found ways to resist and hold off the pernicious effects of proficiency testing on their curriculum. Specifically, they helped students keep parallel sets of notes, one set for the real knowledge and one for the knowledge they would need for the test. They did this rather than give over the entire course to the "fragments and facts" required on the test.

This is only one example of a strategy for resistance. As I continue next to describe productive ways to use assessment in classrooms, I emphasize the need sometimes to "mark" informal assessment occasions for students as they occur within the normal flow of classroom discourse – because this helps students become self-aware about how assessment can help learning. Similarly, I believe we should explicitly address with our teacher education students how they might cope with the contesting forces of good and evil assessment as they compete in classrooms to control curriculum, time, and student attitudes about learning.

Using Assessment in the Process of Learning

A learning culture

Improving the content of assessments is important but not sufficient to ensure that assessment will be used to enhance learning. In this section, I consider the changes in classroom practices that are also needed to make it possible for assessment to be used as part of the learning process. How might the culture of classrooms be shifted so that students no longer feign competence or work to perform well on the test as an end separate from real learning? Could we create a learning culture where students and teachers would have a shared expectation that finding out what makes sense and what doesn't is a joint and worthwhile project, essential to taking the next steps in learning?

I believe that our international colleagues are ahead of us in thinking about the difficulties in making these cultural changes. Sadler (1998) in Australia, for example, writes about "the long-term exposure of students to defective patterns of formative[2] assessment" (p. 77). Perrenoud in Switzerland (1991) notes that there are always certain students in a class who are willing to work harder to learn more and who, therefore, go along with formative assessment. But other children and adolescents are "imprisoned in the identity of a bad pupil and an opponent" (p. 92). According to Perrenoud, "every teacher who wants to practice formative assessment must reconstruct the teaching contract so as to counteract the habits acquired by his pupils" (p. 92). Tunstall and Gipps (1996) have studied classrooms in Great Britain where teachers have developed more interactive ways of discussing work and criteria with students as a means to redistribute power and establish more collaborative relationships with students.

To accomplish the kind of transformation envisioned, we have not only to make assessment more informative, more insightfully tied to learning steps, but at the same time we must change the social meaning of evaluation. Our aim should be to change our cultural practices so that students and teachers look to assessment as a source of insight and help instead of an occasion for meting out rewards and punishments. In the paragraphs that follow, I summarize briefly several specific assessment strategies: dynamic assessment, assessment of prior knowledge, the use of feedback, teaching for transfer, explicit criteria, student self-assessment, and evaluation of teaching. Each of these strategies serves a social, motivational purpose as well as a cognitive, informational one. None of these strategies by themselves will be effective if they are not part of a more fundamental shift in classroom practices and expectations about learning.

Dynamic, On-going Assessment

In order for assessment to play a more useful role in helping students learn it should be moved into the middle of the teaching and learning process instead of being postponed as only the end-point of instruction. Dynamic assessment – finding out what a student is able to do independently as well as what can be done with adult guidance – is integral to Vygotsky's (1978) idea of a zone of proximal development. This type of interactive assessment, which allows teachers to provide assistance as part of assessment, does more than help teachers gain valuable insights about how understanding might be extended. It also creates perfectly targeted occasions to teach and provides the means to scaffold next steps. Although formal dynamic assessments are assumed to involve an adult working with only one child, these ideas about social mediation of learning can be extended to groups, especially if students are socialized into the ways of talking in a community of practice and become accustomed to explaining their reasoning and offering and receiving feedback about their developing competence as part of a social group.

Note that these ideas, based on activity theory and Lave and Wenger's (1991) concept of legitimate peripheral participation, provide a profoundly different view of motivation from behaviorist reinforcement and create no separation between cognitive and motivational goals. According to Lave and Wenger's theory, learning and development of an identity of mastery occur together as a newcomer becomes increasingly adept at participating in a community of practice. If one's identity is tied to group membership, then it is natural to work to become a more competent and full-fledged member of the group.

Prior knowledge

Prior knowledge and feedback are two well-established ideas, the meaning of which may have to be reexamined as learning theories are changed to take better account of social and cultural contexts. For example, assessing my prior knowledge using a checklist or pre-test version of the intended end-of-unit test may not be very accurate unless I already have sophisticated experience with the teacher's measures and conceptual categories. Open discussion or "instructional conversations" (Tharp & Gallimore, 1988) are more likely to elicit a more coherent version of students' reasoning and relevant experiences and can be a much more productive way for novice teachers to learn about the resources brought by students from diverse communities.

In my own experience working in schools, I have noticed two divergent sets of teaching practices that address students' prior knowledge. First, many teachers rely on a traditional, pretest-posttest design to document student progress, but then do not use information from the pretest in instruction. At the same time, a significant number of teachers, especially in reading and language arts, use prior knowledge activation techniques, such as Ogle's (1986) KWL strategy, but without necessarily attending to the assessment insights provided.

We have a great deal of work to do to develop and model effective assessment strategies, for starting points as well as for other stages of learning. One question we may want to consider is whether assessment should become so much a part of normal classroom discourse patterns that scaffolding and ongoing checks for understanding are embedded (and therefore disguised); or whether assessment steps should be marked and made visible to students as an essential step in learning. In our efforts to change the culture of the classroom, it may be helpful, at least in the short term, to label prior knowledge activation techniques as instances of "assessment." What safer time to admit what you don't know than at the start of an instructional activity?

Feedback

We take it for granted that providing feedback to the learner about performance will lead to self-correction and improvement. For the most part, however, the existing literature on feedback will be of limited value to us in reconceptualizing assessment from a constructivist perspective, because the great majority of existing studies are based on behaviorist assumptions. Typically, the outcome measures are narrowly defined, feedback consists of reporting of right and wrong answers to the learner, and the end-of-study test may differ only slightly from the prior measure and from instructional materials.

More promising are studies of scaffolding and naturalistic studies of expert tutoring – but these studies also reveal how much we have to learn about effective use of feedback. For example, Lepper, Drake and O'Donnell-Johnson (1997) found that the most effective tutors do not routinely correct student errors directly. Instead they *ignore* errors when they are inconsequential to the solution process and *forestall* errors that the student has made previously by offering hints or asking leading questions. Only when the forestalling tactic fails do expert tutors *intervene* with a direct question intended to force the student to self-correct, or they may engage in *de-bugging*, using a series of increasingly direct questions to guide the student through the solution process. According to Lepper et al.'s analysis, the tendency of expert tutors to use indirect forms of feedback when possible was influenced by their desire to maintain student motivation and self-confidence while not ignoring student errors. This is a balancing act that new teachers must learn to perform as well.

Transfer

There is a close relationship between truly *understanding* a concept and being able to *transfer* knowledge and use it in new situations. In contrast to memorization – and in contrast to the behaviorist assumption that each application must be taught as a separate learning objective – true understanding is flexible, connected, and generalizable. Not surprisingly, research studies demonstrate that learning is more likely to transfer if students have the opportunity to practice with a variety of applications while learning. Although there appears to be disagreement between cognitivists and situativists regarding knowledge generalization (Anderson, Reder, & Simon, 1996), in fact, both groups of researchers acknowledge the importance of being able to use what one has learned in new situations. Cognitivists focus more on cognitive structures, abstract representations, and generalized principles that enable knowledge use in new situations, while situativists are concerned about "learning to participate in interactions in ways that succeed over a broad range of situations" (Greeno, 1996, p. 3).

In working with pre-service teachers, I have suggested that a goal of teaching should be to help students develop "robust" understandings (Shepard, 1997). The term was prompted by Marilyn Burns's (1993) reference to children's understandings as being "fragile" –

they appear to know a concept in one context but not to know it when asked in another way or in another setting. Sometimes this fragility occurs because students are still in the process of learning and sometimes because the framing of the problem, clues, and other supports available in the familiar context are not available in another. All too often, however, mastery appears pat and certain but does not travel to new situations because students have mastered classroom routines and not the underlying concepts. To support generalization and ensure transfer, that is, to support robust understandings, "Good teaching constantly asks about old understandings in new ways, calls for new applications, and draws new connections" (Shepard, 1997, p. 27). And good assessment does the same. We should not, for example, agree to a contract with our students which says that the only fair test is one with familiar and well-rehearsed problems.

Explicit criteria

Frederiksen and Collins (1989) used the term *transparency* to express the idea that students must have a clear understanding of the criteria by which their work will be assessed. In fact, the features of excellent performance should be so transparent that students can learn to evaluate their own work in the same way that their teachers would. According to Frederiksen and Collins,

> The assessment system (should) provide a basis for developing a meta-cognitive awareness of what are important characteristics of good problem solving, good writing, good experimentation, good historical analysis, and so on. Moreover, such an assessment can address not only the product one is trying to achieve, but also the process of achieving it, that is, the habits of mind that contribute to successful writing, painting, and problem solving (Wiggins, 1989). (Frederikson & Collins, 1989, p. 30)

Having access to evaluation criteria satisfies a basic fairness principle (we should know the rules for how our work will be judged). More importantly, however, giving students the opportunity to get good at what it is that the standards require speaks to a different and even more fundamental sense of fairness, which is what Wolf and Reardon (1996) had in mind when they talked about "making thinking visible" and "making excellence attainable."

Self-assessment

Student self-assessment serves cognitive purposes, then, but it also promises to increase students' responsibility for their own learning and to make the relationship between teachers and students more collaborative. As Caroline Gipps (1999) has suggested, this does not mean that the teacher gives up responsibility, but that rather, by sharing it, she gains greater student ownership, less distrust, and more appreciation that standards are not capricious or arbitrary. In case studies of student self-evaluation practices in both an Australian and English site, Klenowski (1995) found that students participating in self-evaluation became more interested in the criteria and substantive feedback than in their grade *per se*. Students also reported that they had to be more honest about their own work as well as being fair with other students, and they had to be prepared to defend their opinions in terms of the evidence. Klenowski's (1995) data support Wiggins's (1992) earlier assertion that involving students in analyzing their own work builds ownership of the evaluation process and "makes it possible to hold students to higher standards because the criteria are clear and reasonable" (p. 30).

Evaluation of teaching

In addition to using assessment to monitor and promote individual students' learning, classroom assessment should also be used to examine and improve teaching practices. This includes both ongoing, informal assessments of students' understandings to adjust lessons and teaching plans as well as more formal and critical action-research studies. As I have suggested with other assessment strategies, here again I believe it will be helpful for teachers to make their investigations of teaching visible to students, for example, by discussing with them decisions to redirect instruction, stop for a mini-lesson, and so forth. This seems to be fundamentally important to the idea of transforming the culture of the classroom. If we want to develop a community of learners – where students naturally seek feedback and critique their own work – then it is reasonable that teachers would model this same commitment to using data systematically as it applies to their own role in the teaching and learning process.

Notes

1 A more detailed discussion of this framework and supporting literature review are provided in Shepard (in press).
2 Sadler (1998) uses the term *formative assessment* to mean assessment "that is specifically intended to provide feedback on performance to improve and accelerate learning" (p. 77). He acknowledges that teachers may have difficulty using feedback in positive ways because of students' negative coping strategies developed in response to past practices.

References and further reading

Anderson, J. R., Reder, L. M., & Simon, H. A. (1996). Situated learning and education. *Educational Researcher, 25*, 5–11.

Assessment Reform Group. (1999). *Assessment for learning: Beyond the black box*. Cambridge: University of Cambridge School of Education.

Au, K. H., & Jordan, C. (1981). Teaching reading to Hawaiian children: Finding a culturally appropriate solution. In H. Trueba, G. P. Guthrie, & K. H. Au (Eds.), *Culture in the bilingual classroom: Studies in classroom ethnography* (pp. 139–152). Rowley, MA: Newbury House.

Ayers, L. P. (1918). History and present status of educational measurements. *Seventeenth Yearbook of the National Society for the Study of Education, Part II*, 9–15.

Black, P., & Wiliam, D. (1998a). Assessment and classroom learning. *Assessment in Education: Principles, Policy, and Practice, 5*(1), 7–74.

Black, P., & Wiliam, D. (1998b). *Inside the black box: Raising standards through classroom assessment*. London: School of Education, King's College.

Bliem, C. L., & Davinroy, K. H. (1997). *Teachers' beliefs about assessment and instruction in literacy*. Unpublished manuscript, University of Colorado at Boulder.

Bobbitt, F. (1912). The elimination of waste in education. *The Elementary School Teacher, 12*, 259–271.

Bransford, J. D. (1979). *Human cognition: Learning, understanding, and remembering*. Belmont, CA: Wadsworth.

Bransford, J. D., Brown, A. L., & Cocking, R. R. (1999). *How people learn: Brain, mind, experience, and school*. Washington, DC: National Academy Press.

Brown, A. L. (1994). The advancement of learning. *Educational Researcher, 23,* 4–12.

Burns, M. (1993). *Mathematics: Assessing understanding.* White Plains, NY: Cuisenaire Company of America.

California Learning Assessment System. (1994). *A sampler of science assessment – elementary.* Sacramento: California Department of Education.

Cremin, L. (1961). *The transformation of the school: Progressivism in American education, 1876–1957.* New York: Vintage Books.

Darling-Hammond, L. (1988). Accountability and teacher professionalism. *American Educator, 12,* 8–13.

Darling-Hammond, L. (1996). The right to learn and the advancement of teaching: Research, policy, and practice for democratic education. *Educational Researcher, 25,* 5–17.

Frederiksen, J. R., & Collins, A. (1989). A systems approach to educational testing. *Educational Researcher, 18,* 27–32.

Gagne, R. M. (1965). *The conditions of learning.* New York: Rinehard & Winston.

Gipps, C. V. (1999). Socio-cultural aspects of assessment. In P. D. Pearson & A. Iran-Nejad (Eds.), *Review of Research in Education* (Vol. 24, pp. 355–392). Washington, DC: American Educational Research Association.

Graue, M. E. (1993). Integrating theory and practice through instructional assessment. *Educational Assessment, 1,* 293–309.

Greeno, J. G. (1996, July). *On claims that answer the wrong questions.* Stanford, CA: Institute for Research on Learning.

Heath, S. B. (1983). *Ways with words: Language, life, and work in communities and classrooms.* Cambridge: Cambridge University Press.

Hull, C. L. (1943). *Principles of behavior: An introduction to behavior theory.* New York: Appleton-Century.

Klenowski, V. (1995). Student self-evaluation process in student-centered teaching and learning contexts of Australia and England. *Assessment in Education, 2,* 145–163.

Kliebard, H. M. (1995). *The struggle for the American curriculum: 1893–1958* (2nd ed.). New York: Routledge.

Lave, J., & Wenger, E. (1991). *Situated learning: Legitimate peripheral participation.* Cambridge, England: Cambridge University Press.

Lepper, M. R., Drake, M. F., O'Donnell-Johnson, T. (1997). Scaffolding techniques of expert human tutors. In K. Hogan & M. Pressley (Eds.), *Scaffolding student learning: Instructional approaches & issues.* Cambridge, MA: Brookline Books.

Madaus, G. F., West, M. M., Harmon, M. C., Lomax, R. G., & Viator, K. A. (1992). *The influence of testing on teaching math and science in grades 4–12.* Chestnut Hill, MA: Center of Study of Testing, Evaluation, and Educational Policy, Boston College.

Mathematical Sciences Education Board. (1993). *Measuring up: Prototypes for mathematics assessment.* Washington, DC: National Academy Press.

McLaughlin, M. W., & Shepard, L. A. (1995). *Improving education through standards-based reform: A report of the National Academy of Education panel on standards-based educational reform.* Stanford, CA: National Academy of Education.

McNeil, L. M. (1988). *Contradictions of control: School structure and school knowledge.* New York: Routledge.

National Academy of Education. (1999, March). *Recommendations regarding research priorities: An advisory report to the National Educational Research Policy and Priorities Board.* New York: New York University.

National Research Council. (1999). *Improving student learning: A strategic plan for education research and its utilization.* Washington, DC: National Academy Press.

Ogle, D. M. (1986). K-W-L: A teaching model that develops active reading of expository test. *The Reading Teacher, 39*(6), 564–570.

Perrenoud, P. (1991). Towards a pragmatic approach to formative evaluation. In P. Weston (Ed.), *Assessment of pupils' achievement: Motivation and school success* (pp. 77–101). Amsterdam: Swets and Zeitlinger.

Putnam, R. T., & Borko, H. (1997). Teacher learning: Implications of new views of cognition. In B. J. Biddle, T. L. Good, & I. F. Goodson (Eds.), *International handbook of teachers and teaching* (Vol. 2, pp. 1223–1296). Dordecht, The Netherlands: Kluwer.

Ross, C. C. (1941). *Measurement in today's schools.* New York: Prentice-Hall.

Ruch, G. M. (1929). *The objective or new-type examination.* Chicago: Scott Foresman.

Sadler, D. R. (1998). Formative assessment: Revisiting the territory. *Assessment in Education: Principles, Policy and Practice, 5,* 77–84.

Schoenfeld, A. H. (1999). Looking toward the 21st century: Challenges of educational theory and practice. *Educational Researcher, 28*(7), 4–14.

Shepard, L. A. (1997). *Measuring achievement: What does it mean to test for robust understanding?* Princeton, NJ: Policy Information Center, Educational Testing Service.

Shepard, L. A. (in press). The role of classroom assessment in teaching and learning. In V. Richardson (Ed.), *Handbook of research on teaching* (4th ed). Washington, DC: American Educational Research Association.

Skinner, B. F. (1938). *The behavior of organisms: An experimental analysis.* New York: Appleton-Century-Crofts.

Skinner, B. F. (1954). The science of learning and the art of teaching. *Harvard Educational Review, 24,* 86–97.

Tharp, R. G., & Gallimore, R. (1988). *Rousing minds to life: Teaching, learning, and schooling in social context.* New York: Cambridge University Press.

Thompson, P. W. (1995). Notation, convention, and quantity in elementary mathematics. In J. T. Sowder & B. P. Schappelle (Eds.), *Providing a foundation for teaching mathematics in the middle grades* (pp. 199–221). New York: State University of New York Press.

Thorndike, E. L. (1922). *The psychology of arithmetic.* New York: Macmillan.

Tunstall, P. & Gipps, C. (1996). Teacher feedback to young children in formative assessment: A typology. *British Educational Research Journal, 22,* 389–404.

Vygotsky, L. S. (1978). *Mind in society: The development of higher psychological processes.* Cambridge, MA: Harvard University Press.

Whitford, B. L., & Jones, K. (2000). Kentucky lesson: How high stakes school accountability undermines a performance-based curriculum vision. In B. L. Whitford & K. Jones (Eds.), *Accountability, assessment and teacher commitment: Lessons from Kentucky's reform efforts.* Albany NY: State University of New York Press.

Wiggins, G. (1989). A true test: Toward more authentic and equitable assessment. *Phi Delta Kappan, 70,* 703–713.

Wiggins, G. (1992). Creating tests worth taking. *Educational Leadership, 49,* 26–33.

Wolf, D. P., & Reardon, S. F. (1996). Access to excellence through new forms of student assessment. In J. B. Baron & Wolf, D. P. (Eds.) *Performance-based student assessment: Challenges and possibilities* (pp. 1–31). Chicago: University of Chicago Press.

Index